The Dream Discourse Today

Freud's own high opinion of the discoveries disclosed in *The Inter-pretation of Dreams* has meant that further thought about the dream poses a poignant challenge for all psychoanalysts. Throughout the history of the psychoanalytical movement — now approaching the 100th anniversary of Freud's great discovery — many analysts have tried to link later psychoanalytic perspectives with Freud's original discovery.

The Dream Discourse Today brings together some of the most significant essays on the dream of the last twenty-five years. The papers come from a broad spectrum of analytical schools of thought from Europe and America. All are inspired by Freud but add a new dimension to the understanding of the dream in clinical practice. Different writers see the dream as developmental testimony to the progress of a psychoanalysis, as a variety of self experience, as a method of adaptive mastery, as an indicator of a particular form of mental disturbance, as perversion of a meaning it is meant to process.

The Dream Discourse Today will not only serve the reader as a valuable reference, but will stimulate renewed consideration of the mental event that Freud regarded as the cornerstone of psychoanalysis. For teacher and clinician alike, this is a thought-provoking collection, enhanced by an informative introduction and lucid editorial commentary to each essay.

Sara Flanders received her doctorate in English Literature at the State University of New York at Buffalo. She is a member of the British Psycho-Analytical Society and a psychoanalyst in private practice.

The New Library of Psychoanalysis was launched in 1987 in association with the Institute of Psycho-Analysis, London. Its purpose is to facilitate a greater and more widespread appreciation of what psychoanalysis is really about and to provide a forum for increasing mutual understanding between psychoanalysts and those working in other disciplines such as history, linguistics, literature, medicine, philosophy, psychology, and the social sciences. It is intended that the titles selected for publication in the series should deepen and develop psychoanalytic thinking and technique, contribute to psychoanalysis from outside or contribute to other disciplines from a psychoanalytical perspective.

The Institute, together with the British Psycho-Analytical Society, runs a low-fee psychoanalytic clinic, organizes lectures and scientific events concerned with psychoanalysis, publishes the *International Journal of Psycho-Analysis*, and runs the only training course in the UK in psychoanalysis leading to membership of the International Psychoanalytical Association – the body which preserves internationally agreed standards of training, of professional entry, and of professional ethics and practice for psychoanalysis as initiated and developed by Sigmund Freud. Distinguished members of the Institute have included Michael Balint, Wilfred Bion, Ronald Fairbairn, Anna Freud, Ernest Jones, Melanie Klein, John Rickman, and Donald Winnicott.

Volumes 1–11 in the series have been prepared under the general editorship of David Tuckett, with Ronald Britton and Eglé Laufer as associate editors. Subsequent volumes are under the general editorship of Elizabeth Bott Spillius, with, from Volume 17, Donald Campbell, Michael Parsons, Rosine Jozef Perelberg and David Taylor as associate editors.

IN THE SAME SERIES

NEW LIBRARY OF PSYCHOANALYSIS
17

General editor: Elizabeth Bott Spillius

The Dream
Discourse Today

Edited and introduced by
SARA FLANDERS

LONDON AND NEW YORK

First published in 1993
by Routledge
11 New Fetter Lane, London EC4P 4EE

Simultaneously published in the USA and Canada
by Routledge
29 West 35th Street, New York, NY 10001

Phototypeset in 11pt Bembo by
Mews Photosetting, Beckenham, Kent
Printed and bound in Great Britain
by Mackays of Chatham PLC, Chatham, Kent

British Library Cataloguing in Publication Data
A catalogue record for this book is available from the British Library.

Library of Congress Cataloging in Publication Data
The Dream Discourse Today / edited by Sara Flanders.
p.   cm. — (New library of psychoanalysis : 17)
Reprint of works originally published 1962—1985.
1. Dreams. 2. Psychoanalysis. I. Flanders, Sara, 1944—
II. Series.
BF175.5.D74D74   1993   92-37649
154.6'3–dc20   CIP
ISBN 0-415-09354-6
0-415-09355-4 (pbk)

Contents

Contents

Acknowledgements

'Dream psychology and the evolution of the psychoanalytic situation' by M. Masud R. Khan

This paper first appeared in *The International Journal of Psycho-Analysis*, 1962, vol. 43. It is an enlarged version of the paper read in the Symposium 'The Psycho-analytic Situation: The Setting and the Process of Cure' at the 22nd Congress of the International Psychoanalytical Association, Edinburgh, August 1961.

'Dreams in clinical psychoanalytic practice' by Charles Brenner

This paper first appeared in the *Journal of Nervous and Mental Disease*, 1969, vol. 149.

'The exceptional position of the dream in psychoanalytic practice' by R.R. Greenson

This paper appeared in *The Psychoanalytic Quarterly*, 1970, vol. 39.

'The use and abuse of dream in psychic experience' by M. Masud R. Khan

Published in *The Privacy of the Self*, 1974, this is a revised version of a paper first published in the *International Journal of Psychoanalytic Psychotherapy*, 1972, vol. 1.

'The function of dreams' by Hanna Segal

This paper was first published in *The Work of Hanna Segal*, 1980.

'Dream as an object' by J-B. Pontalis

This paper appeared in *The International Review of Psycho-Analysis*, 1974, vol. 1.

'The experiencing of the dream and the transference' by Harold Stewart

This appeared first in the *International Journal of Psycho-Analysis* in 1973, vol. 54. The paper was read at a Symposium on 'The Role of Dreams in Psychoanalysis' given to the British Psycho-Analytical Society on 15 November 1972.

'Some reflections on analytic listening and the dream screen' by James Gammill

This paper appeared in the *International Journal of Psycho-Analysis* in 1980. It was presented at the 31st International Psychoanalytical Congress, New York, August 1979.

'The film of the dream' by Didier Anzieu

This paper constitutes a chapter in the book *The Skin Ego*, published in English in 1989 by Yale. It was published in French in 1985 in *Le Moi-Peau*.

'The manifest dream content and its significance for the interpretation of dreams' by Jacob Spanjaard

This paper was published in the *International Journal of Psycho-Analysis*, 1969, vol. 50.

'A psychoanalytic-dream continuum: the source and function of dreams' by R. Greenberg and C. Pearlman

This paper appeared in the *International Review of Psycho-Analysis*, 1975, vol. 2.

'Dreaming and the organizing function of the ego' by Cecily de Monchaux

This paper appeared first in the *International Journal of Psycho-Analysis*, 1978, vol. 59.

'Psychoanalytic phenomenology of the dream' by Robert D. Stolorow and George E. Atwood

This paper was published in *The Annual of Psychoanalysis*, 1982, vol. 10.

Introduction

Today, nearly a century after Freud's great breakthrough in the understanding of dreams and the functioning of the unconscious mind, the
dream no longer occupies the centre of psychoanalytical debate. Although
dreams remain the classical illustrative evidence in psychoanalytic clinical
papers, the pendulum which Ella Freeman Sharpe observed swinging away
from psychoanalytic interest in dream interpretation in 1937 has never
swung back (Sharpe 1937: 67). Nor does it today obey a single driving
force or current of professional opinion. Psychoanalysts today speak what
André Green has called a polyglot tongue (Green 1975), potentially
confusing even for the mature and theoretically sophisticated analyst.
Further complicating if also enriching the heterogeneity of an international psychoanalytic view of dreams is the impact of neurological
research into the dreaming function, influencing sometimes directly and
sometimes indirectly the uncertain psychoanalytic consensus. It is,
however, hoped that the cumulative effect of the articles collected here
will be to leave the reader with both a sense of the range of current
perspectives on the dream in psychoanalytic thinking and a confidence
strengthened by the often converging implications of thinking predicated
quite differently.

   In this Introduction I will first briefly present Freud's views on dreams,
then selected developments in later thinking about dreams and their place
in the psychoanalytic process. I have divided the chapters which follow
into four parts. In Part One, a paper by Masud Khan lays the foundation
for this collection by examining the relationship between classical dream
theory and the psychoanalytic process. Part Two includes the central papers
of a classic debate over whether and how the dream is still 'special' in
clinical practice. Part Three includes papers expressing British and French
views on the dreaming process, and Part Four describes developments
which come from the traditions of classical ego and later self psychoanalysis,

1

principally but not only in the United States. The reader will note that there is an historical element in the ordering of these papers which, I believe, is useful in conveying the developing trends as they have materialized in psychoanalytic discourse. Finally, this is a limited selection, by no means complete, but one in which each contribution introduces or furthers a point of view. There is little repetition, and much distinguished, sometimes quite difficult argument.

The historical background

In 1932 Freud wrote of the theory of dreams, 'It occupies a special place in the history of psychoanalysis and marks a turning point; it was with it that analysis took the step from being a psychotherapeutic procedure to being a depth psychology' (Freud 1932: 7). In this same publication he lamented the waning of interest in the dream, as measured by the disappearance of a special section 'On dream interpretation', from the *International Journal of Psycho-Analysis* (1932: 8). A sense of loss, therefore, informs the claim made in the previous year, 1931, when, in the preface to the third English edition of *The Interpretation of Dreams*, he assessed his early work:

> It contains, even according to my present day judgment, the most valuable of all the discoveries it has been my good fortune to make. Insight such as this falls to one's lot but once in a lifetime.
>
> (Freud 1931)

If the psychoanalytic movement was, by the 1920s and 1930s, marching to a different tune, it was still Freud who led them, and into matters of enduring interest: the origins of psychosis, the formulation of the structural theory, the exploration of early object relations, the problem of anxiety, the increased awareness of the transference. As many present-day analysts lament (see Brenner, this volume), Freud never fully re-wrote the theory of dream interpretation to bring it in its entirety within the framework of later conceptualizations, most specifically the structural model of the mind. He remained loyal to his original conceptualization, made without benefit of the later theory, although he added elaborative footnotes over a lifetime of publication. Moreover, as he wrote in 1932, the theory of dreams was his 'sheet anchor':

> When I began to have doubts of the correctness of my wavering conclusions, the successful transformation of a senseless and muddled dream into a logical and intelligible mental process in the dreamer would renew my confidence of being on the right track.
>
> (Freud 1932: 7)

There is a nice irony in this most labile and mysterious area of the mind providing Freud with his 'sheet anchor', his reassurance and support in the potentially chaotic climate of the consulting room. His loyalty to his work, his affirmation of its centrality are no doubt related to the process of its writing, and to its place in his own personal self-analysis (Anzieu 1986). But Freud is not alone in his evaluation of the importance of *The Interpretation of Dreams*. Some of the most innovative and difficult contributors to the post-Freudian canon have agreed with his assessment, Lacan and, more recently, Matte-Blanco (1988) among them.

It is in *The Interpretation of Dreams* that Freud located and disclosed to an unresponsive scientific world the nature of unconscious mental processes. He arrived at the understanding, he wrote, 'in the following manner':

> I have been engaged for many years (with a therapeutic aim in view) in unravelling certain psychopathological structures – hysterical phobias, obsessional ideas, and so on. I have been doing so, in fact, ever since I learnt from an important communication by Josef Breuer that as regards these structures (which are looked upon as pathological symptoms) unravelling them coincides with removing them. [Cf. Breuer and Freud 1895.] If a pathological idea of this sort can be traced back to the elements in the patient's mental life from which it originated, it simultaneously crumbles away and the patient is freed from it . . . .
>
> . . . It was in the course of these psycho-analytic studies that I came upon dream interpretation. My patients were pledged to communicate to me every idea or thought that occurred to them in connection with some particular subject; amongst other things they told me their dreams and so taught me that a dream can be inserted into the psychical chain that has to be traced backwards in the memory from a pathological idea. It was then only a short step to treating the dream itself as a symptom and to applying to dreams the method of interpretation that had been worked out for symptoms.
>
> (Freud 1900: 100–1)

Symptoms have meaning and a place in an individual's personal history, and so do dreams. When the work of interpretation has been completed, the Freudian dream is disclosed to be the disguised fulfilment of a wish, a wish provoked by encounters with reality on the previous day. Something in the day has awakened and united with unconscious infantile drives, urges that press for hallucinatory satisfaction in the dream state. The work of the dream is to satisfy but also disguise the unconscious wish, which otherwise would threaten to disturb the dreamer and end both sleep and dream. Interpretation of a dream is by its very nature a disturbing activity; it is the undoing of the dream-work, the unravelling of the disguise, the translation of the manifest content of the dream hallucination back into the thoughts which lie behind it, the thoughts which are latent. The translation is possible because Freud had discovered that the dream-work operates according to its own mechanisms, condensing and displacing meanings, representing and disguising multiple layers of significance, giving visual shape to overlapping thoughts, memories, desires. Freud maintained consistently when stating the theory of the dream that the manifest or surface content of the remembered dream, the bizarre or commonplace narrative in its entirety, is not where the meaning of the dream lies. The surface of the dream can never be entirely trusted, never swallowed whole. The appearance of a narrative, a story, is 'secondary elaboration', a yoking together of fragments, not a dramatic action. Freud's dream is, in this way, less than art. The dream's meaning is discovered only after more work is done, after the dreamer makes his own associations to its imagery and to the events and thoughts of the previous day that are suggested by the dream, and so begins to locate the elaborated dream in the context of personal experience.

Ten years after publishing the first edition of *The Interpretation of Dreams*, Freud added a privileged form of dream imagery to his theory of disguised meaning (Freud 1900: 350–80). Along with other psychoanalysts involved in dream analysis, he discovered some imagery to be recurrent and constant in its meaning, and to yield little in the way of associations. These are the dream 'symbols', more representations than disguises for a vein of meaning Freud said was not wide, but which is in fact almost infinitely inclusive: the human body as a whole, parents, children, brothers and sisters, birth, death, nakedness, and most commonly, the field of sexual life (Freud 1916: 153). The place of symbolic representation in dreaming reinforces the idea of the dream as creative, synthetic, in psychoanalytic discourses, revealing, rather than concealing, disguising, defending. The dream symbol binds manifest and latent content, contains connections instead of splitting them off.

Yet, in spite of the accumulated number of symbols claimed to be constant and to be interpretable without associations, Freud's most consistent argument, like a leitmotif running through his work on dreams, is the insistence on the first importance of opening up the network of the dreamer's associations. Over and over, Freud admonishes the dream interpreter not to be misled by the manifest content, but to seek out the latent dream thought through the dreamer's associations to fragments of the dream. This is Freudian dogma, or would become so. Never trust what might be obvious about a dream, even if Freud himself patently disobeys his own dictum (Spanjaard, this volume). It is one of the most awkward of the lessons taught to psychoanalytic candidates (Erikson 1954), who, struggling to follow a bombardment of material, must also remember that even if a reported dream seems to be the only lucid communication, it is not in itself the 'sheet anchor' to which to cling. Rather it is the procedure, founded on the respect for the dreamer's unconscious processes and arguably, on the dreamer's capacity for self-discovery, to wait for the associations which may, though not necessarily, disclose the very opposite of the obvious. It is on this basis that Freud made his claim, both for the dream and for psychoanalysis, that the interpretation of dreams is the 'royal road to a knowledge of the unconscious activities of the mind' (1900: 608). Freud's insistence on the need for associations to uncover the disguised or latent meaning of the dream coupled with his less emphatic but clear recognition of the expressive meaningfulness of symbolic imagery constitutes a problematic around which succeeding generations of analysts have struggled.

Twenty years after the publication of *The Interpretation of Dreams*, in *Beyond the Pleasure Principle*, Freud addressed what he regarded as the single exception to his fundamental notion of the dream-creating process. He addressed the observed compulsion to repeat, in the transference, in life and in 'traumatic dreams', replicas of undisguised painful experience. In returning over and over to realistic depiction of a situation in which a trauma occurred, dreams are 'endeavouring to master the stimulus retrospectively, by developing the anxiety whose omission was the cause of the traumatic neurosis' (Freud 1920: 32). It is therefore 'impossible to classify as wish fulfilments' the dreams which occur in either the 'traumatic neurosis' *or* the 'dreams during psychoanalyses which bring to memory the physical trauma of childhood' (Freud 1920: 32). If there is, he writes, a 'beyond the pleasure principle it is only consistent to grant that there was also a time before the purpose of dreams was the fulfilment of wishes' (p. 33).

The repetition of traumatic experience in the material of the dream is an idea, like that of the symbolic representation in dreams, which can be stretched almost indefinitely. Ferenczi was the first to do so:

> it strikes us more and more that the so-called day's [and as we may add, life's] residues are indeed repetition symptoms of traumata . . . .
> Thus instead of 'the dream is a wish-fulfilment' a more complete definition of the dream function would be: every dream, even an unpleasurable one, is an attempt at a better mastery and settling of traumatic experiences, so to speak, in the sense of an *esprit d'escalier* which is made easier in most dreams because of the diminution of the critical faculty and the predominance of the pleasure principle.
> (Ferenczi 1931: 238)

Indeed, it is possible to discover in the regression implicit in every dream a potential trauma (Garma 1966; see Curtis and Sachs 1976). Given the nature of unconscious intentions, trauma is likewise implicit in every-day life (Sandler 1976), in the apparent banalities of social intercourse, as well as the emotional intensities of intimacy. Freud himself, as he pursued his enquiry into the origins of psychic structure, emphasized more and more the 'positive Hell' (Freud 1916: 43) of instinctual life, as well as the potential cruelty of the archaic superego, the dangers to develop-ment implicit in the helplessness of the human infant. As Freud later pointed out, no one escapes in the infancy that returns to us in our dreams, the traumas of childhood experience (Freud 1932: 27–30). The self psychologists (Kohut 1971, 1977) have recently made particular use of the linking of trauma to relatively undisguised symbolic dream material in which they see disclosed in a manifest content understood metaphorically an insecure self about to be overwhelmed to the point of distintegration, the visual imagery itself being utilized to bind nameless anxiety or dread. Socarides, in 1980, sees the same process in dreams of perversion.

Although Freud himself linked the dream to thought processes generally (Freud 1925: 112), and traumatic dreams to mastery of anxiety, he consistently portrayed the dream-work as specific to the function of maintaining sleep, to the prevention of an overwhelming of the ego which would result in awakening. Regarding the wider adaptive function of the dream, he was cautious, more cautious than most analysts are today.

> It is misleading to say that dreams are concerned with the tasks of life before us, or seek to find a solution for the problems of our daily work. That is the business of preconscious thought. Useful work of this kind is as remote from dreams as is any intention of conveying information to another person. When a dream deals with a problem of actual life, it solves it in the manner of an irrational wish.
>
> (Freud 1925: 127)

There is, of course, a difference between a view of dreams as problem-solving, which is one extreme of the revisionist spectrum within psychoanalysis (French and Fromm 1964) and the view of the integrative function of normal dreams, potentially reflecting and even advancing the internal strength of the ego (Segal, this volume), or integrating new perceptions with established structures (Palombo 1978; Greenberg and Pearlman, this volume), or dreams viewed as preserving and even facilitating developmental structure (Fosshage 1983; Stolorow and Atwood, this volume). Certainly, a fuller regard for the integrative function of the dream has been informed by the confluence of REM research and the tradition of ego psychology (see Greenberg and Pearlman, this volume). In recent decades researchers have found in the laboratory many dreams manifestly related to problems confronting the subject, in his life and in an ongoing psychoanalysis.

6

Within the body of Freud's writing, the advent of the structural model, the enlarged conceptualizations of an ego fulfilling a synthesizing or integrating function both day and night, both consciously and unconsciously, led finally to a more direct articulation of a dream continuum. There are 'dreams from above and dreams from below' (Freud 1925: 113) or later, dreams which 'arise either from the id or from the ego'. However, Freud's dream always 'finds reinforcement during sleep from an unconscious element' (Freud 1940: 168). As he wrote in *The Interpretation of Dreams*, the 'entrepreneur' of a daytime thought requires the 'capital' of a wish from the unconscious (Freud 1900: 561).

Writing in 1938, one year before his death, Freud offered a re-worked understanding of the dream from the point of view of the psychoanalytic practitioner:

> every dream that is in process of formation makes a demand upon the ego – for the satisfaction of an instinct, if the dream originates from the id; for the solution of a conflict, the removal of a doubt or the forming of an intention if the dream originates from a residue of preconscious activity in waking life. The sleeping ego, however, is focused on the wish to maintain sleep, it feels this demand as a disturbance and seeks to get rid of the disturbance. The ego succeeds in doing this by what appears to be an act of compliance: it meets the demand with what is in the circumstances a harmless fulfilment of a wish and so gets rid of it.
>
> (Freud 1940: 169–70)

Freud thus discloses how far he has come towards conceding theoretically the possibility of the ego's conflict-solving role in the formation of the dream, and how far he maintains that the central theme of every dream is disguised wish fulfilment. That is, Freud's dream is less than integration or synthesis or creativity or realistic problem solving. Nevertheless, the ground of dream interpretation has shifted: the dream, seen to reproduce conflict between dynamic agencies in the mind, corresponds with a psychoanalytic treatment no longer conceived as the unravelling of the unconscious desire but the strengthening of the ego against the claims of both the id and the superego (see Brenner, this volume).

For instruction on the use of dream interpretation within the process of psychoanalytic treatment, which is not the intention of Freud's major work, there can be no more useful introduction than Ella Freeman Sharpe's slim but brilliant volume, *Dream Analysis*. Gathered together from lectures to the British Society in the 1930s, she locates the dream within the psychoanalytic task, which she defines, following the later Freud, as the 'enlargement of the ego boundaries' in a 'complicated psychical readjustment achieved through the dynamics of transference'. A successful analysis results in an ego equipped to 'tolerate and deal with instinctual impulses in a rational and effective way within a socialized community, this being achieved proportionally to the modification of the unconscious super-ego' (Sharpe 1937: 17). Dream analysis is crucial to the process because 'assimilation of knowledge of the unconscious mind through the ego is an essential part of the psychical process'. More evocatively, bringing to her task the interpretive skills of literary appreciation, she describes the principle underlying all dream interpretation, 'the revelation of the unknown, implicit in the known, in terms of the individual' (p. 18). That is, the imagery of the dream derives from the experience it therefore discloses.

But this is not the only link between the dream and poetry. Ella Freeman Sharpe was the first to make the leap made famous by Lacan, locating in the imagery of the dream, in the mechanisms of the dream-work, the laws of poetic diction. Equating condensation and displacement with metaphor and metonymy as Lacan was to do later, she likened the dream to poetry and drama, therefore preservative and expressive of meaning. Condensation, like metaphor, implies sameness or likenesses, while displacement, like metonymy, implies a 'change of name' from one thing to another, from a whole to a part. In spite of this acknowledge-ment of the potential meaningfulness of dream imagery, she is none the less scrupulous in insisting on attention to the latent content, the thoughts hidden behind the visual image of the manifest content (p. 75). Like Freud, she is explicit in her suspicion of the use of the dream as resistance to psychoanalytic treatment. Although drawing a comparison between dream and art, she specifically alerts against the reading of the dream as a whole, therefore confirming, like Freud, the difference between a dream and a work of art. Adding to her continued relevance is Sharpe's clinically modern focus on the function of the dream within the unfolding transference, an emphasis which is consistent with most of the papers included here.

Writing her lectures for a British Society already well exposed to Melanie Klein's innovative use of play in the psychoanalysis of children, Sharpe likens the dream to children's play and to drama. Drawing on both Freud (1917: 223) and Klein, she equates the dream phenomenon with projections of the self (Sharpe 1937: 59), relating this to the objectification of an inner drama. The dream story and the patient's transference to the analyst are clearly linked, the dream personae and the process that Klein eventually called 'projective identification' (Klein 1946).

Having advanced an invitation to consider the revelatory function of the dream, Sharpe reminds the reader constantly of the duplicity fostered by the dream censor, and the obscurity deriving from the necessary translation of thought into visual imagery in the dreaming process.

8

These are the challenges to the interpreter: What in the dreaming process and in the dream telling leads to emotional growth, to an expanding awareness, and what is thrown up to protect whatever the present *modus vivendi* might be? The double task marks the privileged burden of the psychoanalyst: to achieve the often difficult balance between the 'willingness to suspect, the willingness to listen; the vow of rigour, the vow of obedience' (Ricoeur 1970). And of course, these are the reasons why the dreamer's associations are such important clues to the understanding of the dream.

Suspicion of the manifest content of the dream, such a consistent leitmotif in Freud's writing, became routinized in much psychoanalytic thinking. Against a potentially hackneyed failure to appreciate the positively adaptive ego functions usefully disclosed in the dream, therefore to miss important communication, Erik Erikson addressed his justly famous 1954 paper, 'The dream specimen in psychoanalysis'. Looking at Freud's Irma Dream, the first dream analyzed in *The Interpretation of Dreams*, the dream used to disclose the meaningfulness hidden beneath the fragments of the dream, Erikson examined the manifest content for what it revealed. Calling it more than a mere 'shell to the kernel', rather a 'reflection of the individual ego's peculiar time-space, the frame of reference for all its defenses, compromises and achievements' (Erikson 1954: 21), he argues for an aesthetic receptivity to the surface of the dream, the product of the dreaming ego. Bringing to the dream the ego psychologist's emphasis on the integrating and adaptive function of the ego, he discloses a dreaming ego struggling with the stress of creative work, conflicts of loyalty, the bearing of powerful conflicting emotions. Since Erikson's time, the Irma dream has been re-examined, by Shur (1966), by Greenberg (1978), by Mahoney (1977), each finding in the manifest content, or, in Mahoney's case, in the language of the dream telling, deep meaning in what is contained and expressed rather than in what is hidden by the dream imagery.

Writing in America in the 1940s and 1950s, Bertram Lewin, drawing on Freud's notion of the temporal as well as the topographical regression implicit in sleep and dream (Freud 1917: 22), opened up the exploration of the formal features of the dream, linking it to mental and emotional development in a way that continues to inspire psychoanalytic thought. As Freud drew the analogy between sleep and return to the womb, Lewin linked the dream and the 'screen' onto which it is projected with an internalized maternal breast, the individual's first object (Lewin 1946). With resonant effect, Lewin also linked the psychoanalytic situation to the phenomena of dreaming (1955). Again, following Freud, who has now been corroborated by the REM researchers, he noted the high level of arousal associated with dreaming (Jones 1970), and compared the rhythms of wakefulness and sleep, dreaming and non-dreaming sleep with the potentially awakening impact of the psychoanalyst. 'Inescapably', he wrote, 'the analyst is an arouser as well as a day residue ... the analyst continuously operates either to wake the patient somewhat or to put him to sleep a little, to soothe or to arouse' (Lewin 1955). Further, 'to be wakened is to be weaned, and as a variant, to be brought back to this world'.

The history of the analyst as hypnotist is perhaps controversially embedded in the language utilized here to describe the analytic role. However, the degree of internal safety necessary to sleep, to dream, then to awaken restored, like the degree of safety required to use the dream-telling experience constructively in the analytic setting, to depend creatively on the analyst, is implicit in this formulation. Likewise, the centrality of the transference is clarified and historically reconstructed, as is the idea of the analyst as protector of the unfolding disclosure which includes the progress of dream interpretation within the psychoanalytic process. Lewin's inspired notion of the dream screen remains a fertile conceptualization, advanced in this volume by Khan, Pontalis and Gammill. Lewin located the thread linking dream, psychoanalytic process, regression in the service of the ego, and creativity, with particular attention to the *boundaries* containing these processes. He is a key figure in the history of psychoanalytic attention to the phenomenon of dreaming: Unlike most other authors, Lewin's touchstone is the dream. In this way he differs from Klein, Winnicott, Bion, Lacan, all of whom have had a great influence on the development of psychoanalytic thinking but have focused more generally on the evolution and nature of symbolic processes and less specifically on dreaming.

Although he wrote relatively little about dreams directly, Winnicott wrote much and influentially about the evolution of the capacity to play, and his thinking on the development of this symbolic capacity has influenced the way many psychoanalysts attend to dream. The fact that the play of children is rich with emotional and symbolic significance was an important contribution to Melanie Klein's, one which has broadly supported the understanding of the communicative potential of the dream, the meaning contained in the imagery. Winnicott's subsequent enquiry into the development and function of play illuminates the dreaming function, its place in emotional and mental life, and in the psychoanalytic process. The capacity to play develops out of the child's relation to the mother, her original 'holding' of the infant's emotional intensity, her reflexive recognition or mirroring of the child's need, his psychic reality. This holding, together with the meeting of the infant's needs, leads in Winnicott's view to a temporary illusion of fusion which paradoxically sustains a growing capacity to bear the reality of separateness and the loss of omnipotence. The crucial step in Winnicott's view is attachment to concrete objects or special sounds or sights which come to stand for possession and union with the mother. The 'transitional object' sustains this illusion. From this experience develops the transitional activity or play, and the transitional space (Winnicott 1971) in which the evolving child can play.

Winnicott's emphasis, like Marion Milner's (Milner 1952) is on the creative necessity of illusion, the learning to play and dream within a transitional space that is protected, at least temporarily, from the invasion of reality. All cultural phenomena take place in transitional space, all creativity, either in a formally defined space, the boundaries of the page, the canvas, the stage, or internally, through the capacity to stage an inner play. The ability to suspend disbelief momentarily, to give the self up to sleep and dream or reverie or free association, depends on safety, on boundaries, on what Didier Anzieu has called a 'psychic envelope' (1989). Similarly, a capacity to own and reflect on a dream depends on the capacity for differentiation between the state of sleep and wakefulness, dream and reality, the symbolic and the concrete. The achievement in the analytic setting of the ability to use a dream becomes the focus of much of the writing in this volume.

Winnicott's enquiry into the development of the capacity to play is complemented by Bion's hypothesis regarding the development of a capacity to contain feelings and thought (Bion 1962a). Bion begins with the Kleinian concept of projective identification, and adds the idea of a mother who is receptive, can receive the raw intensity of the baby's projections, empathize and bear with them and so render them bearable and eventually containable by the baby. The baby internalizes the containing function, with it the mental space to think, to elaborate symbolically, or to perform what Bion calls alpha function (Bion 1962a). If the raw, distressed feelings are not attended to, received, contained and transformed by maternal attention, then the baby does not internalize the capacity to bear feeling, but is at the mercy of raw, unprocessed psychic events which later appear as psychotic thinking. The emphasis in Bion's view, following Klein, has much to do with the bearing of painful experience, rather less to do with pleasure, and this may be in keeping with the general trajectory of Freud's own thinking about the development of the ego, the importance of aggression, and the perils of dependency in the evolution of the psyche.

From this perspective on the dreaming function, best expressed in this volume by Hanna Segal, the power of wish fulfilment in dream or in the ego's relation to its objects is not denied, but is frequently evaluated along a continuum measuring the extremity of projective processes aimed at getting rid of, finally evacuating unacceptable or unbearable feeling.

11

Avoiding disturbing recognition is of course, according to Freud, the motive for much of the dream-work. Disguise, however, is a qualitatively different concept from the extreme projective evacuative processes observed by many Kleinians. Ultimately, these processes attack the differentiation between sleep and wakefulness, reality and phantasy,[1] primary and secondary process, and, in psychosis, shatter the fragile boundaries which fail to contain the dream-space.

The shift, therefore, in psychoanalytic attention to the early stages of ego development, particularly to the acquisition of the capacity to symbolize, has led to a greater focus on the potential achievement of the dreaming function. Generally psychoanalysts locate the dream-telling process on a better understood continuum of ego development, and in treatment, within a context attuned above all to these developments as they are manifest in the patient's transference and the analyst's counter-transference. This transference is understood in terms of earlier as well as later object relations, the dreads and desires which inform the very capacity to sleep, to dream, and then to recollect and tell the dream in a good-enough psychoanalytic situation. It is the psychoanalyst's privilege to bear witness to this remarkable achievement, to facilitate the reconstruction of the capacity when it is damaged, when the boundaries of the ego or 'psychic envelope' (Anzieu 1989) are too rigid or fragile or damaged to contain the dreaming process.

Why these papers?

This collection of papers, most of which first appeared in journals, have been gathered on historical and conceptual lines, and have been chosen either because in themselves they offer a specific contribution to the subject of dream interpretation, or because they offer a useful and relatively contemporary synthesis of a particular point of view.

M. Masud R. Khan begins this collection with an essay written in 1962, a concise examination of the relationship between the analytic process and classical dream psychology, the correspondence between the project of the analysis and the use of the dream in daily life. Drawing on Lewin and Kris, he gives a useful and rich summary of the ego strengths required both to produce a 'good' dream, which he proceeds to identify, and to surrender to the analytic process, to produce a 'good analytic hour' (Kris 1956). He lays a firm foundation on which to build an understanding of the propensity of the more disturbed patient to abuse or subvert the function of the dream and, correspondingly, to pervert or flee or attack the boundaries of the analytic setting and the project of the analysis. Many of the papers in the third and fourth parts of this collection derive from analytic experience with more disturbed and vulnerable patients. The writers consider the place of the dreaming function as it appears in the analyses of patients for whom the capacity to produce a 'good dream' or a 'good analytic hour' is only painstakingly won.

Although a number of instructive papers have been necessarily excluded from this limited collection, it is also the case that relatively few papers on dreaming have been produced in the last quarter century. As the state of the patient's ego has become more and more the focus of psychoanalytic thinking, and as the transference to the analyst has become the royal road to the understanding of the patient's emotional and mental life, the lessening centrality of dream interpretation to analytic practice has been reflected in a diminished number of papers devoted to it in the journals. In 1967, a distinguished group of American analysts, the Kris Study Group under the chairmanship of Charles Brenner, reported by Herbert Waldhorn, considered the place of dream in clinical practice (Waldhorn 1967). They came to the conclusion that the dream report is not such a unique form of communication. The logic of the structural theory of the personality, the differention of an id, ego and superego, all held in constant tension, implies the ubiquity of unconscious phantasy. Because unconscious phantasy is constantly pressurizing the ego, it informs all activity in everyday life, and every analytic communication (Waldhorn 1967).

Part Two presents two papers crucial to the argument about whether or not the dream should retain its special place in psychoanalysis. The findings of the Kris Study antedate the article by Brenner included here, which clearly puts the case for the demotion of the dream, along with the topographical model of the mind, as the foundation for psychoanalytical thinking. This point of view had its dissenters, perhaps none so distinguished as R.R. Greenson, whose paper included here represents a sharp rebuttal to the position so lucidly argued by Brenner. Greenson tackles what he regards as a recoiling from the disturbing richness of unconscious mentation. All communications are not equal: the best window into the internal world is the dream, the freest form of free association is the dream, the best access to early childhood experience and the best hope of awakening childhood memories come from the dream.

In this paper, Greenson turns his critical attention not only towards the analysts whom he regards as too fearful of the unconscious but also to those, here identified as Kleinian, who are in his view too convinced of their own understanding of unconscious phantasy, too sure of the dream symbolism, and, at least in written accounts, neglectful of the patient's associations, and therefore neglectful of the patient's own developing relationship to his unconscious processses. The patient's dream, whatever the analytic day residue, whatever the transference meaning, however familiar its symbolism might appear to the veteran analyst, is personal, the patient's own creation, an elaboration of his experience, the understanding of which an analysis attempts to build rather than impose. He quotes from Freud, who frequently inveighed against unscientific virtuosity in the interpretations of dream (Freud 1916: 151). Freud also observed that with knowledge of the dreamer's personality, knowledge of his life situation as well as the impressions of the day preceding a dream, dream interpretations could be made straightaway, with the aid of the analyst's familiarity with unconscious symbolism (Freud 1916: 151–2). Freud explicitly states, however, that such 'virtuosity' does not facilitate a patient's active engagement in the process of analysis, however much it might illuminate the journey for the analyst.

The papers grouped in Part Three are linked by preoccupation with symbolic processes in general, the relationship of these processes to the state of the ego and, particularly, to the relationship of dream interpretation to the psychoanlaysis of the dreamer. Informing the thinking of most of the writers in this section is familiarity with and, in some cases, a creative conflict with the work of Melanie Klein. Her investigation into the meaning of children's play provides the background not only to her contribution to the understanding of primitive anxieties and primitive defensive impediments to mental and emotional growth (Klein 1955), but also to the different and to some extent corrective contributions of Winnicott and Bion, who have in turn influenced the writers included here. To Klein's understanding of the rich symbolic significance of the child at play, Winnicott and Bion have added, crucially, a developmental understanding of this capacity, its evolution through primary relationship to the 'good enough' mother. What the child internalizes or learns through experience is the capacity to contain, to process instinctual elements, to think, wait, play and dream. Influenced by Winnicott, Masud Khan coined the term 'dream-space', and describes the evolution of the concept in an article included in this collection. It

> gradually crystallised from watching and studying Winnicott's therapeutic consultations with children where he uses the squiggle-game and which he has reported with such veracity and vividness in his book *Therapeutic Consultations in Child Psychiatry*. I began to discover in my clinical work with adults that they can use the dream-space in exactly the same way as the child uses the transitional space of the paper to doodle on. Furthermore, it was important for me to distinguish between the process of dreaming which articulated unconscious impulses and conflicts from the dream-space in which the dream actualises this experience.

The ability to own and use dream-space becomes an aim of the psychoanalytic process, and a sign of developing psychic health. Learning to use the dream-space is part of a process, a learning to accept and live with the privacy of the self, in Winnicottean terms, the 'true self'. The dreaming patient, like the playing child, is in this perspective sacred and separate, expressive as the Kleinian child, but valued above all for the individuality which it is the aim of the analysis simultaneously to recognize and bring alive.

Hanna Segal's paper emphasizes the constructive, 'working through' potential of the dream, and then from her Kleinian perspective she discloses the potential misuse of the dreaming function, notably in the analysis of very seriously disturbed borderline patients, those struggling with large psychotic elements in their personalities. For example, she shows how the dream-space can be used for splitting off and 'evacuating' significant emotional recognitions. She uses, to illuminating effect, the antithesis developed by Bion between projection and containment, thinking and acting out, working through and evacuation, and adds her own useful distinction between symbolism and symbolic equation. Informing her analysis of the dream in the analytic situation is the Kleinian emphasis on growth towards the 'depressive position', the fundamental emotional acceptance of the boundaries of self, the limitations of projective possibilities, the recognition of internal and external reality. To bring a dream to the analyst for analysis, not for evacuation is to accept the analytic project, including its limitations, its boundaries and, within it, the creative potential of its space. Such acceptance presents even the good neurotic with a considerable task of mourning, even as it offers the hope of realistic enrichment and growth.

The introduction and elaboration of the spatial metaphor in relation to thought, dream, play, emotional growth, marks a significant evolution in the history of psychoanalytic thought. It adds an important formal dimension to the understanding of the analytic process, and supports a claim for the particular usefulness of the analytic setting, as Masud Khan articulates so well in the first paper in this collection. To be privileged to use what Marion Milner calls the 'framed space' of the analytic setting (Milner 1952, 1957) is to be provided with the opportunity to re-engage with the fundamental task of investigating and mending the containing capacity of the ego within a context which itself supplies a model. Pontalis's paper 'Dream as object', carries this formal, fundamentally aesthetic preoccupation one step further. He emphasizes the added boundaries as well as the reconnection with the experience of boundlessness realized in the bringing of a dream to the analyst. The dream brought, which is never the dream in itself, binds and separates the analyst in an important way, one which 'protects' both analyst and analysand from too

15

much interpenetration. The dream insists on the patient's privacy and mystery, the limits of interpretation, even of the transference. Here Pontalis, repeating Winnicott's emphasis on the space between mother and child, analyst and patient, argues against the interpretive terrorism he thinks endangers the Kleinian way of knowing transference manifestations. It is interesting that he never refers to Bion in this article, whose concept of the maternal, then internalized containing function restores the boundaries to intersubjectivity.

Implicit in Pontalis's paper is the history of the concept of cultural and mental space as it has evolved in psychoanalysis out of observations of children playing. Indeed, the article by Pontalis is saturated with allusion, rarely explicitly noted, to the history of dream interpretation within the analytic process. He has his own ideas to offer about the potential for perverting the process of dream interpretation, which in itself, he reminds us, following Freud, might be an abuse of the dreaming function. The necessary ambiguity of the dream's meaning is related to Pontalis's hypothesis, that 'every dream refers to the maternal body in so far as it is an object in the analysis', and of course an object suffused with the dangers of the infinite and the incestuous. The dream screen and the modality of the visible image have facilitating and defensive properties: the visible implies distance, object–relatedness rather than objectlessness. The dream screen inscribes the boundary that is the 'protective shield' to traumatic overwhelming, the boundary which the analyst, it is implied, must observe or, as Segal, Khan, Stewart, Gammill and Anzieu disclose, must help to bring into being or repair.

Two papers in this section describe analyses in which the dream reclaims its potential function: Harold Stewart's paper describes the evolution of the capacity to dream in conjunction with the patient's developing dependency on her analyst. The relationship between the dreaming capacity corresponds to the entirely convincing growth of the ego which mirrors the shift in the transference. It is a very concise description of an analytic process, illuminating the interrelationship between the patient's growing involvement with her analyst and her relationship to her dreams.

Gammill's later paper casts a wide theoretical net in his exploration of the ego growth of a young schizoid man who was unable to dream until after his analyst helped him to reclaim the parts of himself he had been unable to bear. Analytic listening and interpreting, operating along the lines of Bion's conception of maternal containment, fosters the internalization of a containing function in the patient. Here Gammill links this container to Lewin's concept of a dream screen which he also enriches by understanding it in relation to the skin experiences of the early mother–child relationship. As Gammill points out, Lewin touched on all these

16

elements in his writing on dreams and the analytic situation. There is much scope for elaboration, as Anzieu indicates in the last paper in this section.

Entitled 'The film of the dream', Didier Anzieu's contribution is a chapter out of his book translated as *The Skin Ego*. He draws the analogy between the 'psychic envelope' of the skin ego, a concept which he has very profoundly elaborated, and the dream screen, called dream–film, which he terms a 'visual envelope'. Its function, as he sees it, is to provide for the repair of ruptures made in the skin ego during the day, damage which he postulates, like Ferenczi, to be implicit in daily functioning. He describes an analysis in which the appearance of dreams follows a recognition of the patient's confused and impinged–upon boundaries. Following an important realization in her analysis, the dreams of this patient suddenly proliferate, significantly excluding even her analyst from what he views as an important moment in her psychic growth. The boundaries of intersubjectivity are re-established, or, in the body language which is Anzieu's particular contribution, her dreams weave a 'new psychical skin to replace her deficient protective shield'. He thus describes the return of the self and the dream to a conceptually enriched body ego (Freud 1923), as well as to a conceptually enriched 'protective shield' (Freud 1920).

The papers in the fourth part of this volume are marked by the tradition of ego psychology. I am including the self psychologists' contribution within this frame of reference, as this is the context out of which self psychology developed. Significantly, both ego and self psychologists have moved towards appreciation of the meaning contained rather than disguised in the manifest content of the dream. Hartmann's emphasis on the importance of the ego's adaptive function with specific reference to reality, so influential in America, informs this intellectual development (Hartmann 1939; Greenberg and Mitchell 1983). Greenson's paper from Part Two clearly protests against this shift in psychoanalytic thinking, towards the ego's function in the mastering of reality, and arguably away from the id, the instinctual life, the deeper layers of the mind. The shift, whatever its potential for distorting a fundamental psychoanalytical preoccupation, has provided the basis for fresh thinking about dreams.

Perhaps most relevant to the papers included in the last part of this collection is Erikson's watershed article on 'The dream specimen of psychoanalysis' (1954), in which he shows the rich adaptive allusions in the manifest content of Freud's 'Irma' dream. Erikson also placed the problem of identity at the centre of psychoanalytic consideration. Although this thread of concern carries into that stream of psychoanalytic thinking which takes the integrity of the self as a central focus of the analytic process and an important factor in thinking about the meaning and function of dreams, this aspect of Erikson's perspective is not rewarded with reference in this collection. Kohut's more radical orientation to the self appears to have superseded it (see Stolorow and Atwood, this collection). Likewise, Mark Kanzer's intriguingly object-relational approach to the dreaming phenomenon, linking the importance of the internal object both to the formation of the dream and to the communication of the dream to the analyst (1955) relates more directly to the papers in Part Three than to those which have appeared in America in the last twenty-five years.

If attention to internalized object relations and to symbolic and communicative processes does not link the papers in Part Four as it does so markedly in the preceding selection, the directly related question of the manifest content of the dream, in particular its expressive and integrative function, is a remarkably consistent feature. It is worth noting that Erikson, an artist, was impressed like his English counterparts with the rich symbolic meaningfulness of children's play (Erikson 1954). Erikson's analytic training came, however, from Anna Freud, rather than Melanie Klein (Young-Bruehl 1989: 176), and he practised in America, where ego psychology and its emphasis on adaptive ego functioning dominated the psychoanalytic culture. His thesis on the significance of manifest content, informed by his artistic receptivity to the meaningfulness of children's play, amounts to an open argument with Freud, who emphasized so consistently the dangers of being seduced into analyzing directly from manifest content.

The first two papers in this section take some aspect of the manifest dream and its usefulness in the clinical situation as the starting point. Spanjaard's admirably thorough paper offers a very useful history of Freud's attitude to manifest content and of subsequent developments, including the extreme, problem-solving approach to dream interpretation, which, however remote from psychoanalytical preoccupations, has had a major influence in America (French and Fromm 1964). Spanjaard argues that the surface of the dream is the place from which the patient is starting, therefore the most accessible point of contact with the current conflict. He supports his argument with a careful assessment of the contradictions within Freud's analysis of his own dreams, noting the central presence, for example, of meaningful ego feeling in all Freud's dreams. Spanjaard calls upon the evidence of the dream laboratory to substantiate the attention paid to the meaning disclosed rather than disguised by manifest content, and this trend is continued in the paper by Greenberg and Pearlman. They utilize evidence from the material of a man who spends nights in the dream laboratory and hours in analysis. To their analytic eyes the night and day tasks of the ego look remarkably similar, although the language of the dream is different, uniquely personal. Following Joffe and Sandler (1968), Greenberg and Pearlman see the ego at work in the dream to create

18

new organizations of the ideal state of self in order to preserve a feeling of safety and to avoid the experience of being traumatically overwhelmed . . . . That these previous ideal states are not always so easily abandoned contributes to the appearance of infantile wishes and the wish fulfilment aspect of dreaming.

When Cecily de Monchaux asks why patients bring dreams, her answers, cast again in the ego psychologist's terms of organization and mastery, find all kinds of good, adaptive reasons. As one patient put it to her, dreams, because of their dissociative characteristics, can bear the unbearable, take some of the 'load', push transference feeling into the past of last night, constructively split off meaning until re-integration is possible. It is a good and useful form of splitting, a creative disassociation, a modification of responsibility and a distancing of emotional experience which makes for recognizing 'en route to reconciling, the two sides which are intrinsic to any argument in the unconscious'. Cecily de Monchaux's paper has taken many of the defensive and potentially negative features of ego activity as identified by Kleinian thinkers – in particular, the evacuative function of the dream – and found its constructive, adaptive uses. She views it as a step in progressive integration, in Winnicott's terms, a transitional activity. Her paper provides, I think, a nice comparison with the paper by Pontalis, who uses very different language and references to emphasize similarly the usefulness of the dream's distance from the psychoanalyst and the psychoanalysis, however suffused with the analytic experience it may be.

The concept of mastery has become linked in the thinking of the self psychologists to the idea of binding, literally into the shape of a manifest dream image, the otherwise nameless dread of traumatic psychic dissolution, psychosis. This idea has born some fruit amongst more classical psychoanalytic thinkers, nowhere in more accessible form than in a paper by Socarides (1980) on 'Perverse symptoms and the manifest dream of perversion', which appears in a relatively recent and very variable collection of American papers on dream (Natterson 1980). In a later and theoretically ambitious paper, Stolorow and Atwood address this phenomenon as an intensification of something generally true of dreaming, the adaptive function of the hallucinatory vividness of the dream image. Looking for a psychological purpose in the dream hallucination itself, they conjecture that the function of the imagery, which is experienced as real, is to 'solidify the nuclear organising structures of the dreamer's subjective life'. This function overcomes all others, including the elaboration of conflicted wishes when the self is threatened with disintegration or psychosis. That is, perceiving, as does, for example, Hanna Segal (this volume) the confluence of concretized dream imagery and disintegration of ego boundaries, they identify a different function for the concretization. They see this phenomenon as an attempt at intensifying a sense of identity, or self, not as a product of the breakdown of the relationship between self and object, the symbol and the symbolized. For the self psychologist, repetitive dreams, like ritualized, masochistic or bizarre actions, are viewed as efforts to shore up a disintegrated sense of self, however omnipotently or compulsively or cruelly. Following the progress of a psychoanalytic psychotherapy, Stolorow and Atwood observe a patient's evolution toward a capacity to give up some of her omnipotence and cruelty, to symbolize, to use words in a therapeutic relationship. Interestingly, this paper does not identify how the analyst is used by the patient, what in the process of the psychoanalytic therapy facilitates this movement, nor do the authors make much of the violently destructive nature of the patient's material.

In conclusion

If the articles collected here testify to the heterogeneity of psychoanalytical thinking on the subject of the uses of the dream in the unfolding process of a psychoanalysis, they do not, I think, produce a chaos of intellectually indigestible material. Although the papers are selected from different psychoanalytic traditions, shaped by different historical developments and intellectual climates, all are rooted in the work of Freud. All share a chronological distance from the time, long before the death of Freud, when psychoanalysis could almost be equated with a technique of dream interpretation, when an analyst waited expectantly for the dream's exclusive message from the unconscious without which no analysis seemed possible (Sharpe 1937: 66). Today, few would disagree with Brenner's observation that unconscious phantasy is ubiquitous and expressed through symptoms, language, gesture – indeed, in every sphere of everyday life. Moreover, the focus of a contemporary analysis is emphatically the dreamer, not the dream. The aim of an analysis is to facilitate emotional growth through understanding derived principally from the interplay of the transference and counter-transference. Stated more classically, the psychoanalytic process fosters the development and resolution of a transference neurosis, and it is this process which is the fundamental concern of the analyst.

It was Freud who located in the interpretation of the transference the essential psychoanalytic activity, the context into which the dream report is inserted and becomes meaningful. It was also Freud who established the developmental conceptualization of the ego which has been so fruitful in subsequent thinking about the capacity to use the analytic situation, as well as to dream a 'good', or analytically useful, dream. Finally, it was Freud who recognized the impingement of trauma and the centrality of anxiety in the structuring of the psychic organization. It is that structure which reveals itself in an analysis, in the dreams disclosed within it, or not, and in the patient's use of the dreaming function within the unfolding process.

Although most analysts would agree that the dream has lost its unequivocal centrality in the analytic endeavour, it remains true not only that most analysts pay particular attention to a dream report, but that the dream has a special place in the professional discourse: very few psychoanalytic papers which use illustrative clinical material do not include the analysis of a dream. Writers of such papers know that their colleagues want to hear about dreams: psychoanalysts understand that the patient locates himself in a particular way in a psychoanalysis by his way of bringing a dream and that through that dream, the patient is most likely to speak for himself, often to the detriment of an impressively marshalled clinical argument.

Regarding Freud's classical insistence on associations prior to interpretation, the ground has shifted, although the principles behind this dictum are still stoutly defended (Greenson, this volume; Blum 1976). There are few examples in the literature of the kind of analysis Freud recommended chiefly for self-analysis, which is to 'proceed chronologically and get the dreamer to bring up his associations to the elements of the dream in the order in which those elements occurred in the account of the dream' (Freud 1923: 109). By 1923, this was for Freud only one of several approaches, the freest of which was to leave the patient to make whatever association came to mind. This, of course, is not to understand the transference situation or psychoanalytical context as the most fundamental association, a common procedure today, though lamented by some (Greenson, this volume), particularly if it precludes associations to memories of childhood events which are more likely to be awakened by asking for associations to specific dream material (Palombo 1984).

The English and continental papers on dream included here disclose with some consistency a dream understood to be relevatory of the object relations lived out between analyst and patient in the psychoanalytic process. The dream in the psychoanalytic context reveals fundamental strengths and weaknesses in the patient's capacity to bear the burden of emotional life, to accept the boundaries of separate identity, to symbolize, to use the analytic setting, to regress in the service of the ego (Kris 1950, 1956). The papers in Part Three address these problems directly and fruitfully. For the clinician they offer satisfying illustrations of theoretical and therapeutic interplay. We see how the psychoanalysis is moving; we discover the links between an understanding of the dreaming process and the psychoanalysis itself. We observe the developing capacity for intrapsychic communication and, with it, a healthier, less omnipotent ego.

There has been less consistency in the evolution of thinking about dream in America, and this in spite of the pioneering centrality of Lewin, the American trained in Berlin in the 1920s. His concern for the relation between dream psychology and the potentialities of the psychoanalytic situation has migrated back to the Old World and settled more deeply into the synthesis which has developed there (see Khan, this volume).

The American development has been influenced most by the ego psychology which flourished in the 1950s and 1960s, and it is the effect of this development which is tackled by Greenson in his paper of 1970. In the debate between Brenner and Greenson, we see the tension polarized between Greenson's insistence on the uniqueness of the dream report, 'the freest free association', its closeness to the instinctual derivatives of early childhood, and the cooler logic of Brenner. Against Greenson's emphasis on the instinctual life and the unconscious, Brenner argues that the dream is but another product of the ubiquitous balancing act of the ego, the beleaguered master of both id and superego. Greenson's influential paper, essentially conservative of the richness of psychoanalytic tradition and the special place of the dream in psychoanalysis, spawned little fresh development in the American canon. He was apparently supportive of European efforts to look again at the dream phenomena (Curtis and Sachs 1976).

The ego-psychological viewpoint, centring on the synthesizing ego and its adaptive relation to reality, informs the respect, introduced by Erikson, for the manifest content of dream. Spanjaard's essay, included in this volume, develops this theme, as does the paper by Greenberg and Pearlman. Like so much of the other REM-related laboratory research (Jones 1970; Palombo 1978), Greenberg and Pearlman's paper testifies to the adaptive mental work of the ego in dream, as disclosed in the manifest material. Arrayed against these advances, the strong classical tradition in America regularly reaffirms the danger, as did Freud, of over-emphasizing the manifest content at the expense of the latent concerns (Blum 1976), the defensive disguises and the wish-fulfilling function of dreaming.

However, it is in the attention to the manifest content of the dream, as well as to the variety of constructive or organizing uses made by the ego of the dreaming capacity, that the ego and later the self psychologists included in this volume make their separate way to an enriched understanding of the uses of the dream, both in the mastery of anxiety and in the maintenance of identity. Here, as amongst the object-relations analysts who have focused on the dream, there is a reciprocal enrichment in the understanding of the integrative capacities and fundamental weaknesses of the archaic ego which are disclosed in a particular way in the bringing of dreams to analysis.

Having said this, I think it is wise to end on a note in keeping with Pontalis, who reminds us that the dream retains an essential mystery, however demystified its potential. It confronts the analyst with the limits of the knowable, an awareness of the infinite (Matte-Blanco 1975), the ambiguity which the project of a psychoanalysis attempts to frame and to fathom. It is better done with respect for its inevitable incompleteness.

Note

1 Generally, the spelling 'phantasy' as opposed to 'fantasy' has been adopted by English but not American writers when referring to 'the imaginative activity which underlies all thought and feeling' (Rycroft 1968). Throughout this collection, the authors' original spellings have been preserved.

References

Anzieu, Didier (1986) *Freud's Self Analysis*, London: Hogarth.

—— (1989) *The Skin Ego*, London: Yale.

Bion, Wilfred (1962a) 'A theory of thinking', *International Journal of Psycho-Analysis* 43: 306–10.

—— (1962b) *Learning from Experience*, London: Heinemann; reprinted in paperback, Maresfield Reprints, London: H. Karnac Books (1984).

Blum, Harold (1976) 'The changing use of dreams in psychoanalytic practice: dreams and free association', *International Journal of Psycho-Analysis* 57: 315–24.

Bollas, Christopher (1987) 'At the other's play: to dream', in *The Shadow of the Object: Psychoanalysis of the Unthought Known*, London: Free Association Books.

Breuer, Joseph and Freud, Sigmund (1895) *Studies on Hysteria*, SE11.

Curtis, Homer and Sachs, David (1976) 'Dialogue on the changing use of dreams in psychoanalytic practice', *International Journal of Psycho-Analysis* 57: 343–54.

Erikson, Erik H. (1950) *Childhood and Society*, New York: W.W. Norton & Co.

—— (1954) 'The dream specimen of psychoanalysis', *Journal of the American Psychoanalytical Association* 2: 5–56.

—— (1959) *Identity and the Life Cycle*, New York: International Universities Press.

Ferenczi, S. (1931) 'On the revision of *The Interpretation of Dreams*', *Final Contributions to the Problems and Methods of Psychoanalysis*, London: Hogarth (1955).

Fosshage, James (1983) 'The psychological function of dreams: a revised psychoanalytic perspective', *Psychoanalysis and Contemporary Thought* 6: 4, 641–69.

French, T.M. and Fromm, E. (1964) *Dream Interpretation*, New York: Basic Books.

Freud, Sigmund (1900) *The Interpretation of Dreams, Standard Edition of the Complete Psychological Works of Sigmund Freud*, SE 4/5, London: Hogarth Press (1950–70).

—— (1916) *Introductory Lectures on Psychoanalysis*, SE 15.

—— (1917) 'Metapsychological supplement to the theory of dreams', SE 14.

—— (1920) *Beyond the Pleasure Principle*, SE 18.

—— (1923) *The Ego and the Id*, SE 19.

—— (1925) 'Some additional notes on dream interpretation as a whole', SE 19.

—— (1931) Preface to the third (revised) English edition of *The Interpretation of Dreams*, SE 4: xxxi.

—— (1932) 'Revision of *The Interpretation of Dreams*', Lecture XXLV, New Introductory Lectures, SE 22.

—— (1940) *An Outline of Psycho-analysis*, SE 23.

Garma, Angel (1966) *The Psychoanalysis of Dreams*, London: Pall Mall Press.

—— (1974) *The Psychoanalysis of Dreams*, New York: Jason Aronson.

Green, André (1975) 'The analyst, symbolization and absence in the analytic setting (on changes in analytic practice and analytic experience)', *International Journal of Psycho-Analysis* 56: 1–21.

Greenberg, Jay R. and Mitchell, Stephen A. (1983) *Object Relations in Psychoanalytic Theory*, Cambridge, MA: Harvard University Press.

Greenberg, R. and Pearlman, C. (1978) 'If Freud only knew: a reconsideration of psychoanalytic dream theory', *International Review of Psycho-Analysis* 5: 71–5.

Hartmann, H. (1939) *Ego Psychology and the Problem of Adaptation*, New York: International Universities Press.

Joffe, W.G. and Sandler, J. (1968) 'Comments on the psychoanalytic psychology of adaptation', *International Journal of Psycho-Analysis* 49: 445–54.

Jones, R.M. (1970) *The New Psychology of Dreaming*, New York: Grune & Stratton.

Kanzer, Mark (1955) 'The communicative function of the dream', *International Journal of Psycho-Analysis* 36: 260–6.

Khan, Masud (1974) *The Privacy of the Self*, London: Hogarth.

Klein, Melanie (1946) 'Notes on some schizoid mechanisms', in *The Writings of Melanie Klein*, vol. III, London: Hogarth.

—— (1955) 'The psycho-analytic play technique: its history and significance', in *Envy and Gratitude and Other Works*, London: Hogarth.

Kohut, H. (1971) *The Analysis of the Self*, New York: International Universities Press.

—— (1977) *The Restoration of the Self*, New York: International Universities Press.

Kris, Ernst (1950) 'On preconscious mental processes', *The Psychoanalytic Quarterly* 19: 540–56.

—— (1956) 'On some vicissitudes of insight in psychoanalysis', *International Journal of Psycho-Analysis* 37: 445–55.

Laplanche, J. and Pontalis, J.B. (1973) *The Language of Psycho-Analysis*, London: Hogarth.

Lewin, Bertram (1946) 'Sleep, the mouth and the dream screen', *The Psychoanalytic Quarterly* 15: 419–34.

—— (1955) 'Dream psychology and the analytic situation', *The Psychoanalytic Quarterly* 25: 169–99.

Mahoney, Patrick (1977) 'Towards a formalist approach to dreams', *International Review of Psycho-Analysis* 4: 83–98.

Matte-Blanco, Ignacia (1975) *The Unconscious as Infinite Sets*, London: Duckworth.

—— (1988) *Thinking, Feeling and Being*, London: New Library of Psychoanalysis.

Milner, Marion (1952) 'The role of illusion in symbol formation', in *New Directions in Psychoanalysis*, London: Tavistock.

—— (1957) *On Not Being Able to Paint*, London: Heinemann.

Natterson, Joseph (1980) *The Dream in Clinical Practice*, New York: Jason Aronson.

Palombo, Stanley (1978) 'The adaptive function of dreams', *Psychoanalysis and Contemporary Thought* 1.

—— (1984) 'Deconstructing the manifest dream', *Journal of the American Psychoanalytic Association* 32: 405–20.

Ricoeur, Paul (1970) *Freud and Philosophy*, London: Yale University Press.

Rycroft, Charles (1968) *A Critical Dictionary of Psychoanalysis*, London: Thomas Nelson & Sons.

Sandler, Joseph (1976) 'Dreams, unconscious fantasies and identity of perception', *International Review of Psycho-analysis* 3: 33–41.

Sharpe, Ella Freeman (1937) *Dream Analysis*, London: Hogarth (1978).

Shur, M. (1966) 'Some additional "day residues" of the specimen dream of psychoanalysis', on R. Loewenstein *et al.* (eds) *Psychoanalysis: A General Psychology*, New York: International Universities Press.

Socarides, Charles (1980) 'Perverse symptoms and the manifest dream of perversion', in *Joseph Natterson (ed.) The Dream in Clinical Practice*, New York: Jason Aronson.

Tolpin, Paul (1983) 'Self psychology and the Interpretation of Dreams', in Arnold Goldberg (ed.), *The Future of Psychoanalysis*, New York: International Universities Press.

Waldhorn, Herbert F. (1967) *Reporter: Indications for Psychoanalysis: The Place of Dreams in Clinical Psychoanalysis*. Monograph II of the Kris Study Group of the New York Psychoanalytic Institute, Edward P. Joseph (ed.) New York: International Universities Press.

Winnicott, D.W. (1971) *Playing and Reality*, London: Tavistock Publications.

Young-Bruehl, Elisabeth (1989) *Anna Freud*, London: Macmillan.

PART ONE

The psychoanalytic dream:
the psychoanalytic process

Masud Khan's paper of 1962, Chapter 1, the earliest in this collection, describes the conceptual relationship between Freud's dream psychology and the psychoanalytical situation. He develops Bertram Lewin's analogy of analysand and dreamer, the regression implicit in sleep and in the submission to analytic endeavour, and the opposing correspondence between the awakening process contained by the dream and the arousal caused by the stirring of the transference. Drawing on Kris's concept of the 'good analytic hour', he enumerates the ego's complex achievement in producing a 'good' dream, a dream which facilitates intrapsychic communication and, in treatment, analytic work. At the end of the chapter, he touches on a theme which surfaces in many of the chapters which follow, a much more primitive use of dream, both intraphysically and within the psychoanalytic process.

---- 1 ----

Dream psychology and the evolution of the psychoanalytic situation

M. MASUD R. KHAN

Freud's self-analysis and the discovery of the analytic situation

Jones (1953) in his biography of Freud tells us: 'Two important parts of Freud's researches are intimately connected with his self-analysis: the interpretation of dreams, and his growing appreciation of infantile sexuality' (p. 320). Kris also stressed this in his introduction to the Fliess Letters (p. 33). What has not been sufficiently pointed out is that the unique gain to the science of psychoanalysis from Freud's self-analysis, which he undertook in the summer of 1897 and kept up for a lifetime, was the invention of the analytic situation as the therapeutic and research instrument towards the understanding and resolution of another person's intrapsychic unconscious conflicts, which are symbolized and epitomized in his symptoms and illness. Freud's self-analysis was conducted on two parallel lines: (a) through interpretation of his dreams; and (b) through empathy and insight into his clinical experience with patients. This latter was an old bias of Freud's temperament. As early as 29 October 1882 he had written to his fiancée: 'I always find it uncanny when I can't understand someone in terms of myself' (Jones 1953: 320).

Freud's self-analysis not only gave us his monumental work on dreams and the theories of infantile sexuality as well as hypotheses on the aetiology of neuroses in infantile psychic life, but it essentially and irreversibly changed the aim of therapeutic endeavours. The invention of the analytic situation changed the goal of analytic process. As Szasz (1957) pertinently states: 'The goal of helping the patient became subsidiary to the goal of scientific understanding.' It was this shift in the direction and intention of Freud's therapeutic procedure that was in time going to earn him as much hostility and criticism from his own disciples as earlier on his theories

29

of dream-mechanisms and infantile sexuality had laid him open to from society at large. Most, if not all, of the later defections amongst his disciples (Jung, Adler, Rank, Reich, Reik, and so on) in one way or another centred round the therapist's eagerness to help the patient at the cost of sponsoring insight and understanding. Freud himself was most acutely aware of this resistance among his followers, and with this in view, in his address to the 5th International Psycho-Analytic Congress at Budapest in 1919, he explicitly formulated the basic task of the analytic situation as being

> to bring to the patient's knowledge the unconscious, repressed impulses existing in him, and for that purpose to uncover the resistances that oppose this extension of his knowledge about himself . . . our hope is to achieve this by exploiting the patient's transference to the person of the physician, so as to induce him to adopt our conviction of the inexpediency of the repressive process established in childhood and of the impossibility of conducting life on the pleasure principle. . . . Analytic process should be carried through, as far as is possible, under privation – in a state of abstinence. . . . As far as his rela-tions with the physicians are concerned, the patient must be left with unfulfilled wishes in abundance. It is expedient to deny him precisely those satisfactions which he desires most intensely and expresses most importunately.

> (Freud 1919)

For a comparison of the therapeutic aims one has only to glance at the concluding paragraph of *Studies on Hysteria* (Freud and Breuer 1893–5), where Freud promises the patient 'help or improvement' by means of a cathartic treatment' towards transforming 'hysterical misery into common unhappiness' (p. 305).

If it is true that it was Freud's self-analysis that led him to the invention of the analytic situation, then we should look more carefully for clues in that direction for a clearer understanding of the analytic situation. I hasten to add that I am not proposing a re-analysis of Freud's subjective data. That would be not only impertinent but utterly futile. Freud has done that for us, and in Jones's apt phrase, 'once it is done forever'.

How hard Freud had to struggle to maintain the determination to understand the mysterious workings of his own psyche has been most vividly described by Eissler (1951):

> Freud was able to lift his own repressions solely by his own efforts. . . . It is therefore true of Freud's self-analysis that as a type of psychological and historical event it can never be duplicated; it is a type of event which is represented only by a single occurrence

unique in its kind, and incapable of being repeated by any other person. ... The process of self-analysis, at the point of human history when Freud conducted it, was, so to speak, against human nature.

What enabled Freud to transform this heroic subjective experience of self-analysis ('this analysis is harder than any other' (Freud 1954)) into a therapeutic procedure was his genius for abstraction, which led him to recreate all the vital elements of the dreamer's situation in the analytic setting, so that in a wakeful conscious state the person in analysis can psychically *re-experience* through transference-neurosis the unconscious psychic disturbances and states of arrest that are distorting his ego-functioning and affective freedom.

Furthermore, it was Freud's most fateful discovery from his own experience of self-analysis, and from his insight into the use he had made of his relation with Fliess during this period, that this re-experience through transference-neurosis is only possible if there is another person available who, by lending himself as an object and his ego-support, can help the patient to express and work through personal conflicts to a therapeutic point of self-integration. One could almost put it that Freud's self-analysis revealed to him the impossibility of such a self-analysis for most human beings and compelled him to create a setting and the means of a relationship where this could be achieved.

The hypothesis that I am offering towards the genetic sources of the analytic setting in terms of Freud's self-analysis is that through the analysis of his own dreams and empathy with the clinical experiences of his patients in the hypnotic and cathartic situations of treatment, Freud intuitively recreated a physical and psychic ambience in the analytic setting which corresponds significantly to that intrapsychic state in the dreamer which is conducive to a 'good dream'. I shall later detail the ego-aspects of this intrapsychic state.

Hypnotic situation, dream psychology and the analytic situation

The regressive incentive of the analytic situation and its relation to the hypnotic situation and sleep states has been discussed often (cf. Lewin, Fisher, Gill and Brenman, Macalpine, Fliess, and so on). Lewin, in particular, in a series of stimulating and provocative papers has discussed the bearing of the derivation of the analytic situation for the hypnotic one. He has attempted (1955) 'to project upon the couch and the analytic situation the idea that the patient is as if somewhat asleep' and elaborated:

genetically, the analytic situation is an altered hypnotic situation ...
sleep, excluded by agreement from the analytic situation, gained access
to it in another form — the method of free associations ... the wish
to be put to sleep, which the patient brought to the hypnotic situation,
has been supplanted by the wish to associate freely in the analytic
situation. The patient lies down, not to sleep, but to associate. ...
The narcissism of sleep ... coincides with narcissism on the couch.
The manifest dream text coincides with the manifest analytic material.
... Dream-formation is to be compared with 'analytic-situation'
formation.

Lewin, following Rank (but judiciously) sees in this regressive repetition
'the direct experience of the baby in the nursing situation'. Lewin pointed
out, however (as had Kris), that 'attention to the interpretation of contents
and the dream world has distracted us, here too, from the problem of
sleep and from a consideration of the analytic subject as a fractional dreamer
or sleeper. ... The patient on the couch was prima facie a neurotic person
and only incidentally a dreamer.'

In psychoanalytic literature three aspects of sleep have been often
discussed:

1 Sleep as a biological need (Freud (1900–1917) and the dream's function
   of maintaining sleep.
2 Sleep as a regressive defence reaction in the analytic situation against
   aggressive, masochistic and passive impulses which threaten the ego's
   equilibrium of defences (cf. Bird (1954); Ferenczi (1914); Stone (1947),
   etc.).
3 Regression in sleep as recapturing the ontological phases of infancy
   development and the infant's primary relation to the breast (Isakower
   (1938); Lewin (1955), Spitz (1955), etc.).

The relation of the sleep-wish and its regressive defence derivatives to
the wish for cure and ego's cathexis of consciousness (self-awareness) have
been relatively neglected. Lewin (1955), discussing the evolution of the
analytic situation from the hypnotic treatment, pertinently states:

It was during the transition from hypnotic treatment to catharsis and
analysis that the neurotic patient changed from being a hypnotic subject
to being a confider, and the therapist *pari passu* became a psycho-analyst.
... The magical sleep-maker became a confidant, and the analytic
situation arrived in history. ... The inference is that the analyst is
a waker.

It is my impression that we have not, as yet, done full justice to the
implications of this most significant change in the therapist's rôle, from

hynotizer to 'the arouser' (Lewin 1955). When Freud respected the patient's resistances, rather than magically getting them out of the way through hypnotic sleep, he was starting a new process in the development of human consciousness, a process which bridged the split between the conscious and the unconscious. By crediting that in the patient's ego there was more co-operativeness available for cure besides the wish to be hypnotized, and guided by his observations in self-analysis, he created the analytic situation where the patient through the analyst's help could become just as receptive as in his sleep to dreams or as in the hypnotic state to the repressed content. To express it cryptically, whereas the rationale of the hypnotic therapy had been to induce 'dream-states' which the patient could then be confronted with – namely, where the patient was put to sleep in order to 'dream' and in the final stages to be woken up and be enabled to recall and remember 'the dream' of the hypnotic state – in the altered and new analytic situation the analyst helped the patient's conscious ego in its task of reclaiming the repressed and the unconscious. Once Freud had changed the basic tool of the therapeutic process from hypnotic sleep to conscious recall, with all the attendant resistances in the ego against relaxing its repressions, the very nature of the therapeutic situation and the analyst's rôle changed. New areas of psychic activity became available to the therapeutic process. For example, what had so far been seen only as the restricting influence of the censor in dream formation (Freud 1900) now became clinically accessible as the resistances in the patient to the analytic process. In due course this was to yield us profound insight into the pathogenic functions of the archaic and sadistic superego in severely disturbed character-neuroses.

Wakefulness, sleep and the analytic situation

Dream psychology, which has taught us so much about the unconscious processes and primitive id contents of the human psyche, has, however, left us relatively in the dark about the nature of sleep itself and its psychological meaning for the human being. The wish to go to sleep and the wish to wake up have been somewhat taken for granted as man's natural necessities, both by the psychoanalysts and by the biologists. Here I can only briefly refer to the valuable researches of a few analysts who have given this complex and mysterious problem their attention; namely, those of Jekels (1945), Federn (1934), Grotjahn (1942) and Scott (1956). For us what is significant to point out here is the clinical fact that observations of the oscillations of sleep and wakefulness in the analytic situation have thrown some valuable light on the wish for cure and the willingness to keep awake and free-associate in the analytic situation. Clifford Scott's contributions (1952, 1960) towards the understanding of this problem are particularly valuable, since he has extended the hypotheses of Jekels, Isakower and Federn to the direct examination of rhythms of sleep and wakefulness in the analytic situation. Scott's hypothesis is: 'The total satisfaction of sleep is waking or the art of waking up' (1952a). He further postulates the existence of a 'wake-wish' in the psyche which operates as the motivation for the act of waking up.

It is interesting to compare Scott's researches with those of Lewin (1954) and Jekels (1945). Jekels has postulated: 'I assume that the awakening function is inherent in all dreams and that it constitutes their quintessence, their fundamental task.' Lewin has ascribed the rôle of 'a waker' to the analyst. From this it would follow that one function of the dream has been taken over by the analyst in the analytic situation, that of an awakener. Jekels, in his most interesting discussion of schizophrenic states, ego–activity in dreams and process of falling asleep arrived at the conclusion: 'The restitution of the ego, identical with awakening, is started by the mental ego; it is carried out just as in schizophrenia by means of hallucinosis, that is, by means of the dream.' If my inference is correct, then the analyst's ego takes on this 'restitutive' rôle in relation to the more regressive states of severely ill patients (cf. Winnicott, 1954a and b; and Bion, 1958, 1959). Only in the analytic situation the analyst does not work through hallucinosis but with interpretations. His capacity to interpret relies very much on his ego–strength, which involves controlled experimental preconscious activity in the service of the patient. This is what we normally describe as empathy and intuition. Therefore, if the narcissism of sleep is replaced by the narcissism of the couch (Lewin 1955), then the awaking function of the dream is apportioned to the analyst. It is he who keeps awake and guides the regressive drift of the patient's affective processes and gives them meaning and shape through his interpretations. It is our frequent clinical experience that during the acute regressive states of severely disturbed cases, it is the analyst's wakefulness and ego-activity, expressed through his body-aliveness and interpretations, that keeps the patient going and stops irreversible surrender to primary process activity.

I would like briefly to draw attention here to the more severe and profound disturbances of the quality and subjective experience of both sleep and consciousness in a certain type of schizoid regressive patient. With these patients, who present in their overt behaviour manic over-elated hyperactivity or extreme forms of inertia and apathy, it often transpires that only when they can gradually begin to rely and depend on the analyst's wakeful and embodied presence and functioning in the analytic setting are they able to get to sleep without anxiety. And only then can they wake up in an affective state that does not compel primitive splitting mechanisms in the ego. In these patients it is only when this very primitive rhythm of sleep and wakefulness has been re-established that one can see the capacity for a good dream and free association coming into operation.

I have made this long digression to show how the analytic situation, once it was established, has made it possible to observe the very processes from which it has derived: namely, the wish to sleep and the wish to wake up and the capacity to dream.

By rejecting hypnotic sleep as the therapeutic agent and redistributing the total psychic forces operating in the dreamer in the analytic situation, Freud made it possible to evaluate the rôle and function of sleep and wakefulness both in the therapeutic situation and in ontological development (cf. Fliess 1953; Isakower 1938; Lewin 1954; Federn 1934; Gifford 1960; Hoffer 1952; Spitz 1955; Scott 1960; Winnicott 1954a and b).

Hypothesis of 'the good dream'

A vast amount of our literature, myths, social customs, rituals and intellectual discoveries are either based on or derived from the capacity to dream (cf. Sharpe 1937; Lewin 1958; Róheim 1952). In this sense dreaming is prototypic of all psychic creativity in the human adult. I am here proposing the concept of a 'good dream' on the lines of Kris's concept of the 'good analytic hour'. I shall now schematically state some salient features of the sleeper's intrapsychic situation which enables a 'good dream' to materialize.

1 A secure and restful physical ambience where the ego can withdraw safely its cathexes of the external world and reinforce the sleep-wish.
2 A state of trust in the ego that this external world will be there to return to after the satisfaction of sleep-wish.
3 Ego's capacity to be in touch with the wish to sleep.
4 An unconscious internal source of disturbance which is the motive force of the dream and is articulated through the dream-work.
5 Availability to the ego of the day-residues for formal structuring of the latent 'dream-wish'.
6 Capacity to tolerate the regressive process in the psychic apparatus: away from motility to hallucination (Kris 1952).
7 Reliability of the integrative processes in the ego. This reliability presupposes that the earliest stages of psyche-soma integration in the nascent ego (Winnicott 1949) have been established firmly.
8 Ego's narcissistic capacity for gratification from dream-world in lieu of either the pure narcissism of sleep or the concrete satisfaction of

reality. This implies a capacity to tolerate frustration by the ego and accept symbolic satisfactions.

9 A capacity in the ego for symbolization and dream-work, in which sufficient counter-cathexis against primary process is sustained for the dream to become an experience of intrapsychic communication.

10 A capacity for benign distancing from primitive and sadistic superego elements so as to allow for relaxing of the repression-barrier.

11 A capacity in the ego for receptiveness and surrender to the id wishes with a corresponding confidence in being able to 'resist' their chaotic and excessive influx.

12 A reliable time-space unit of experience in which all this can be undertaken and repeated at fairly predictable intervals.

13 Availability in ego of enough neutralized energy to be able to harness and harmonize the intruding id-impulses: both libidinal and aggressive (Hartmann 1954).

14 The capacity to retain an 'after-image' of the dream in waking state should this be felt necessary.

Given some such intrapsychic state a person can have a 'good dream'. By a 'good dream' I mean a dream which incorporates through successful dream-work an unconscious wish and can thus enable sleep to be sustained on the one hand and can be available for psychic experience to the ego when the person wakes up. In this context it is interesting to compare the ego-activity of the sleeper in relation to the 'good dream' with what Winnicott (1951) has described as the primitive psychic functions utilized by the infant in relation to transitional object (also cf. Milner 1957, 1952).

The capacity for a 'good dream', though a prerequisite for psychic health, is however, not a guarantee of it. It is a measure of a psychic capacity in an individual, or as Dr Valenstein suggested, it is the dream increment of ego-strength.

The classical analytic situation and its functions

Let us now examine briefly the concept 'the analytic situation'. The total analytic situation can be somewhat arbitrarily divided into three component parts:

1 the patient;
2 the analyst;
3 the analytic setting.

The interplay between these three constitutes the analytic process and procedure.

The patient brings to it a wish for cure, which forms the basis of therapeutic alliance. In terms of dream psychology, his capacity to surrender to the couch-situation is a derivative of the narcissistic sleep-wish (Lewin 1955). His symptom is the expression of the 'latent dream-wish', that is, the unconscious repressed conflicts and wishes. He also brings a capacity for analytic work which is intimately dependent on his capacity for dream-work in sleep (cf. Kris 1956). Where a patient's 'dream-work' capacities are grossly disturbed by ego-distortions, primitive defence mechanisms or psychotic anxieties (cf. Bion 1958, 1959), we invariably find they cannot comply with the fundamental rule and free-associate. In such cases acute defensive or regressive use of sleep and silence is a characteristic feature of their behaviour in the analytic situation. Conversely, hypomanic states of elation and acting out can disrupt the transference working through (cf. Klein 1946, and Winnicott 1935, on manic defence).

The analyst in his person provides a receptiveness towards the material of the patient; namely his free associations. In this way he reinforces both the 'wake wish' ('analyst is a waker' — Lewin), and also occupies the rôle of the sleeper's ego that articulates the dream-work. He helps to release and organize the unconscious wishes through his interpretation of the resistances in the patient and alleviation of primitive guilt feelings. He operates as an 'auxiliary ego' (Heimann 1950) in the analytic situation. He also lends his freer capacity for symbolic associations to the patient. He holds the patient's material 'alive' and in focus over time. He sees to it that there are no false and precipitate defensive closures of the psychic and affective process. Thus he establishes a movement in the analytic situation (Glover 1928).

The analyst, like the dreaming ego, does not gratify concretely any of the unconscious wishes of the patient as they find expression in the transference-neurosis, but restricts his rôle to that of sympathy, support and understanding. These are the symbolic satisfactions he offers.

In order to facilitate the expression of the patient's wishes and behaviour as well as to operate creatively and freely himself, he establishes a physical ambience: *the analytic setting.* By analytic setting I mean the physical ambience in which an analyst undertakes to initiate and carry out the analytic process with a patient. In our vast literature, exhaustive discussions of the patient and the analyst are readily available. It is only in the post-war years that the setting as such has come in for closer scrutiny and examination (cf. Winnicott, Spitz, Scott and others). How and why Freud established the physical attributes of the analytic setting are generally taken for granted. I would like to reiterate here that I am not concerned with the subjective reasons for Freud's choice of certain elements in this setting, such as his personal dislike for being stared at and hence choosing to sit behind a patient (1913). It was Freud's genius that, starting from subjective data, he invariably succeeded in abstracting a general and valid therapeutic procedure (cf. Eissler 1951). The analytic setting consists of a room, with privacy and guaranteed protection against intrusions and infringements from the outside world. Also a comfortably warm temperature, light and air, and a couch to lie on in a relaxed way. He provides a predictably repetitive span of time with a beginning and an end. He also undertakes to keep awake, receptively alert and capable of action, and remains unintrusive (Rycroft 1956a; Winnicott 1954a).

Even a casual comparison shows how ingeniously Freud redistributed the intrapsychic state of the sleeper between three elements in the analytic situation: namely, the patient, the analyst and the analytic setting. How well these three constituents of the total analytic situation lend themselves for the displacement and projection of the tripartite structuring of the human personality – for example in terms of id, ego and superego – has been detailed exhaustively and ingeniously by various analysts (cf. Fenichel, Bion, Fairbairn, Klein, Strachey and so on).

One very significant and crucial difference from the state of the sleeper is that the analyst through his person makes available a relationship (the transference) which is at the extreme opposite of the isolation of the dreaming ego. And it is precisely this transference relationship which makes the analysis, in contradistinction to dreaming, therapeutic. One further distinguishing feature of the analyst's activity (interpretations) as compared with the ego's dream-work is that he deals with the unconscious impulses not through regressive mechanisms which the sleeper's ego uses – for example, displacement, condensation, hallucination and so on – but through dealing with both the resistances and the pathogenic use of primitive defence mechanisms. He does not obviate the resistances, as in hypnosis, but works with them and at them, thus gradually enabling the patient's ego to have access to new sources of energy and more effective psychic processes. Through the transference relationship Freud enabled the human ego to achieve its maximum conquests of the unconscious into conscious and reclaimed to self-awareness, insight and communication vast areas of affectivity and psychic inner life (phantasy) which had been so far available only metaphorically through the products of poets, artists and gifted dreamers. In a century which was to devote itself almost exclusively to the exploration and conquest of the physical environment, Freud established the techniques for the exploration of the inner life and what man has done to man. He made it possible creatively and patiently to enquire into the forces and factors that make us human, namely our emotions, instincts, psyche and consciousness. In him the human ego found its first true ally and not yet another inspired prophet or an intellectual or therapeutic tyrant. It is now conceded even by the opponents of Freud that he enabled us to make therapeutic inroads into the unconscious; what is not so clearly seen is that after him and through his work the very function and scope of human consciousness have changed and widened, inwards and outwards (Trilling 1955). What Freud has attributed to Michelangelo in his creation of Moses, in spirit, is even more aptly true of Freud's struggle with himself which led to his creation of the analytic situation:

> But Michelangelo has placed a different Moses on the tomb of the Pope, one superior to the historical or traditional Moses. He has modified the theme of the broken Tables; he does not let Moses break them in his wrath, *but makes him be influenced by the danger that they will be broken and makes him calm that wrath, or at any rate prevent it from becoming an act.* In this way he has added something new and more than human to the figure of Moses; so that the giant frame with its tremendous physical power becomes only a concrete expression of the highest mental achievement that is possible in a man, that *of struggling successfully against an inward passion for the sake of a cause to which he has devoted himself . . .* thus, *in self-criticism, rising superior to his own nature.*
> (Freud 1914: 233–4; italics mine)

To shift our attention to the clinical aspects of the analytic situation: this situation, during the first two decades of psychoanalysis, was intended to meet the needs and requirements of hysterics (Freud 1919). In other words, the patient who was considered suitable for analysis was supposed to have reached a fair degree of ego-integration and libidinal development. The conflicts were in the nature of unresolved tensions between the ego, the superego and pre-genital impulses and object relationships. The ego-functions of these patients were more or less intact, and their symptoms were the result of involvement of these intact ego-functions with primitive id-impulses and guilt feelings. The conflicts had not sapped or distorted in any acute degree the ego-functions themselves. Because of this these patients could be relied upon to use the transference function of the analytic setting. As in 'the good dream' neither does the disturbing id-impulse break through the ego's regressive control of the dream-work into motility (otherwise the sleeper would wake up), nor has the ego to use primitive total defences to deal with the dream (as in psychosis, cf. Nunberg 1920, and Bion 1958). Similarly, for these patients the analytic situation's transference-potential for carrying regressive thought and wish cathexes and their expression through words is sufficient for the therapeutic process. They do not 'act out' in analysis or their social life in any harmful or intense way. Conversely, it is my clinical experience that patients who cannot have a 'good dream' also cannot creatively use the analytic situation.

Borderline cases, regression, and the new demands from the analytic situation

In the past three decades a variety of patients have come for treatment who, because of the very nature of their illness, have not been able to use the classical analytic situation constructively. They are compelled by their personality disorders to fail to fulfil the 'expectancy' and rules of the analytic situation. They come to treatment without specifically identifiable symptoms or even a well-organized wish for cure. Though intellectually they can all too easily grasp the requirements of the analytic situation, affectively and in terms of ego-process they fail to make any use of it. They freeze up, instead of free-associate; regressively cling to various elements of the setting and the person of the analyst (Fliess 1953) and can establish neither a therapeutic alliance (Zetzel 1956) nor transference-neurosis (Sterba 1957; Stone 1947) that is workable. In their experience of the analytic situation a regressive confusion and blurring of the boundaries of self, analyst and setting continuously takes place. These patients have been variously defined as borderline cases (Greenacre 1954; Stone 1954), schizoid personalities (Fairbairn 1940; Khan 1960b), narcissistic neuroses (Reich 1933–49), 'as if personalities (Deutsch 1942), identify disorders (Erikson 1959; Greenson 1958), suffering from 'ego-specific' defect (Gitelson 1958), 'false personality' (Winnicott 1956; Laing 1960) and 'basic fault' (Balint 1960), and so forth. The primitive ego-distortions in these patients do not lend themselves to the establishment of that 'benign split' which is a prerequisite for the success of the clinical process in the classic analytic situation. In these cases confusions of self and object, urgent wishes to control regressive psychic affective experiences through motility and intellectual defence (A. Freud 1952), delusional transference (Little 1960; Stone 1954) and symbiotic dependency states precipitately take hold of the analytic situation (Sterba 1957). And they try desperately with all varieties of bizarre and primitive defence mechanisms to bring this charged analytic situation within the range of their omnipotence (Winnicott 1960).

The various new technical procedures, amendments and innovations that have been offered during the past three decades by analysts, with varying degrees of certainty and assurance, have all resulted from an honest clinical attempt to meet these clinical states.

And yet even a casual examination convinces us that they contradict each other (cf. Balint 1950). Some analysts are inclined to exploit the regressive processes in the patient and the analytic situations towards a recreation of the patient's personality (cf. Little 1960). Others distrust the regressive potential of the transference and the analytic situation and impose upon it and the patient wisely selected restrictions and obligations and with these hope to guide the patient through 'corrective emotional experiences' to a new freedom and vitality of ego-functions and psychic health (cf. Alexander 1950; Macalpine 1950), and so on. By and large, most of us are agreed today that for the aetiology of these disorders we have to look much further back than the Oedipal situation and pregenital id-conflicts and object relationships. In the words of Gitelson, in the consideration of these cases 'our thinking is channelled in a direction which assumes an ego-specific defect'. We are more and more inclined to account for these disorders in terms of the disturbance of the primitive stage of ego-differentiation and its emergence from the ambience of infant care into a self-unit. With this, by definition, the very nature of our therapeutic task, and the function of the analytic setting, changes. No longer can we exclusively devote our skill towards the evolution of a transference-neurosis in the analytic setting which will express the latent conflicts of the patient and through interpretation and working through resolve it. I have not the time to discuss them separately in detail (cf. Eissler (1950) and Khan (1960a)). All I can briefly indicate here is that once the clinical process goes beyond the 'transference limits' of the analytic situation and the patient compulsively acts out in a concrete way his *needs* (as against wishes, for which the symbolic speech idiom was sufficient) and primitive ego-distortions, then the analogy of the sleep and dream-situation with the analytic situation is no longer feasible. In chapter 7 of *The Interpretation of Dreams* (pp. 565–6), Freud makes it quite explicit that wish fulfilment in dreams is only possible of the mnemic images of the previous satisfaction of needs are available for cathexis. He succinctly sums it up on page 598: 'The first wishing seems to have been a hallucinatory cathecting of the memory of satisfaction.' We can elaborate on this to say where in a person's experience of infant-care such *satisfactions* have not been either reliable and consistent or have been too inadequate, the capacity to use these 'mnemic images of satisfaction' for mobilization of dream-wish must by definition be lacking or distorted (cf. Winnicott 1945). In these circumstances later ego-development can be used as a magical way of making good the deficiency of early satisfaction experiences. Intrapsychically this can mean an *abuse* of dreaming to create a magical omnipotent dream-world which aims at creating the illusion of satisfying actual needs with an omnipotent denial of the necessity of external objects for satisfaction and the dependence on them. We see this most vividly in certain psychotic illnesses. My experience clinically is that patients who have very primitive ego-distortions cannot work with the symbolic transference value of the analytic situation. They either deny their *dependence* on it altogether or try to compel it into a magical omnipotence of thought or regress to making actual need-demands that are totally beyond the scope of the analyst or his setting. The clinical

41

crises of these patients demand a different capacity from the analytic situation, and if we are not to get lost in this situation, we must keep clearly in mind that it is not the analytic situation that has created this state of affairs, as Macalpine, Alexander and Fairbairn suggest, but the *need* in the patient. The one saving grace of these clinical crises is that Freud's instrument of the analytic siutation is resilient and pliable enough to meet these 'needs' and can withstand all the primitive 'delusions' (Little) and distortions to which the patient subjects it. As Winnicott, Spitz, Milner, Scott and others have reported, in these circumstances the 'transference' idiom of the analytic situation changes into a more primitive and primary mode of experience, very much in the nature of the infant-care situation. And once this comes to pass clinically, how metapsychologically valid a specific therapeutic procedure would be depends upon the 'theory' with which the analyst is working. And the more we can openly discuss the theories, expectancies and anticipatory attitudes with which we approach these clinical crises, the greater will be our benefit from each other and the more shall we correct our procedures into true analytic focus.

Meantime, it is best for us to heed Freud's cautionary words to his audience at the 5th International Congress at Budapest in 1919:

> We refused most emphatically to turn a patient who puts himself into our hands in search of help into our private property, to decide his fate for him, to force our own ideals upon him, and with the pride of a Creator to form him in our own image and see that it is good.

References

Alexander, F. (1950). 'Analysis of the Therapeutic Factors in Psychoanalytic Treatment.' *Psychoanal. Quart.*, 19.

Alexander, F., and French, T.M. *Psychoanalytic Therapy, Principles and Application.* (New York: Ronald Press, 1946.)

Balint, M. (1950). 'Changing Therapeutic Aims and Techniques in Psycho-Analysis.' *Int. J. Psycho-Anal.*, 31.

—— (1960). 'The Regressed Patient and his Analyst.' *Psychiatry*, 23, 3.

Bion, W.R. (1958). 'On Hallucination.' *Int. J. Psycho-Anal.*, 39.

—— (1959). 'Attacks on Linking.' *Int. J. Psycho-Anal.*, 40.

Bird, B. (1954). 'Pathological Sleep.' *Int. J. Psycho-Anal.*, 35.

Deutsch, H. (1942). 'Some Forms of Emotional Disturbance and their Relationship to Schizophrenia.' *Psychoanal. Quart.*, 11.

Eissler, K.R. (1950). 'The Chicago Institute of Psychoanalysis and the Sixth Period of the Development of Psychoanalytic Technique.' *J. General Psychol.*, 42.

—— (1951). 'An Unknown Autobiographical Letter by Freud and a Short Comment.' *Int. J. Psycho-Anal.*, 32.

—— (1953). 'The Effect of the Structure of the Ego on Psychoanalytic Technique.' *J. Amer. Psychoanal. Assoc.*, 1.

Erikson, E.H. (1954). 'The Dream Specimen of Psychoanalysis.' *J. Amer. Psychoanal. Assoc.*, 2.

—— *Identity and the Life Cycle*. (New York: Int. Univ. Press, 1959.)

Fairbairn, W.R.D. (1940). 'Schizoid Factors in the Personality.' In: *Psycho-Analytic Studies of the Personality*. (London: Tavistock, 1952.)

—— (1957). 'Freud, the Psycho-Analytical Method and Mental Health.' *Brit.J. Med. Psychol.*, 30.

—— (1958). 'On the Nature and Aims of Psycho-Analytic Treatment.' *Int. J. Psycho-Anal.*, 39.

Federn, P. (1932). 'Ego-Feeling in Dreams.' *Psychoanal. Quart.*, 1.

—— (1934). 'The Awakening of the Ego in Dreams.' *Int. J. Psycho-Anal.*, 15.

Fenichel, O. *Problems of Psychoanalytic Technique*. (New York: Psychoanal. Quart. Inc., 1941.)

Ferenczi, S. (1914). 'On Falling Asleep during Analysis.' In: *Further Contributions to the Theory and Technique of Psycho-Analysis*. (London: Hogarth, 1926.)

—— (1927). Review of Rank's *Technik der Psychoanalyse: I. Die Analytische Situation, Int. J. Psycho-Anal.*, 8.

Ferenczi, S., and Rank, O. (1925). *The Development of Psychoanalysis*. Nerv. and Ment. Dis. Mono. No. 40.

Fliess, R. (1953). 'The Hypnotic Evasion: A Clinical Observation.' *Psychoanal. Quart.*, 22.

Freud, A. (1952). 'A Connection between the States of Negativism and of Emotional Surrender.' Author's Abstract. *Int. J. Psycho-Anal.*, 33.

Freud, S. *The Origins of Psycho-Analysis*. (London: Imago, 1954.)

—— (1900). *The Interpretation of Dreams*. SE, 4 and 5.

—— (1913). 'On Beginning the Treatment (Further Recommendations on the Technique of Psycho-Analysis, I)' SE, 12.

—— (1914). 'The Moses of Michelangelo.' SE, 13.

—— (1917). 'Metapsychological Supplement to the Theory of Dreams.' SE, 14.

—— (1919). 'Lines of Advance in Psycho-Analytic Therapy.' SE, 17.

Freud, S., and Breuer, J. (1893–1895). *Studies on Hysteria*, SE, 2.

Gifford, S. (1960). 'Sleep, Time and the Early Ego.' *J. Amer. Psychoanal. Assoc.*, 8.

Gill, M. and Brenman, M. *Hypnosis and Related States*. (New York: Int. Univ. Press, 1959.)

Gitelson, M. (1952). 'The Emotional Position of the Analyst in the Psycho-Analytic Situation.' *Int. J. Psycho-Anal.*, 33.

—— (1958). 'On Ego Distortion.' *Int. J. Psycho-Anal.*, 39.

Glover, E. *The Technique of Psycho-Analysis*. (London: Baillière, 1928.)

Greenacre, Phyllis. (1954). 'The Rôle of Transference: Practical Considerations in Relation to Psychoanalytic Therapy.' *J. Amer. Psychoanal. Assoc.*, 2.

Greenson, R. (1958). 'Screen Defenses, Screen Hunger and Screen Identity.' *J. Amer. Psychoanal. Assoc.*, 6.

—— (1960). 'Empathy and its Vicissitudes.' *Int. J. Psycho-Anal.*, 41.

Grotjahn, M. (1942). 'The Process of Awakening.' *Psychoanal. Rev.*, 29.

Hartmann, H. (1954). 'Problems of Infantile Neurosis.' *Psychoanal. Study Child*, 9.

Heimann, P. (1950). 'On Counter-Transference.' *Int. J. Psycho-Anal.*, 31.

—— (1956). 'Dynamics of Transference Interpretation.' *Int. J. Psycho-Anal.*, 37.

Hoffer, W. (1952). 'The Mutual Influences in the Development of Ego and Id: Earliest Stages.' *Psychoanal. Study Child*, 7.

Isakower, O. (1938). 'A Contribution to the Psychopathology of Phenomena associated with Falling Asleep.' *Int. J. Psycho-Anal.*, 19.

Jekels, L. (1945). 'A Bioanalytic Contribution to the Problem of Sleep and Wakefulness.' *Psychoanal. Quart.*, 14.

Jones, E. *The Life and Works of Sigmund Freud*, Vol. I. (London: Hogarth, 1953.) *Journal of the American Psychoanalytic Association* (1954), 2, part 4.

Khan, M.M.R. (1960a). 'Regression and Integration in the Analytic Setting.' *Int. J. Psycho-Anal.*, 41.

—— (1960b). 'The Schizoid Personality: Affects and Techniques.' *Int. J. Psycho-Anal.*, 41.

Klein, M. (1946). 'Notes on Some Schizoid Mechanisms.' *Int. J. Psycho-Anal.*, 27.

—— (1955). 'The Psycho-Analytic Play Technique: Its History and Significance.' In: *New Directions in Psycho-Analysis*. (London: Tavistock, 1955.)

Kris, E. (1950). 'On Preconscious Mental Processes.' *Psychoanal. Quart.*, 19.

—— *Psychoanalytic Explorations in Art.*(New York: Int. Univ. Press, 1952.)

—— (1954). Introduction to Freud: *The Origins of Psycho-Analysis*. See Freud (1954).

—— (1956). 'On Some Vicissitudes of Insight in Psycho-Analysis.' *Int. J. Psycho-Anal.*, 38.

Laing, R.D. *The Divided Self.* (London: Tavistock, 1960.)

Lewin, B. *The Psycho-Analysis of Elation.* (London: Hogarth, 1950.)

—— (1953). 'Reconsideration of the Dream Screen.' *Psychoanal. Quart.*, 22.

—— (1954). 'Sleep, Narcissistic Neurosis and the Analytic Situation.' *Psychoanal. Quart.*, 23

—— (1955). 'Dream Psychology and the Analytic Situation.' *Psychoanal. Quart.*, 24.

—— *Dreams and the Uses of Regression.* (New York: Int. Univ. Press, 1958.)

—— (1959). 'The Analytic Situation: Topographic Consideration.' *Psychoanal. Quart.*, 28.

Little, M. (1960). 'On Basic Unity.' *Int. J. Psycho-Anal.*, 41.

Macalpine, I. (1950). 'The Development of the Transference.' *Psychoanal. Quart.*, 19.

Milner, M. *On Not Being Able to Paint.* (London: Heinemann, 1957.)

—— (1952). 'Aspects of Symbolism in Comprehension of the Not-Self'. *Int. J. Psycho-Anal.*, 33.

—— (1956). 'The Communication of Primary Sensual Experience.' *Int. J. Psycho-Anal.*, 37.

Nacht, S. (1957). 'Technical Remarks on the Handling of the Transference Neurosis.' *Int. J. Psycho-Anal.*, 38.

—— (1958). 'Variations in Technique.' *Int. J. Psycho-Anal.*, 39.

Nacht, S. and Viderman, S. (1960). 'The Pre-Object Universe in the Transference Situation.' *Int. J. Psycho-Anal.*, 41.

Nunberg, H. (1920). 'On the Catatonic Attack.' In: *Practice and Theory of Psychoanalysis.* (New York: Nerv. and Ment. Dis. Mono., 1948.)

Orr, D.W. (1954a). 'Transference and Countertransference. A Historical Survey.' *J. Amer. Psychoanal. Assoc.*, 2.

—— (1954b). 'Problems of Infantile Neurosis. A Discussion.' *Psychoanal. Study Child*, 9.

Rank, O. (1924). *The Trauma of Birth.* (London: Kegan Paul, 1929.)

Reich, W. (1933–1949). *Character Analysis.* (London: Vision Press, 1950.)

Róheim, G. *The Gates of the Dream.* (New York: Int. Univ. Press, 1952.)

Rycroft, C. (1956a). 'Symbolism and its Relationship to the Primary and Secondary Processes.' *Int. J. Psycho-Anal.*, 37.

—— (1956b). 'The Nature and Function of the Analyst's Communication to the Patient.' *Int. J. Psycho-Anal.*, 37.

Scott, W.C.M. (1952a). 'Patients who Sleep or Look at the Psycho-Analyst during Treatment. Technical Considerations.' *Int. J. Psycho-Anal.*, 33.

—— (1952b). 'The Mutual Influences in the Development of Ego and Id.' *Psychoanal. Study Child*, 7.

—— (1954). 'A New Hypothesis concerning the Relationship of Libidinal and Aggressive Instinct.' *Int. J. Psycho-Anal.*, 35.

——– (1956). 'Sleep in Psychoanalysis.' *Bull. Philadelphia Assoc.*, 6.

—— (1960). 'Depression, Confusion and Multivalence.' *Int. J. Psycho-Anal.*, 41.

Séchehaye, M.A. (1956). 'The Transference in Symbolic Realization. *Int. J. Psycho-Anal.*, 37.

Sharpe, E. *Dream Analysis.* (London: Hogarth, 1937.)

Spitz, R.A. (1955). 'The Primal Cavity.' *Psychoanal. Study Child*, 10.

—— (1956a). 'Countertransference. Comments on its Varying Rôle in the Analytic Situation.' *J. Amer. Psychoanal. Assoc.*, 4.

—— (1956b). 'Transference: The Analytic Settings and its Prototype.' *Int. J. Psycho-Anal.*, 37.

Sterba, R.F. (1957). 'Oral Invasion and Self-Defence.' *Int. J. Psycho-Anal.*, 38.

Stone, L.(1947). 'Transference Sleep in a Neurosis with Duodenal Ulcer.' *Int. J. Psycho-Anal.*, 28.

—— (1954). 'The Widening Scope of Indications for Psycho-Analysis.' *J. Amer. Psychoanal. Assoc.*, 2.

Strachey, J. (1934). 'The Nature of the Therapeutic Action of Psycho-Analysis.' *Int. J. Psycho-Anal.*, 15.

—— (1937). 'Symposium on the Therapeutic Results in Psycho-Analysis.' *Int. J. Psycho-Anal.*, 18.

Szasz, T.S. (1956). 'On the Experiences of the Analyst in the Psychoanalytic Situation. A Contribution to the Theory of Psychoanalytic Treatment.' *J. Amer. Psychoanal. Assoc.*, 4.

—— (1957). 'On the Theory of Psycho-Analytic Treatment.' *Int. J. Psycho-Anal.*, 38.

Trilling, L. *Freud and the Crisis of our Culture.* (Boston: Beacon, 1955.)

Winnicott, C. (1959). 'The Development of Insight.' *Sociological Rev.*, Mono. No. 2.

Winnicott, D.W. (1935). 'The Manic Defence.' In Winnicott, D.W. (1958).

—— (1945). 'Primitive Emotional Development.' In Winnicott, D.W. (1958).

—— (1949). 'Mind and its Relation to the Psyche-Soma.' In Winnicott, D.W. (1958).

—— (1951). 'Transitional Objects and Transitional Phenomena.' In Winnicott, D.W. (1958).

—— (1954a). 'Metapsychological and Clinical Aspects of Regression within the Psycho-Analytical Set-up.' In Winnicott, D.W. (1958).

—— (1954b). 'Withdrawal and Regression.' In Winnicott, D.W. (1958).

—— (1956). 'Clinical Varieties of Transference.' In Winnicott, D.W. (1958).

—— *Collected Papers.* (London: Tavistock, 1958.)

—— (1958). 'On the Capacity to be Alone.' *Int. J. Psycho-Anal.*, 39.

—— (1960). 'The Theory of the Parent-Infant Relationship.' *Int. J. Psycho-Anal.*, 41.

Zetzel, E.R. (1956). 'Current Concepts of Transference.' *Int. J. Psycho-Anal.*, 37.

PART TWO

The dream controversy:
is it the royal road today?

Charles Brenner's paper of 1969 and R.R. Greenson's of 1970, the latter conceived as an argument to a monograph titled *The Place of the Dream in Clinical Practice* (Waldhorn 1967), are placed together as representing two poles of a classical debate on the centrality of the dream in the psychoanalytic process. With characteristic lucidity Charles Brenner justifies the displacement of the dream from the centre of psychoanalytic practice. Re-formulating the psychology of dreams within the parameters of the structural model of the mind, he argues that the psychological tension between wish and realistic thinking, more fully conceptualized as an intrapsychic conflict between the structural agencies of the mind, the id, the ego and superego, is ubiquitous in psychic life. Symptoms, jokes, social and aesthetic experience are all informed by phantasy, always the product of conflict, and can be used by analyst and patient to gain information about the unconscious workings of the mind.

Greenson disagrees. He argues that there is no window like the dream into the unconscious mind, and no alliance between analyst and patient comparable to that forged when working on the patient's dream. He attacks what he regards as the prosaic and defensive avoidance of the unconscious by ego psychologists exemplified by the Waldhorn report. He is likewise critical of dream interpretation which does not adequately utilize the patient's associations, in effect leaving the patient out of the discovering process.

2

Dreams in clinical psychoanalytic practice

CHARLES BRENNER

Freud began his psychotherapeutic attempts to cure hysterical patients of their symptoms by attempting to undo the patients' amnesia concerning the origin of their symptoms with the help of hypnotic suggestion. He was not, at that time, particularly interested in his patients' dreams, and his earliest articles on hysteria, particularly the *Studies in Hysteria*, which he wrote together with J. Breuer (1895), contain no special references to the subject of dreams or dream interpretation. It was not long after he gave up hypnosis and began to develop the psychoanalytic method, however, that Freud's attention was directed to his patients' dreams and to his own dreams. His quick and brilliant success in elucidating so much of dream psychology contributed substantially toward convincing him of the value of his newly discovered method of investigation and treatment — the psychoanalytic method. More than likely it helped give him the courage to persist in his devotion to psychoanalysis in the face of the disdain and disapproval it engendered, obstacles which would have discouraged a man who was less confident of himself and of the work he was doing. As Freud (1900) himself wrote, in the preface to one of the later editions of *The Interpretation of Dreams*, such a discovery comes only once in a lifetime.

The publication of that monumental work in 1900 aroused little interest in either the medical or the scientific world at first. In 1905 Freud published a case history, *Fragment of the Analysis of a Case of Hysteria*, the 'Dora' case, which was intended primarily to illustrate the practical value of dream analysis in psychoanalytic work. As analysts other than Freud began to appear on the scene, they accepted, or were soon convinced of, the correctness of Freud's emphasis on the usefulness of analyzing patients' dreams. The clinical use of dream analysis very early became one of the hallmarks of genuine, Freudian analysis. It is still so viewed by many, although it is now less often referred to explicitly in this regard, particularly in the psychoanalytic literature proper. As psychoanalysts, we take it for granted today as a part of psychoanalytic practice, but it is interesting to see evidences in the early psychoanalytic literature of very explicit emphasis on the clinical importance of dream interpretation. For example, if one refers to early volumes of the *Internationale Zeitschrift für Psychoanalyse*, one finds a special section in each issue devoted to short communications concerning dream interpretation: a new symbol, an unusual dream, an interesting latent content, and so on.

Psychoanalytic journals do not currently have such a section, to the best of my knowledge, but it is still usual, if not universal, for the curricula of psychoanalytic institutes to devote a considerable amount of time to the study of dream interpretation. In the United States, at any rate, our curricula devote no such amount of time to the study of the interpretation of symptoms, or of character traits, or of parapraxes or jokes. Dreams and their interpretation still occupy a special place in our minds – our professional minds – whether we acknowledge it explicitly or not.

I recall a panel discussion at the Edinburgh Congress, in 1961, at which Dr M. Balint and Miss A. Freud participated. In the course of the discussion, Dr Balint said that it is his practice to insist that every psychoanalytic candidate whom he analyzes stick with at least one of his dreams until it has been thoroughly analyzed, no matter how many analytic sessions it may take. Dr Balint explained that, in this way, he assured himself that every one of his candidates had at least one opportunity to understand a dream thoroughly and to learn what the unconscious mind is really like. Miss Freud, to my surprise, expressed enthusiasm for the idea, although she said that she had never done such a thing and, on being pressed, admitted that it might be undesirable to do so, even in a training analysis. I might add that, in one of the courses I took with him in the early 1940s, Dr H. Sachs described it as his usual practice to continue the analysis of a patient's dream over two or more sessions; that is, to tell a patient at the end of a session, 'Well, we still don't understand that dream. We'll have to spend more time on it tomorrow.' At that time, I was too early in my analytic career for Dr Sachs' comment to make any particular impression on me, but what I heard in Edinburgh did stimulate a lively response, since it differed so markedly from my own practice and was so at variance with what I had until then assumed to be generally accepted procedure among analysts today.

I shall begin my presentation by a brief discussion of dream psychology – of dream theory, if you will.

In the seventh chapter of his *Interpretation of Dreams*, Freud (1900) proposed a theory of mental organization and functioning which seemed to him to explain satisfactorily the diverse phenomena of dream psychology, of neurotic symptom formation of parapraxes and of jokes.

All of these psychic phenomena, both normal and pathological, Freud believed could be explained only if one assumed the operation of a mental apparatus, much of whose workings are unconscious, and, indeed, inaccessible to consciousness as such. This theory was reviewed and expanded somewhat in the paper which he published in 1915 as *The Unconscious*, without, however, being substantially altered. As a matter of convenience, it is often referred to as the 'topographic theory'. Subsequently Freud revised his theories about the mental apparatus and its functioning in rather substantial ways. His revised theory, again for the sake of convenience, is referred to generally as the 'structural theory'.

I do not propose to enter into a discussion of the revisions of Freud's earlier theories which constitute the differences between the topographic and the structural theories; for such a discussion I shall merely refer to *Psychoanalytic Concepts and the Structural Theory*, by Arlow and myself (1964). There has rarely been any discussion of the question whether these theoretical revisions imply, or entail, any new view of dream psychology.

We are familiar with the fact that the revisions have had such an effect with respect to certain pathological phenomena. We have a very different view today from that which analysts had some fifty years ago concerning the psychology (psychopathology) of neurotic symptom formation as well as of the unconscious determinants of many character traits. In particular, we have a different view of the relationship between symptom and anxiety, as well as a much different, and, we believe, more accurate view of the role of conflict, or defense, and of superego tendencies in the production of both neurotic symptoms and normal as well as abnormal character traits. In fact, it was the accumulation of new data from the application of the psychoanalytic method to clinical work with these very phenomena and the reassessment of those data, both new and old, that led to the theoretical revisions to which I refer. Moreover, as we know, it is the theoretical revisions in question which have made possible what we call defense analysis and character analysis in a systematic and effective way, thus enlarging the scope of psychoanalysis therapeutically as well as improving its therapeutic efficacy and diminishing the dangers previously attendant on its use.

It is all the more interesting, therefore, that there have been so few attempts to revise psychoanalytic theories of dream psychology in the light of the structural theory; that is, in the light of the theoretical revisions in the theory of the mental apparatus and its functioning which have proved so valuable clinically. As far as I am aware, the first such attempt was the one I made myself in the chapter on dreams in my *Elementary Textbook of Psychoanalysis* (1955). In that chapter I presented an exposition of dream psychology which included reference to Freud's later theoretical revisions. In 1964 Arlow and I reviewed in detail the psychoanalytic data acquired since 1900 which speak in favor of revising dream theory and presented the suggested, necessary revisions in concise form.

The present chapter offers a revised theory of dream psychology which is based on the structural theory of the mind. Like the structural theory, this dream theory is more consonant with the facts of mental functioning available through application of the psychoanalytic method than is the dream theory outlined by Freud in 1900. Like the structural theory also, it widens the range of our clinical work with dreams and refines our ability to use dream analysis to our patients' best advantage.

The new theory, like the old, begins with the assumption, that, despite the general quiescence of mental functioning during sleep, there are certain energies of the mind which remain active, at least during those times when dreaming − that is, the dream-work − is going on. It is these energies which initiate dreaming. They, or more exactly, the mental representations which are associated with them, constitute the latent content of the ensuing dream. This latent content stems from the instinctual derivatives of the id on the one hand and from the impressions and cares of the preceding day on the other. So far, we are on familiar ground. However, when we leave the questions of the initiation of a dream and of its latent content and turn instead to the dream-work, the new theory shows some significant differences from its predecessor.

To be specific, the new theory assumes that the mental energy which is associated with the latent dream content activates various unconscious ego and superego functions, just as might happen during waking life. Some of the ego-functions assist or guide the instinctual energies toward satisfaction. Other ego-functions, to which we refer as defenses (counter-instinctual ego-functions), oppose the gratification just referred to, acting in accordance with superego demands. It may be added parenthetically that the instinctual gratification which is characteristic of dreaming is a gratification in fantasy − what Freud called an 'hallucinated wish-fulfilment'. At times, however, somatic gratification may occur as well; for example, a sexual orgasm.

To continue with our description of the dream-work, the interplay among instinctual (id) derivatives, ego-functions and superego demands and prohibitions is not always as simple as we have just outlined. For example, defenses (ego-functions) may be directed against superego demands as well as against instinctual derivatives. Moreover, on occasion, superego demands may join forces with an id impulse; for example, a masochistic or a sadistic one. Our theory assumes, therefore, that the dream-work consists of an interplay among id, ego and superego. This interplay may be quite simple or extremely complex. In any case, its final result is the manifest dream — what the dreamer experiences consciously during his sleep.

I should like to emphasize that the description I have just given of the dream-work is not essentially different from what we understand to be the way in which the mental apparatus operates during waking life. In waking life, too, we have reason to assume that conscious thoughts, ideas, fantasies, and so on are the end result of a compromise, an interplay, among instinctual forces, ego-functions and superego demands and prohibitions. This is what is meant by the principle of 'multiple functioning', a term first introduced by Waelder (1936). To be sure, it was Freud who introduced the notion of compromise formation into psychoanalytic theories of mental functioning. He recognized very early that hysterical symptoms are, in fact, a compromise between the gratification of a sexual wish and the infliction by the patient of punishment on himself for permitting himself to gratify such a forbidden wish while, at the same time, the wish itself is barred from consciousness by repression. It was not until many years later, however, that it was clearly recognized that the tendency to compromise formation among id, ego and superego is as characteristic for normal mental functioning as it is for neurotic symptom formation. It may be added, again parenthetically, that the full significance of the principle of mental functioning is still often overlooked. A conscious fantasy, a thought, an action, much less a symptom is never *purely* a defense, a self-punishment or an instinctual gratification. It may be predominantly one or the other, to be sure. It may be proper, as a matter of analytic technique, to draw a given patient's attention to one or another of the several determinants just mentioned. However, it is essential to be clear in one's own mind that whatever one *observes* of the conscious mental life of any person, whether a patient or not, is the result of an interaction among the various forces and trends in the mind, forces which are most conveniently subsumed under the headings of id, ego and superego.

So far, then, we have postulated that during dreaming, as during waking mental life, instinctual energies plus the influences of the outer world — day residues in dreaming, perceptions in waking life — impel or drive the mind in the direction of compromise formation. In other words, the principle of multiple functioning is operative during dreaming just as it is during waking life. Yet we know that the net result of an interplay among the conflicting and co-operating tendencies of id, ego and superego during waking life is not a dream. A dream occurs only when one is asleep. How can one account for the difference?

Our answer is as follows. 1) there is a regressive alteration in many of the functions of the ego during dreaming. 2) there is a similar regressive alteration in superego functioning during dream. 3) instinctual wishes and fantasies stemming from the id play a larger role in dreaming than they do in most adult, waking, mental phenomena. Each of these points will be discussed in turn.

First, with respect to regression of ego-functions during dreaming, we must assume that it is a consequence of the sleeping state (Freud 1917). More than this we cannot say at the present time. We can say much more, however, by way of description of the nature of these regressive alterations and of their consequences. Let us begin by specifying, as far as possible, just what regressive changes characterize ego-functions during sleep.

In any list of the ego-functions which are regressively altered during sleep, we must certainly include reality testing, thinking, language, defenses, integrative ability, sensory perception and motor control. Some of these obviously overlap, others might be subdivided, but since any list would be subject to some qualification, let us take the one just given and consider each of its items.

We shall begin with reality testing. More specifically, we are concerned with that aspect of reality testing which has to do with the ability to distinguish between what is perceived of the outer world and what is the result of something going on in one's own mind: the ability to distinguish fact from fancy. Generally speaking, the dreamer is unable to do this. His ability to test reality, to distinguish between a stimulus from the outer world and a stimulus from the inner world, has regressed to a stage characteristic of infancy, to a time of life when he was unable to distinguish between events of the outer world and those of the inner one. Traces of this stage normally persist well into childhood, as witnessed by the child's tendency to treat his fantasies and games as real, at least during playtime. As an extreme example of this tendency, one may note that it is by no means rare for a young child to have an imaginary companion for months or even years, a companion who is as real and present to the child as any of the objectively real persons of his environment. To an adult dreamer, the conscious result of the dream-work — that is, the images of the manifest dream — are as real as are waking fantasies (of the sort just mentioned) to a small child. The dreamer's function of reality testing has regressed to a stage characteristic of early childhood.

Since thinking and the use of language are so intimately associated, we may conveniently consider them together. There are numerous manifestations of the regressive alteration of these functions during dreaming. For example, a dreamer tends to think as a child does, in concrete sensory images, usually visual, rather than in words, as is characteristic for adult, waking thought. This regression to an infantile mode of thought accounts for the fact that most manifest dreams consist of visual images. Characteristically, a dream is something that the dreamer sees in his sleep. It will be recalled that Freud (1900) originally accounted

54

for this characteristic of dreams by postulating a need for plastic representability as one of the attributes of the dream-work. In addition to thinking
in visual images to a large extent, the dreamer deals with words and
language in a regressive way. There is a clearly evident tendency in the
dream-work to play with words and to equate words that sound alike,
as there is in childhood. There is likewise clearly evident a regression
in other, closely related aspects of thinking. The dream-work is full of
representation by allusion, representation by the opposite, representation of the whole by the part, or the part by the whole. In a word, the
dream-work is characterized by that type of mentation normally dominant
in childhood which is generally referred to in the psychoanalytic literature
as 'primary-process thinking'. In particular, the dream-work is characterized by the use of symbols in the psychoanalytic sense of the word.

Finally, as Freud pointed out, a realistic attitude toward time, toward
space and toward death, as well as the usual adult requirements of logic
and syntax, are either grossly defective or absent. All of these changes
are attributable to a regressive alteration of various aspects of the ego-
functions of language and of thinking. In each case, we can observe that
the dreamer's mind is functioning in a primitive or infantile manner.

The ego' integrative function is also regressively altered during sleep.
Freud noted the participation of this function in the dream-work from
the start of his researches, identifying it at that time as the tendency to
secondary revision. However, despite many exceptions, dreams are not,
as a rule, harmonized and integrated with respect to their various
component parts to nearly the same degree as we expect ordinary waking
thoughts or even day-dreams, to be. The dreamer, like the child, is less
concerned with unity and consistency than is the waking adult, even
though, as Freud noted, the integrative function of the ego does play
a part in dream formation.

One of the most striking of the changes in ego-functioning during
dreaming, and one of the most significant in clinical work, is the
diminution of the ego's defenses. Freud related this diminution to the
paralysis of motility during sleep: since action is impossible, wishes are
not so dangerous. It seems likely, however, that more is involved than
a realistic appraisal by the dreamer of the defensive value of his own
immobility during sleep. The dreamer's diminished defensive opposition
to his own instinctual wishes does, in fact, resemble the limited defensive
capacities of the ego of a small child. If this resemblance is significant,
the diminution of ego defenses during dreaming should be considered
to be at least in part a regressive alteration of the defensive functions of
the ego.

Finally, as we know, ego-functions of sensory perception and of motor
control are also profoundly altered during sleep. In the case of these two

55

functions, however, it is not so clear that the alterations to be observed are a result of regression. They seem to be caused rather by a diminution or suspension of the particular ego-function in question rather than by regression to patterns of functioning which are characteristic of infancy or early childhood. In any case, the alterations in these particular ego functions are of less interest to us than are the others, since they do not seem to be directly involved in or to influence directly the dream-work proper. For that reason, we need not discuss them in particular detail.

Another aspect of the diminution and regression of ego-functions during sleep is that the degree to which it occurs with respect to any particular function may vary considerably from dream to dream and from one part of a dream to another. This fact should occasion no surprise from analysts, who are accustomed to observing evidences of such alterations from day to day and from minute to minute in their analytic patients. In dreams, the dream-work may regressively utilize non-verbal, visual thinking in one part of a dream, while verbal thoughts, characteristic of mature mental functioning, appear in another part. Indeed, visual elements and verbal thoughts may appear in a manifest dream simultaneously. It is important to remember this fact in utilizing dream interpretations in one's clinical practice. It is as necessary to obtain a patient's associations to dream thoughts expressed verbally as it is to obtain his associations to visual or other sensory elements of the manifest dream if one is to arrive at a satisfactory understanding of the dream's latent content. One must not ignore a manifest dream element simply because it is verbal rather than visual.

One may also conclude from such observations of ego-functioning as those noted here that the dream-work, as waking mentation, is characterized by the simultaneous interplay of mature ego-functioning and primitive or infantile ego-functioning: to use more familiar, although less correct, terms, the simultaneous interplay of primary and secondary process thinking. It is only that, in waking life, the more mature forms of ego-functioning tend to predominate while, in the dream-work, less mature forms of ego-functioning predominate; at least they are more conspicuous and relatively more important than they normally are in waking life. It is apparent from all of these considerations why the mental phenomena of waking life to which dreams bear the closest relationship are those in which ego-functioning of a primitive or infantile sort plays a substantial part: neurotic or psychotic symptoms, parapraxes, and such phenomena as day-dreams, jokes, reverie, and so on.

Superego functions also show clear evidence of regressive alteration during dreaming, although superego regression has attracted less general attention than has regression of such ego-functions as defenses and reality testing. It appears, nevertheless, that superego regressions contribute substantially to the infantile character of the mental processes involved in the dream–work and in the manifest dream as well. For example, when unpleasure accompanies the direct or distorted fantasy of instinctual gratification in a manifest dream, it is far more often anxiety than guilt. What would produce guilt or remorse in waking life is more apt to produce fear or punishment during a dream, just as it normally does during early childhood when the superego is still in process of formation. Similarly, the dreamer, like the child, seems to be more nearly exclusively guided by the principle of an 'eye for an eye and a tooth for a tooth', than is the waking adult. He is also more prone to project his guilty impulses onto the person of others, while he identifies himself, in the dream, with the disapproving and punishing judge. Finally, he is more likely to instinctualize punitive suffering, that is to react masochistically. It is apparent that each of these characteristics of dream life represents a regression on the part of the dreamer to a more childish stage of superego development and functioning.

Finally, one may surmise that the fact that instinctual wishes often find a more direct and conscious expression in dreams than would be permitted in waking life bespeaks a diminution of the superego's functioning to a more childish level as well as a diminution of the ego's defenses. We must remember in this connection that the link between superego functioning and the institution and maintenance of anti-instinctual defenses by the ego is a particularly close one. The defenses against the drives are normally maintained by the ego at the behest of the superego, once the superego has been firmly established as a system of the mind.

Now for the third point that we proposed to discuss; namely the fact that instinctual wishes and fantasies stemming from the id play a larger role in dreaming than they do in most adult, waking, mental phenomena. That this is true seems self-evident. The explanation for it seems equally evident: during sleep, the mental representations of external reality are largely decathected. Broadly speaking, the only things that matter to us in our sleep are our own wishes and needs. This is one aspect of what Freud emphasized as the increase in narcissism during sleep. Since the instinctual fantasies which comprise the id aspect of the latent content of a dream are so largely infantile in content it is understandable that they too impart an infantile character to the dream which they stimulate.

I shall attempt now to summarize the theory of dream psychology which I have just described to you. I shall begin by repeating that, despite the general quiescence of mental functioning during sleep, certain energies of the mind remain active. They, and the mental processes associated with them, constitute the latent content of the dream. This latent content takes its origin, on the one hand, from the instinctual derivatives of the id and on the other from the impressions and cares of the preceding day.

57

The dream-work consists of a mutual interplay among the various tendencies of id, ego and superego, tendencies which may reinforce one another, may cooperate with one another or may oppose one another. Such an interplay occurs as a regular state of affairs during waking life as well. However, during sleep, various ego and superego functions are regressively altered. Moreover, a relatively large part is played in the dream-work by infantile, wish-fulfilling fantasies since a relatively smaller part is played by the claims of external reality, which are largely decathected during sleep. As a result, mental activity during dreaming is much more infantile in many ways than is mental activity during waking life. Condensation, displacement, representation by allusion, by opposites, by symbols, representation in concrete, visual images, disregard for time, space and death, in a word, all of the familiar characteristics of the dream-work are caused by ego and superego regression, plus the infantile nature of much of the latest content from which the dream-work takes its origin. Finally, it is as a result of regressive alteration of the ego function of reality testing that the dreamer belives that what he dreams is not fantasy but reality.

Having presented to you this revised theory of the psychology of dream formation, my next task is to explain what relevance it has for clinical psychoanalytic work. In my opinion, its relevance can best be summarized under two headings. First, it suggests that dream analysis has more to tell than merely the content of the dreamer's unconscious, repressed, sexual childhood wishes or fantasies. Second, it suggests likewise that dream analysis is not as uniquely important as a method of investigating unconscious memories and unconscious mental processes as some psychoanalysts believe it to be.

What do I mean by saying that dream analysis has more to offer than a view of the dreamer's unconscious, infantile wishes? We know that it was to these wishes that Freud pointed when he described every dream as a wish fulfillment. When dreams are described as the highway to the unconscious mind of man, what is usually meant by 'the unconscious' are repressed, infantile wishes. What more is there?

Let me give an example to illustrate what I have in mind. A thirty-five-year-old, unmarried man, who had been in analysis for several months, dreamed that he was on a toboggan, rushing swiftly downhill on an icy slide. At first, the ride was exciting and enjoyable. Soon, however, he grew frightened. He was going too fast. An accident seemed inevitable. He did not awaken, but the dream, or his memory of it, ended.

The following information is pertinent. The patient had come to analysis depressed and unhappy over certain events in his life. During the course of the first few months of analysis, he had become more cheerful, even optimistic. Shortly before the dream just reported, however, he had begun to bring to his analysis memories and fantasies that pointed to conflict over frightening, homosexual wishes which were closely related to his jealousy of a younger sister, the family's favorite, as well as to a prolonged separation from his mother in early childhood. The emergence of this material made him noticeably uneasy, although he was not himself aware that this was so.

In associating to his dream about tobogganing, the patient spoke about a number of experiences he had had in another winter sport: namely, skiing. He was a fairly proficient skier and had never been injured while skiing. Friends of his had been injured, however. He recalled a doctor who had once fallen and fractured his clavicle on a downhill run. The man behaved like a child – like a sissy. No real man would have carried on like that over a little pain. The patient himself would certainly have been ashamed to show such weakness. Other associations had to do with the seating arrangements on a toboggan. Each passenger holds up the legs of the one behind. It's lots of fun if one is between two girls but embarrassing to have a man sitting in front of one, or behind one, either, for that matter, the patient felt.

I assume you will agree with me that part of the latent content of my patient's dream was an unconscious, homosexual wish, originating in childhood and revived in the transference. He wished that I, the man seated behind him, would make love to him as though he were a girl. What I wish to emphasize, however, is how much more the dream has to tell us. We learn from it that the patient is far more than just uneasy about his feminine wishes. He is very frightened that their consequence will be a painful physical injury, presumably the loss of his penis. We learn, also, some of the defenses he used in the dream-work and in his associations to the dream in his effort to avoid, or at least to minimize, his anxiety. For one thing, he projected his expectation of bodily injury, as well as his feeling of unmanliness, onto his skiing companion. For another, he emphasized both his own stoicism and his love of sports. We can infer that both of these character traits serve importantly the function of defending him against frightening, homosexual wishes. Indeed, some months later, in order to reassure himself about his manliness, he undertook, successfully, a hazardous athletic feat, of a sort for which he was quite untrained – a typical, counterphobic bit of acting out.

It is clear, therefore, that analysis of this patient's dream affords a view of unconscious *conflict*, rather than merely an opportunity to identify an unconscious, infantile wish. We learn from the analysis of the dream not only the wish itself but also the fears that it arouses and the defenses which are directed against it. It is necessary to have a clear recognition of this fact in order to make the maximum use of dream analysis in one's clinical work with patients. In the present instance, what seemed to me most

59

useful to interpret to the patient was that he was much more frightened by the recent references to homosexuality that had come up in his analysis than he consciously realized. At the time he reported the dream that we have been discussing, the state of the analytic work was such that it would have been premature to interpret to him that he did, indeed, have frightening homosexual wishes, although unconscious ones, to be sure. It would have been equally inappropriate at that time to have interpreted the defensive function of his athletic prowess. However, the decision as to what was appropriate and useful to interpret at the time is determined by factors other than dream interpretation proper. One is influenced by the previous course of the patient's analysis, by one's knowledge of what has already been interpreted to him, how he has responded to previous interpretations, the state of the transference, the general level of resistance, one's knowledge of special events that may be upsetting in the patient's life outside the analysis; that is under different analytic circumstances, it might have been quite proper to interpret to him not only his fear of homosexuality but also his sexual wishes of a feminine nature toward me, or the fact that his interest in dangerous sports served to reassure him against the castration fears aroused by his wish to be loved as a girl. The point that I wish to make is that dream analysis tells one more than his patient's infantile wishes. It also tells us the anxiety (or guilt) associated with those wishes and the defenses which are directed against them in an effort to avoid anxiety. Not infrequently, it tells one something about the dynamics of character traits, as in the case just cited, or about the psychopathology of a symptom.

My second point is that our present understanding of dream psychology suggests that dream analysis is not as *uniquely* important as a method of investigating unconscious mental processes as some psychoanalysts believe it to be. *All* conscious mental phenomena and all behavior are multiply determined. It is not only the case with dreams that they are a compromise formation among instinctual (id) wishes, defenses motivated by anxiety or guilt, and superego demands or prohibitions. The same is true of neurotic symptoms, parapraxes, slips, jokes, many character traits, one's choice of a profession, one's sexual practices and preferences, day-dreams, conscious childhood memories, including screen memories, one's reactions to a play, film, or book, one's social habits and activities in general and, above all, of every patient's so-called free associations. They are no more free than is a manifest dream. Like every dream, they are the outcome of an unconscious interplay among the various forces and tendencies within the mind, forces which are most conveniently grouped under the headings id, ego and superego. It is not possible to predict in general, I believe, which conscious phenomena will lead most quickly and easily to the fullest knowledge of unconscious mental processes. Nor is it, in my opinion, the same phenomena which are most advantageous for anlaysis at every stage of any one patient's analysis. Sometimes a dream is best; at another time, something else. What I wish to emphasize is the incorrectness of the view that dream analysis is, generally speaking, outstandingly the *best* method for learning about unconscious mental processes. It is essential in analysis to pay attention to patients' dreams; it is important, sometimes very important, to analyze them. It is equally important to pay attention to and to analyze many other aspects of what our analytic patients tell us.

In my experience, it is not rare for students to conclude from their analytic education that dreams are treated differently from other analytic material, in the following sense. When a patient tells a dream, one expects him to associate to it; when a patient tells a day-dream, fantasy or symptom, and so on, one doesn't ask for such associations. Apparently, the idea is not rare that dreams or, rather, dream analysis, is different from the rest of analytic practice. This, I believe, is the basis for what Balint said in Edinburgh, for example. I am firmly of the opinion that this view is wrong. In my experience it is as important for patients to associate to symptoms, to fantasies, to physical sensations and images experienced during an analytic hour, and so forth, as it is for them to associate to a dream. The results are just as likely to be illuminating and rewarding. I might add that I believe it is as risky to interpret the unconscious meaning of a neurotic symptom without the patient's associations to it as it is to interpret the unconscious meaning of a dream without the dreamer's associations. One may do either correctly with the skill born of long experience if one has an intimate knowledge of the psychological context in which the dream was dreamed or the symptom appeared. However, one may also go far astray or miss much of importance.

For example, a few days ago I learned from a young, married woman who had been in treatment for two months that she had been quite uncomfortable a couple of weeks before on a recent trip to a bank. She had been invited to have lunch with a friend who worked in the bank in a windowless dining room below street level but couldn't stay in a room down there with only one door for an exit. It made her anxious; why she didn't know. At that moment she realized that she had thought of this example of her habitual claustrophobia just after telling me about her mixed feelings for a sibling who had died before the patient was born, whose picture had been kept in the patient's room all through her childhood, and with whom she felt she was often unfavorably compared. Her first thought was that her fear of closed spaces, her worry that she would be unable to get out, was a result of her rage at her dead baby sister, whom her parents refused to let be dead and gone. Her second thought was to object that such an explanation couldn't be correct, since her sister's body is not buried; it is in a vault above ground. This reminded her that the underground bank rooms in which she had felt so anxious were next to the bank's vaults. She went on then to tell me for the first time that it frightens her to be in tunnels or elevators, especially if she can't get out, that is, if traffic stops in a tunnel or if an elevator's doors fail to open promptly.

I hope I have given enough material in this very brief vignette to illustrate the point that I wish to make: namely, that associations to a symptom are just as valuable and just as necessary to the understanding of the symptom's unconscious determinants as are associations to a dream for its interpretation. It is just as important for a patient to associate to symptoms, day-dreams or fantasies – in a word, to any of the many consequences of unconscious conflicts – as it is for him to associate to the conscious elements of a dream.

In summary, I have presented a revision of psychoanalytic dream theory. According to the theory that I have presented, dreams, like many other features of mental life, are best understood as the result of an interplay among id, ego and superego. Put into other words, a dream is multiply determined. The consequences of this understanding of dream formation are two-fold. First, dream analysis leads to an understanding not only of the unconscious, infantile wishes which the dream endeavors to fulfill in fantasy but also of other aspects of unconscious mental functioning of which those wishes are a part: to the fears and guilt feelings associated with them, to defenses against them and, often, to related symptoms or character traits. Second, while dream analysis is even more useful clinically than we are accustomed to considering it to be, it is not unique in this respect. Other consequences of inner conflict are as important to analyze as are dreams and may, on occasion, be quite as useful a road to the understanding of a patient's inner conflicts, of his unconscious mind, as a dream would be.

References

Arlow, J.A. and Brenner, C. *Psychoanalytic Concepts and the Structural Theory.* International Universities Press, New York, 1964.

Brenner, C. *An Elementary Textbook of Psychoanalysis.* International Universities Press, New York, 1955.

—— Some commments on technical precepts in psychoanalysis. *J. Amer. Psychoanal. Ass.,* in press.

Breuer, J. and Freud, S. *Studies in Hysteria,* Vol. 2, 1895.

Freud, S. *The Interpretation of Dreams,* Vols 4 and 5, 1900.

—— *Fragment of an Analysis of a Case of Hysteria,* Vol. 7, 1905.

—— *The Unconscious,* Vol. 14, 1915.

—— *Metapsychological Supplement to the Theory of Dreams*, Vol. 14, 1917.

Waelder, R. The principle of multiple function. *Psychoanal. Quart.* 5: 45–62, 1936.

3

The exceptional position of the dream in psychoanalytic practice

RALPH R. GREENSON

Introduction

Freud considered *The Interpretation of Dreams* his major work. He wrote in the third (revised) English edition, published in 1932, 'It contains, even according to my present-day judgement, the most valuable of all the discoveries it has been my good fortune to make. Insight such as this falls to one's lot but once in a lifetime' (SE4: xxxii). At the end of Part E in the seventh chapter Freud said: '*The interpretation of dreams is the royal road to a knowledge of the unconscious activities of the mind*' (p. 608). A further indication of how important Freud considered this work to be is that he revised and amplified the book on dreams on eight different occasions, the last time in 1930 (SE4: xii).[1]

You may wonder why I chose to present a paper on the exceptional position of the dream since all this would seem to be common knowledge. A careful reading of the psychoanalytic literature in recent years, however, reveals that a number of psychoanalysts believe either that the dream has declined in clinical importance over the last forty years and is of no special value for psychoanalytic therapy or they use techniques which indicate that they have disregarded Freud's theory and methods of understanding and using the dream in clinical practice. I am also impressed that some influential psychoanalysts contend that this downgrading of the significance of the dream in clinical practice has come about because, (1) the structural theory was introduced, (2) Freud's great work on dreams has discouraged attempts at emulation or elaboration, and (3) Freud's concept of the topographic theory has become useless (Waldhorn 1967: 52, 53). These conclusions and more can be found in a monograph titled *The Place of the Dream in Clinical Psychoanalysis* (Waldhorn 1967), which is the result of a two-year study of dreams by the Kris Study Group under the Chairmanship of Charles Brenner with Herbert Waldhorn serving as reporter. Most of the members of this group appear to have concluded that (1) the dream is, clinically speaking, a communication in the course of analysis similar to all others; (2) it does not provide access to material otherwise unavailable; (3) it is simply one of many types of material useful for analytic inquiry; (4) it is not particularly useful for the recovery of repressed childhood memories; (5) Freud's theory that the dream-work is governed by the interplay between the primary process and the secondary process is not compatible with the structural theory and ought to be discarded.

I disagree with every one of the conclusions stated above. I am happy to point out that I am not alone in my beliefs, for I have discovered that some members of that section of the Kris Study Group, with Leon Altman as their spokesman, opposed many of those opinions. Altman has recently published a book, *The Dream in Psychoanalysis*, in which he suggests other reasons for the decline in clinical use of the dream. He expressed the opinion that since the coming of the trend toward ego psychology, many analysts have not had the experience of having their own dreams properly analyzed, and the lack of this type of personal experience has deprived the psychoanalyst of the conviction that the interpretation of dreams is of outstanding importance for psychoanalysis (Altman 1969: 1).

Besides that section of the Kris Study Group reported in *The Place of the Dream in Clinical Psychoanalysis*, there are prominent analysts of Kleinian persuasion who also work with patients' dreams in ways which are far removed from what Freud, Isakower (1938, 1954), Sharpe (1949), Lewin (1958, 1968), Erikson (1954), and a host of others have described in their writings on this subject. In this paper I shall attempt to contribute some clinical material and formulations which I hope will demonstrate how those analysts who seem to operate from divergent theoretical and technical convictions differ from analysts who believe in the exceptional position of the dream.

It is my belief, after many years of psychoanalytic therapy with private patients and candidates in psychoanalytic training, that one cannot carry out genuine analysis in sufficient depth if one does not understand the structure of dream formation *as well as the patient's and the analyst's contributions to the technique of dream interpretation.*

Some general formulations

The dream, I believe, is a unique form of mental functioning which is produced during a special phase of sleep. This phase is unlike any other phase of the sleep cycle and differs also from the waking state. The psychophysiological research of Dement and Kleitman (1957), Charles Fisher (1965, 1966), and Ernest Hartmann (1965), among others, has made this emphatically clear. Recent research suggests the likelihood that dream deprivation may be the cause of severe emotional and mental disorders. We may well have to add to Freud's dictum that the dream is the guardian of sleep, that sleep is necessary in order to safeguard our need to dream.

The altered balance of mental forces in the dream is produced by bursts of psychic activity that seek sensory release because sleep diminishes contact with the external world and also cuts off the possibility of voluntary motor action. The dream state allows for a reduction and regression of conscious ego activities and of the censorship function of the superego. It is important to realize, however, that in a sense, one is never fully awake nor fully asleep. These are relative and not absolute terms. Kubie (1966), Lewin (1955) and Stein (1965) have stressed the merits of keeping in mind the sleep—waking ratio in studying any kind of human behavior. This helps explain the fact that in the dream the perceiving function of the ego, being deprived of the external world during sleep, turns its energy toward internal psychic activity. Freud wrote that when people go to sleep they undress their minds and lay aside most of their physical acquisitions (1915: 222). Lewin added that the dreamer generally sheds his body. The dream usually appears to us as a picture and is recorded only by an indefinite 'psychic' eye (Lewin 1968: 86).

If we follow the notion of a variable sleep—waking ratio, we are immediately reminded of phenomena similar to dreams: free association, parapraxes, jokes, symptom formations and acting out. But there are crucial differences. No production of the patient occurs so regularly and reveals so much so graphically of the unconscious forces of the mind as the dream. Dream interpretation can uncover in more immediate and convincing ways not only what is hidden, but how it is hidden and why it is hidden. We gain special access to the interplay and the transitions between the unconscious psychic activities governed by the primary process and conscious phenomena which follow the laws of the secondary process. The proportion between input and output, in terms of reported phenomena and obtained knowledge of unconscious material, is in no other type of psychic phenomena as favorable as it is in dreams (Eissler personal communication).

So long as psychoanalytic therapy focuses on the resolution of neurotic conflicts in which the crucial components are unconscious, it makes no sense to consider every production of the patient of equal potential value. Affects, body language and dreams are all, in most ways, nearer to those almost unreachable depths we search out so persistently in our analytic work. We attempt to present our findings to the patient's conscious and reasonable ego with the hope of providing him with a better understanding of his way of life and an opportunity for change.

These same points can be expressed structurally by stating that the dream reveals with unusual clarity various aspects of the id, the repressed, the unconscious ego and superego, and to a lesser degree certain conscious ego-functions, particularly its observing activities. However, limiting the approach to the dream to the structural point of view is an injustice because it neglects the fact that we also have in the dream more open access to dynamic, genetic and economic data of basic importance. Small wonder then that the dream experience itself, often without interpretation, leads more directly and intensely to the patient's affects and drives than any other clinical material. This makes for a sense of conviction about the reality of unconscious mental activity unequalled by any other clinical experience. This is particularly true of transference dreams.

The dream is in closer proximity to childhood memories by dint of the fact that both make use essentially of pictorial representations. Freud (1900–01, 1923) and Lewin (1968) have emphasized that primitive mentation takes place in pictures and is closer to unconscious processes than verbal representation. Even after the child learns to speak, his thinking is essentially dominated by pictorial representations. Things heard get turned into pictures, as we know from certain screen memories (Lewin 1968; Schur 1966). If an event is to become a memory in early childhood, it has eventually to become concretized, a mental representation, a memory-trace. Lewin states that then we search for lost memories as if they can be found somewhere. This type of memory, the recall of an objectified experience, is a step which seems to occur at the end of the first or beginning of the second year of life (Spitz 1965; Waelder 1937). There are more primitive 'imprintings' which are derived from infantile body and feeling states that are not capable of being remembered but which may give rise to mental images and sensations in dreams. Lewin's ideas on blank dreams and the dream screen and his discussion of related problems are especially worthy of note (1953; 1968: 51–5).

To return briefly to the special importance of the psychic eye for the dreamer and the interpreter of dreams. The dream is essentially a visual experience and most adult recollections of early childhood come to us as pictures or scenes. The analyst interpreting to his patient is often working upon a fragment of historical experience which he hopes will lead to a memory. Such fragments or details may appear in dreams. When the analyst tries to fill in the gaps between single interpretations, he is making a construction, he is trying to recreate a series of interrelated forgotten experiences. Such conjectures may lead to recollections but, even if they do not, they may lead to a sense of probability or conviction that the reconstruction is correct. This may then appear in a dream as an event

(Freud 1937). Lewin describes this as trying to recreate a story in pictures of the patient's forgotten past. By doing so we attempt to get the patient to scan his past along with us; we are engaged in conjoint looking (Lewin 1968: 17). The ultra-clarity of some dream details also indicates that there is a special relationship between the cathexis of looking and the search for memories. This wish to see what actually took place, to be 'in' on it, adds to the special sense of conviction that the correct interpretation of a dream can convey.

Ernst Kris decried the one-sided emphasis on analyzing defenses and stressed the importance of reconstructing past historical events so that the patient could 'recognize' the pictures drawn as familiar (1956a: 59). He believed that memory plays a central role in a circular process which, if integrated, makes it possible for the patient to reconstruct his total biographical picture, change his self-representation and his perspective of the important persons in his world. In Kris's paper on the 'good analytic hour', it is remarkable how often he chose examples of hours which contained dreams and recovered memories (1956b).

The predominant elements in the psychic activities that occur in dreams are heavily weighted on the side of the id, the repressed memories, the primitive defensive mechanisms of the ego, and the infantile forms and functions of the superego. Occasionally one can observe more mature ego-functions, but they are rarely dominant. All this testifies to the high degree of regression that occurs in dreaming, but as in all regressive phenomena, the quality and quantity of regression is uneven and selective in the different psychic structures and functions, as Freud pointed out as early as 1917 (in *A Metapsychological Supplement to the Theory of Dreams*), Fenichel in 1945 (*The Psychoanalytic Theory of Neurosis*), and Arlow and Brenner in 1964 (in *Psychoanalytic Concepts and the Structural Theory*). The clearest and most comprehensive description of the unevenness and selectivity of regression can be found, in my opinion, in Anna Freud's book, *On Normality and Pathology in Childhood* (1965: 93–107).

Free association is a similar regressive phenomenon; it is an attempt to approximate something between wakefulness and sleep. The use of the reclining position, the absence of external distractions, the patient's attempt consciously to suspend his ordinary censorship, to abandon strict logic and coherence in his communications, all attest to that. However, real spontaneous free associations are rarely achieved by most patients and are then defended against with far greater sophistication. The point I wish to make is that the dream is the freest of free associations. Slips of the tongue may quickly reveal some deep unconscious insights but they occur rarely; insight is localized and the old defenses are very readily re-instituted. Acting out is by definition ego-syntonic to the patient, and its infantile origins are strongly rationalized away and defended. By contrast, as bizarre and incomprehensible as the dream may appear, the patient recognizes the dream as his, he knows it is his own creation. Although the strange content of the dream may make it seem alien, nevertheless it is irrevocably his, like his symptoms, and he is quite willing to work on his dreams, provided his analyst has demonstrated how working together on dreams is helpful in achieving greater awareness of the patient's unknown self.

A few words before turning to some clinical examples. In 1923 Freud himself recognized that *some* of his ideas subsumed under the topographic point of view conflicted with the descriptive and dynamic attributes of unconscious mental activities and he introduced the structural point of view (1923). This new division of the psychic apparatus into id, ego and superego clarified the role of the conscious and unconscious ego and the conscious and unconscious superego in its conflicts with the totally unconscious id. I agree with Fenichel (1945), with Rapaport and Gill (1959), as well as with Arlow and Brenner (1964), who stress the superiority of the structural theory in affording a clearer and more logical explanation for the origin and fate of neurotic conflicts. I do not agree with Arlow and Brenner, however, that Freud's hypotheses concerning the primary process, the secondary process, and the preconscious should be discarded or that they are incompatible with the structural point of view. Even Merton Gill (1963), who believes that the topographic point of view is conceptually not on a par with the other metapsychological points of view, agrees that some topographic conceptions have an important place both clinically and theoretically. I find this to be particularly true in working with dreams. It is equally important in dealing with patients who suffer from defects and deficiencies in ego formation and the parallel difficulty in building constant internal object-representations, problems which go below and beyond the conflict theory of the psychoneuroses. I do not wish to dwell on theory — it is not my strong point, but those interested may turn to the writings of Hartman (1951), Loewenstein (1954), Benjamin (1959), Eissler (1962), Schur (1966), Loewald (1966), Mahler (1968), and Fisher's remarks in the panel on *The Psychoanalytic Theory of Thinking* (1958), for a more thorough discussion of the subject.

Clinical examples

Some clinical examples of how different analysts work with dreams illustrate the divergencies in technique and theoretical orientation. I shall begin with clinical material from the publications of psychoanalysts who work with dreams in ways that seem to me to be unproductive, wasteful, and at times even harmful.

A clinical illustration presented in Waldhorn's *The Place of the Dream in Clinical Psychoanalysis* (1967: 59–67) was that of a thirty-year-old writer in the second year of her analysis. Essentially, she seemed to be an as-if character, exceedingly immature and dependent. There was a childhood history of social failure in competition with her younger sister because of the patient's ineptitude and gaucheness. The patient had severe acne of the face, neck and back in adolescence and had occasional recurrent active lesions. She was also thin and flat-chested. She entered treatment because of mild depressions, poor concentration, and inability to sustain an intimate relationship with a man. The patient had several brief affairs accompanied by a dread of losing the man and was always flooded by remorse and loss of self-esteem when the affair ended. In the weeks prior to the dream reported, the patient had had sexual relations with a man named John, whom she had known only a short time. He had left town for several weeks and, in spite of knowing better from past disappointments, she found herself imagining that John loved her and they would be married. During this interval she brought in a dream. Now I quote verbatim from the monograph.

> She began the hour as follows: 'I had a very bad dream. I had cancer of the breast. A doctor, a woman, said it would have to be removed. She said that there would be after-effects which I would feel in my neck. My friend R. had this operation. I was scared and I panicked, and wondered how I could get away, run away, and not have to have this done.' She continued with the following associations: 'I tried to think why I should have such a dream. I thought it must be related to my idea that I am both complete by myself and that I need some sort of union with a remarkable man to make myself complete. This might be related to my worry that John was gone and maybe this was symbolized by my breast being removed. Actually, I am very frightened by things like that. Many people do have an obsession about such fears. For example, Paul does. Some people can face these things with great courage and strength, but not me. I am very frightened when I think about the danger of the scorpions in Mexico [she was planning a trip in a few months].'
>
> (1967: 61, ff.)

The patient awoke, fell asleep and had another dream, but I shall omit it because the presenter and the group did not touch upon it. After a few innocuous associations, the analyst finally spoke and I shall quote his first remarks verbatim.

> At this point the analyst intervened, asking, 'about your dream. What do you associate to the business about the doctor?' The patient

responded: 'She was a matronly type of woman, stern. She didn't seem to feel sorry for me or anything like that, but just said what would have to be done. I was thinking, how could a man make love to me without one breast? I would be terribly self-conscious . . .' After a pause the analyst asked: 'What about the part in the dream about the neck?' She responded: 'Sometimes I make a wrong movement and my neck muscles can hurt. That area is vulnerable for me because of my complexion problems involving my chin and neck, about which I have always felt so self-conscious . . .' The analyst then added: 'When you speak of self-consciousness about your skin and neck, does it remind you of the self-consciousness you have recently been describing when you told me about how terrible you felt before you had any breast development?' The patient said: 'So, do you think that the fact that John did not call me made me re-experience those feelings of inadequacy? They may still be present.'

(1967: 62 ff.)

The analyst then offered a long intellectual interpretation and the patient responded in kind.

The Study Group's discussion of this presentation included the following excerpt.

The discussion of this report was initiated by the remarks of the analyst presenting the data. He maintained that the clinical material supported the belief that dreams can best be treated in the same way as other associations in the hours, and not necessarily accorded extraordinary or exhaustively detailed procedural attention as some would insist. Here, in the hours described, the analytic work is focussed on the problems highlighted by the repetitive life experience of the patient. . . . Accordingly, some portions of the dream can be neglected in favor of others, and a dream need have no specific attention directed to it if spontaneous associations are meager and the work with the dream (as opposed to other material) seems less likely to be rewarding. The rich amount of symbolically understandable elements in the second half of the first dream was not explored at all, but it was the analyst's clinical judgment that nothing was lost in the process.

(1967: 64 ff.)

I shall limit myself to a few remarks about the patient's manifest dream, her associations, the analyst's interventions and the group discussion. In the first dream the patient is terrified upon discovering she has a cancer of the breast. She is told this by a female doctor who warns her there will be after-effects. The patient's associations sound to me intellectualized and a rote repetition of old interpretations given her by her male analyst.

71

There does not seem to be any attempt on the part of the analyst to point out her intellectualization or to get to her terror of this malignant thing growing inside her. The analyst did not pursue the only spontaneous free association the patient produced; namely, her fear of scorpions in Mexico. After the patient reported the second dream and a few innocuous associations, the analyst asked: 'About your dream. What do you associate to the business about the doctor?' To me, the way the question was put gives the impression the analyst is either defensive and hostile or even contemptuous, otherwise he would not use a phrase like 'what about the business about the doctor'. Furthermore, it is all too intellectual. Words like 'what do you associate' push the patient in the direction of intellectual compliance; not the best way to get to feelings or really free, free associations. In general, there was no sign that the therapist was trying to reach or establish contact with the patient's affects; he shows no signs of being 'tuned in' on her feelings; on the contrary, he seems to play right along with her intellectualized defensiveness.

If you read the second dream, it seems to express in obvious symbolic terms the patient's envy of her sister and her aunt, but it was completely ignored. Apparently the analyst and the group did not discern any possible connections between cancer, breast, mother and envy. There also was no apparent awareness of how frequently heterosexual promiscuity is used as a defense against helpless childhood dependency needs with the resultant urges and fears of fusing or becoming reunited with the pre-genital mother. There was also no mention of a hostile transference to her male analyst or a wish to have a female analyst. The analyst and the group seemed content to maintain a highly intellectual contact with the patient, and were reluctant to open up the patient's fantasy life and follow wherever it might lead. Toward the end of this discussion in the monograph, there are a few sentences that deserve special comment.

> Such axiomatic procedures as the desirability of working with transference elements before nontransference material, or affect-laden before nonaffect-laden material, or the necessity of drawing the patient's attention to evident omissions or to an addendum, were all mentioned. The consensus was that these were best considered as tactical maneuvers, subordinated to an overall strategy of the conduct of the analysis, which would, of course, change with the progress of the treatment.
>
> (1967: 66)

In my opinion there is no place for 'axiomatic procedures' in trying to do psychoanalytic therapy. It is true that some of us follow certain time-tested technical guidelines in beginning the exploration of such oft-recurring clinical constellations as may occur in associating to dreams or in free association in general. These approaches are tools for investigation. I find the concept of an 'overall strategy of the conduct of the analysis' an impressive high-sounding phrase but, in reality, with our present state of knowledge, this 'overall strategy' is at best loose, subject to frequent changes and revisions, and full of unknowns. Only psychoanalysts with preconceived and rigid theoretical notions are sure of an 'overall strategy'. And they also have prefabricated interpretations for all types of patients and disregard the fact that each individual human being is unique, as well as the fact that there is still much even the best of us do not know and cannot predict about our patients. Freud had the humility to say that we should let the patient determine the subject matter of the hour (1905); he attached great importance to following the patient's free associations. In 1950 Eissler severely criticized Alexander and his followers for making decisions about the definitive strategy for treatment of a case. Eissler felt that Alexander was more interested in validating his own hypotheses than in really analyzing his patients.

This leads to another type of distortion in working with dreams which can be found in the writings of some of the Kleinian analysts. Hans Thorner in studying the problem of examination anxiety illustrated his ideas by describing a patient, a dream and his interpretations. Again, limitations of space permit me to present only the highlights.

A man of early middle age complained of impotence and that all his love relationships came to a premature end. At times he could begin a relationship but as soon as he felt the woman was interested in him, he had to break off. He was impotent in other spheres of his life as well. Although he had reached a high standard of proficiency in music he was unable to play in public or before his friends. It became clear that all these situations approximated an examination situation. When he applied for a new job he was terrified of being interviewed because of what he considered to be his 'black record', although realistically there was little black in his record. During one of these intervals he reported a dream which shed new light upon the nature of his black record. In the dream red spiders were crawling in and out of the patient's anus. A doctor examined him and told the patient that he was unable to see anything wrong with him. The patient replied, 'Doctor, you may not see anything, but they are there just the same.'

Thorner reports his interpretations to the patient as follows:

Here the patient expresses his conviction that he harbours bad objects (red spiders) and even the doctor's opinion cannot shake this conviction. The associative link between 'black record' and 'red spiders' shows the anal significance of his 'black record'. He himself is afraid of these objects against which he, like the man in the dream, asks for help.

73

This help must be based on a recognition of these objects and not on their denial – in other words he should be helped to control them. It is clear that we are here dealing with a feeling of persecution by bad internal objects.

(1957: 284 ff.)

I believe this a prime example of interpreting the manifest content of a dream according to the analyst's theoretical convictions. The patient's associations are interpreted in a narrow preconceived way. The patient's reproach to the examining physician, 'Doctor, you may not see anything, but they are there all the same' is not recognized as a hostile transference nor is it acknowledged as a possible justifiable reproach to the analyst that he really may be missing something. I wonder if the red spiders drawing in and out of the patient's anus are not the patient's reaction to his analyst's intrusive and painful interpretations. But now I, too, am guilty of interpreting without associations.

Another example of a similar type can be found in Hanna Segal's book (1964). She describes a patient, his dream and her interventions as follows.

Powerful unconscious envy often lies at the root of negative therapeutic reactions and interminable treatments; one can observe this in patients who have a long history of failed previous treatments. It appeared clearly in a patient who came to analysis after many years of varied psychiatric and psychotherapeutic treatments. Each course of treatment would bring about an improvement, but deterioration would set in after its termination. When he began his analysis, it soon appeared that the main problem was the strength of his negative therapeutic reaction. I represented mainly a successful and potent father, and his hatred of and rivalry with this figure was so intense that the analysis, representing my potency as an analyst, was unconsciously attacked and destroyed over and over again. ... In the first year of his analysis he dreamt that he put into the boot of his little car tools belonging to my car (bigger than his), but when he arrived at his destination and opened the boot, all the tools were shattered.

Dr Segal interprets:

This dream symbolized his type of homosexuality; he wanted to take the paternal penis into his anus and steal it, but in the process of doing so his hatred of the penis, even when introjected, was such that he would shatter it and be unable to make use of it. In the same way, interpretations which he felt as complete and helpful were immediately torn to pieces and disintegrated, so that it was particularly following good sessions which brought relief that he would start to feel confused and persecuted as the fragmented, distorted, half-remembered interpretations confused and attacked him internally.

(1964: 29–30)

Here too, I believe one can see how the analyst's conviction about the correctness of her insights and interpretations tempts her to make detailed interpretations without any of the patient's associations for confirmatory clinical evidence. Once again I do not see in this case presentation any evidence of an analyst and patient working together on a dream. I see instead, an analyst forcing a patient to submit to her interpretation. By doing so this analyst is acting in a way which proves she is really like the patient's hated and envied potent father. No wonder he dreams that all his tools are shattered. To quote Freud: 'But dream interpretation of such a kind, without reference to the dreamer's associations, would in the most unfavorable case remain a piece of unscientific virtuosity of very doubtful value' (1925: 128). I must add that many analysts of non-Kleinian affiliation also disregard the patient's associations.

At this point, I will present some work with dreams that I believe exemplifies how an analyst who appreciates the exceptional position of the dream utilizes it in his practice. For the sake of clarity and demonstrability, the dreams I have chosen for illustrations are those from my recent clinical experience with which I was able to work fruitfully. They are not everyday examples of my work with dreams. There are many dreams I can understand only vaguely and partially and some I can hardly understand at all. There are also occasions when the dream is not the most productive material of the hour, but this has been rare in my experience. Freud wrote as far back as 1911 that dream interpretation should not be pursued for its own sake, it must be fitted into the treatment, and all of us agree on this obvious point.

I realize that no clinical demonstration of the value of dream interpretation will change the opinions of those who are predominantly devoted to theory conservation or theoretical innovations. Their theories seem to be more real to them than the memories and reconstructions of their patient's life history. Working with dreams is not only an enlightening experience for the patient, but it may also be a source of new clinical and theoretical insights for the analyst, if he has an open mind. Furthermore, there are some analysts who have no ear or eye for dreams, like people who find it hard to hear and visualize the beauty of poetry, or like the tone-deaf who cannot appreciate the special imagery and language of music, or those who have no facility for wit and humor. Such analysts will lower the importance of dream interpretation, no matter what evidence you present. Finally, there are analysts who, for some other reasons, have never had the opportunity to learn how to listen to, understand and work with dreams.

The two dreams I shall present are from the analysis of the same patient, a thirty-year-old writer, Mr M., who came for analytic treatment because of a constant sense of underlying depressiveness, frequent anxiety in social and sexual relations, and a feeling of being a failure despite considerable success in his profession and what appeared to be a good relationship to his wife and children. He had a great fear that he would not be able to do free association at all, and that if he did I would find him empty or loathsome and send him away. We worked on these resistances for several weeks and he was then able on occasion to do some relatively spontaneous free association on the couch. One of the major sources of his resistances in the beginning was his experience with several friends who were also currently in psychoanalytic treatment. They talked freely and often in social situations about their Oedipus complexes, their positive and negative transference reactions, their castration anxiety, their superegos, their incestuous desires, and so on, all of which my patient felt was 'textbooky', 'artificial' and 'a load of crap'. Mr M. was afraid that he would not be able genuinely to accept such interpretations, and yet also dreaded that unknowingly he too might turn out to be a 'junior psychoanalyst' socially. I want to present the highlights from an hour in the sixth week of his analysis in which he reported his first dream. He had often had the feeling of having dreamed, but until this point could never remember any of his dreams.

One day he began the hour by stating: 'I had a dream but it seems unrelated to anything we have been talking about.'

I was making a phone call to some guy in a men's clothing store. I had ordered some clothes made to order and they didn't fit. I asked the guy to take them back but he said I had to come in myself. I told him I was not going to pay for the clothes until they fit. I said it seems like you just took them off the rack. I repeated, I won't pay for the clothes until they fit. As I said that I began to vomit, so I dropped the phone and ran into the bathroom to wash out my mouth. I left the receiver dangling and I could hear the guy saying, 'What did you say, what? What?'

I remained silent and the patient spontaneously began to speak: 'The most striking thing to me is the vomiting. I just can't vomit, I never, never vomit. I can't even remember the last time I did, probably as a child sometime. It is like a biological thing, it's so strong. Like in yesterday's hour, I couldn't get myself to talk. [Pause] Free association is like vomiting.' I intervened at this point and said, 'Yes, free association becomes like vomiting when things are trying to come up in your mind that you would rather keep inside yourself and away from me. The dream says it has to do with something not fitting you properly.' The patient quickly replied, Yes, it's about clothes, but that is too silly. Why clothes? Clothes not fitting? [Pause] Oh my God, this can't have anything to do with the analysis. The man saying, what is it, what, what, that could be you. [Pause] I leave you talking and go to vomit in the bathroom – but why, why do I do that?' I answered, 'When I give you an interpretation that doesn't seem to fit you, you must resent it and feel that I just took it off my "psychoanalytic rack", like the other "textbooky" analysts you have heard about.' The patient: 'Oh Jesus, I can't believe it, I thought things like this only happened in books. How funny!'

At this point, the patient began to roar with laughter and tears streamed down his face. He gathered himself together and said: 'I never thought things like this would happen to me. You are right. When you say things that don't seem to fit me, sometimes I do get annoyed, but I keep it in. [Pause] I get scared here when I feel angry. It's like being afraid of my father when I was a kid. [Pause] I now suddenly see a vague picture of me vomiting when I was about three or four years old. [Pause] It was with my mother, right on her, she must have been holding me. She was so nice about it, too, she took me to the bathroom and cleaned me up and herself too. Amazing, this whole thing.' I answered: 'Yes, apparently you were not afraid to vomit up things in front of your mother, but you must have been very scared of doing that with your father and now you feel the same way here with me. But you see these kinds of things do tend to come out in dreams or in such things like your forgetting to pay me this month.' The patient was startled and blurted out: 'This is too much. I had your check in my wallet, but in the last minute I decided to change my jacket and left my wallet at home. And I never even thought of it when I was telling you the dream, all about not wanting to pay that man. Something must really be cooking inside of me.' The patient paused, sighed, and after a while I asked him just to try to say what was going on. His associations then drifted to his shame about revealing his toilet activities, masturbation, his hemorrhoids, a history of an anal fistula, and other matters.

I believe this clinical example demonstrates how it is possible to work productively with a first dream, which is contrary to the opinions expressed in the monograph *The Place of the Dream in Clinical Psychoanalysis*. Avoidance of dream interpretation by the analyst can frighten the patient, because the patient may sense the analyst's fear of the dream contents. An analyst's timid approach to a dream may add to a patient's suspicion that he, the patient, is especially full of internal evils or may convince him that he has a frightened analyst. On the other hand, deep interpretations given too early will either frighten the patient into leaving the analysis or it will persuade him that the analyst is omniscient and convert the patient into a devout follower and not a working ally. One has to assess carefully with each patient how much and how little one can do with early dreams and early material in general.[2]

Let us scrutinize more carefully what I tried to do with that first dream. Once the patient was spontaneously able to connect his fear of vomiting with his fear of free association, I first confirmed this representation of his resistance by saying out loud what he had already become conscious of – his dread of losing control over the horrible things inside of himself: vomiting is equated to free association and he vomits into the sink and not into the phone, the analysis. I then felt I could lead him in the direction of trying to discover what was making him vomit. The obvious symbolism of the ill-fitting clothes delivered to him ready-made and not made to order, symbols which he himself could grasp, encouraged me to point out his suppressed anger at me for my ill-fitting, ready-made interpretations, taken off my psychoanalytic rack. His laughter was a relief from the fear that he lacked an unconscious mind and was a freak, and also that I might be harsh with him for such thoughts. It was confirmation of the correctness of my interpretation and also an early sign of conviction that there is an active but unconscious part of his mind which does contain specific and personal meanings and they are not as terrible as he had imagined.

My referring to myself as the 'textbooky guy' who is unable to tailor his interpretations to suit the patient must have given Mr M. enough trust in my motherliness so that he could recall an early childhood memory of vomiting on his mother. Here vomiting is loving and not hating. He was then able to contrast this with his dread of vomiting up things in the presence of his father. His later association to the toilet, masturbation, and so forth, indicated an increase in his ability to let things come up in free association in my presence, a lessening of his resistances. Apparently my way of communicating to him helped me establish a working alliance with his reasonable, observing ego.

There are many elements in this dream which I did not point out to Mr M. but which are of interest to us as examples of the function of the dream-work and of the interaction of the primary process and the secondary process as well as of the interaction of the id, ego and superego. The patient's very first sentence before telling the dream – 'I had a dream but it seems unrelated to anything we have been talking about' – is an attempt to contradict and deny the very essence of the dream; namely, that it concerns his feelings about me and the analysis. The psychoanalytic situation is depicted as a telephone conversation, only a verbal exchange, and even that is held at a distance. The man he speaks to is referred to as a 'guy working in a store', not the most awesome or flattering representation of a psychoanalyst. The insights and interpretations I gave him were represented by clothes, and clothes conceal rather than reveal, an example of reversal and the use of opposites. Psychoanalysis does not strip you, it is supposed to clothe you, a reassurance, a wish fulfilment. His fear of close emotional contact with the analyst is demonstrated by his refusal to come in person to the store. His leaving the phone dangling and hearing the 'guy's voice' saying 'what is it, what, what', is a beautiful and hostile caricature of my analytic technique. It is as well his revenge against me for leaving him dangling hour after hour; it is not he who keeps asking desperately, but I. The vomiting is not only an expression of his forbidden instinctual impulses, but it is also a self-punishment for his hostility. It is as well a rejection of the interpretations I have been forcing him to swallow and also his spiteful obedience: 'You want me to bring things up. OK, here it is.' This is an example of the coexistence of opposites in the primary process.

One can see that the vomiting is derived from both the id and the superego. It also serves the resistances, a defensive function of the ego, by breaking off our line of communication. All this and more is in the dream *and* in the patient's associations, facilitated by the interpretations. Only a fraction of this material can be meaningfully conveyed to the patient in a single hour, but it serves a valuable service for the analyst as source material for clues that will be of use in the future.

Mr M. continued with the theme of clothes and concealment in the next several hours. As a child of impoverished parents he was embarrassed by his shabby, dirty clothing. He was also ashamed of being skinny and had tried to hide this by wearing several sweatshirts and sweaters on top of each other when he was young. When he later became affluent he bought bulky tweed sport coats and often wore turtle-neck sweaters with a leather jacket and boots. During the post-dream interval he recalled stealing money from his father to buy a zoot suit, which was fashionable in his youth, because he wanted to make a good impression at a school dance. He also recalled having severe acne which he attributed to masturbation and which he attempted to cover with various facial creams and lotions. He tried to rationalize his stealing from his father by recalling that his father cheated his customers at times. All this material had the meaning: 'I have to hide my true self. If anyone sees beneath my surface he will find me ugly and unlovable. I am a fraud, but so is most of the world. How do I know you are genuine and sincere in your treatment of me and will it change once I am stripped of all my superficial disguises?' (I was not merely working with the manifest dream in the following days, but with the latent dream thoughts which the patient's associations and my interventions had uncovered.)

The second dream of Mr M. occurred about two and one-half years later. The patient had to interrupt his analysis for six months because of a professional assignment abroad and returned some three months before the dream. During this three-month interval of analytic work Mr M. was in a chronic state of quiet, passive depression. I had interpreted this as a reaction to his wife's fourth pregnancy, which must have stirred up memories and feelings in regard to his mother's three pregnancies after his birth. It seemed clear to me that he was re-experiencing the loss of the feeling and fantasies of being his mother's favorite, the only child and the favorite child. The patient accepted my interpretations submissively and conceded they had merit, but he could recall nothing about the birth of his three siblings nor his reactions, although he was over six when the youngest was born. My interpretations had no appreciable influence on his mood.

Mr M. came to the hour I shall now present, sadly and quietly, and in a somewhat mournful tone recounted the following dream:

I am in a huge store, a department store. There are lots of shiny orange and green plastic raincoats on display. A middle-aged Jewish woman is arranging other articles of clothing. Nearby is a female manikin dressed in a gray flannel dress. I go outside and see a woman who looks very familiar but I can't say specifically who she is. She is waiting expectantly and eagerly for me near a small surrey, putting clothes in it. I feel sorry for the poor horse and then realize the surrey is detached from the horse. I lift up the surrey to connect it and I am surprised how light the surrey is, but I don't know how to hitch it up to the horse. I also realize then that I was silly to feel sorry for the horse.

Mr M.'s associations were as follows: 'The three women in the dream were so different from one another. The older Jewish woman was a motherly type, working, doing, arranging, like my own mother used to before she became bedridden. The manikin reminds me of how I used to think of gentile girls when I was a kid; beautiful, pure, and cold, like my wife. But they taught me different. The best sex I have ever experienced was only with gentile girls. Jewish women just don't turn me on. They never did. Since my wife's pregnancy our sex life is practically nil. She isn't feeling well and I must say I'm in no mood for sex. I would like to be close to her in bed, but I don't want her to think it is a sexual demand so there is no talking even. I'd like to just be close and cuddle. My wife is so quiet of late. I feel she is getting revenge on me for all my past wrongs. I never realized before I had had such a bad temper and that she had been and still is so afraid of me. [Pause] I feel so alone in that big house of ours. I work like a horse to pay for it. Maybe I am the horse in the dream that I felt sorry for.'

I intervened. 'It might be so. You think he had such a big load to carry, but then you lift up the buggy and you are surprised to discover how light it is.' The patient interrupted me. 'That buggy is so light, it's a baby buggy, it's a baby carriage. No wonder it was so light, it was so tiny, and the woman was putting clothes on it, like diapers.' [Pause] I interrupted. 'A baby buggy is very heavy for a little boy, he has to work like a horse to push it.' Mr M. burst in with, 'I can remember trying to push my baby sister in her buggy but it was too heavy for me. Now I see my father carrying the baby carriage downstairs as if it were a toy. I can even remember my brother and me together trying to push it.' I interpreted and reconstructed: 'I believe you have been depressed ever since your wife got pregnant because it stirred up memories of how you reacted when you were a small boy and your mother got pregnant and delivered your brother and sisters. You didn't want to face the fact that your father was hitched up to the coming of the babies. You wished you could have been the father of the babies. But you weren't – you didn't know how to do it as a little boy and you felt left out in the cold, detached. You have been depressed about this ever since.' After a pause, Mr M. said, 'I've always felt I'm not a real man. I act like one, but inside I still feel a real man should be like my father; strong physically, tough, and unafraid. I can fly airplanes but my hands sweat whenever I want to screw my own wife.'

In the next hour the meaning of the green and orange raincoats became clear. The patient spontaneously recalled some dirty jokes from early puberty in which the terms 'raincoat' and 'rubbers' were used to refer to condoms. He then remembered finding condoms in his father's chest of drawers and later stealing some for his own use, just in case an opportunity presented itself, which, he wistfully said, 'didn't occur for several years'. By that time the 'rubbers', the raincoats, had disintegrated in his wallet. It is worth noting how the hidden old shreds of 'rubbers' in the patient's associations were changed into the shiny new raincoats on display in the dream. Here you can see the attempt at wish fulfilment in the manifest content of the dream: 'I can buy conspicuous sexual potency in a store or in analysis.' Later it also became clear that I too was the poor horse who had him as a big load to carry and also I was the 'horse's ass' who could not help him make proper sexual connections with his wife or any other woman.

To me the outstanding element in the manifest dream was the surrey which turned out to be so tiny and light. My translation of the word 'surrey' into 'buggy' was the crucial technical point. I got from surrey to buggy by visualizing a surrey, which I have never seen in actual life but which brought to mind a popular song, 'A Surrey with a Fringe on Top'. This led me to baby buggies with fringes on top. Not wanting to push the patient into *my* association of baby buggy, I dropped the baby part and said just buggy, to see where it would lead him. (All this flashed through my mind quickly and was not as carefully thought out as it sounds here.) But I believe I was on the right track as it helped the patient pictorialize a baby buggy. And this enabled him to recall early childhood memories that had been repressed. Once his associations became freer, I could see how the dream-work had condensed, reversed, and disguised the agony of feeling abandoned, unloved, inept, and depressed, by pictorializing an attractive woman waiting eagerly for him to join her. The tininess and lightness transforms the surrey into a baby buggy and changes the adult Mr M. into a jealous, rivalrous small boy who cannot make babies as his big father can. The dream-work tries to negate the fact that the father is connected with the mother's pregnancies: the surrey and horse are not hitched together – the patient is unable to hitch a male and female together. The familiar but unrecognizable woman is the mother of his childhood years, whom he has tried to ward off in his memories, in his sexual life and in the analysis. The hugeness of the department store is a plastic representation of him as a little boy in a situation too big for him, as his present big house makes him feel like a tired old horse. He is full of jealous, envy, and depression, and sorry for himself.

It was not possible to work on all these points in one hour, but the surrey–baby-buggy dream led in the next hours to the conviction that his present depression and the old underlying depression from childhood, which had brought him into the analysis, were directly connected, hitched up, to his mother's pregnancies and deliveries. The repression, isolation and denial were temporarily broken through by our work with this dream and there were several tearful and angry hours in contrast to the quiet sadness of the previous months. Making available to the patient's conscious ego the memories and affects related to trying to push the baby carriage made it possible to reconstruct a crucial phase of this man's conflicts in early childhood, which were emotionally inaccessible to him until our work on the dream.

I believe this clinical vignette demonstrates the exceptional position of the dream. Months of what I believe to have been good psychoanalytic work on the patient's acting out or re-enactment of the childhood depression provided insight and some understanding, but no emotional or behavioral change although I am fairly sure that it prepared the way for the surrey–buggy dream. It was the dream, however, plus the patient's and analyst's work on it, that made possible the breakthrough to the hidden memories and affects. Only then did the patient develop a conviction and certainty about the re-construction – and when he clearly understood and felt the connection between the seemingly strange, remote and symbolic elements of the dream and the events in his present and past life. For me this is convincing evidence of the special proximity between the dream, childhood memories and affects. To a great extent this depends on whether the patient and the analyst can use their capacity to oscillate between the primary and secondary processes in helping each other reach the latent dream thoughts hidden beneath the manifest dream. The patient contributes by his free associations; the analyst contributes by associating as if he were the patient and then translating his findings in ways that provide links or bridges to the vital and alive psychic activities in the patient which are capable of becoming conscious at the moment. This is dependent on the analyst's capacity for empathy, his ability to visualize the verbal productions of his patient, and then to translate his findings at a time and in a style and form which are real and plausible to the patient (Greenson 1960, 1966, 1967).

Conclusion

The dream is an exceptional and unique production of the patient. It is his special creation but can only be fully understood if the analyst and the patient work together by means of the patient's free associations and the analyst's interpretations. To work effectively with a patient's dream the analyst must subordinate his own theoretical interest, his own personal curiosity, and attempt to make contact with what is living, accessible and dominant in the patient's psychic life at the time. He must associate empathically with the patient's material, as if he had lived the patient's life. Then he must translate the pictures he gets from the patient's verbal rendering of the dream back into thoughts, ideas and words. Finally, he must ask himself what of all of this will be valuable to the patient's conscious and reasonable ego and how he can say it effectively to the patient.

This can be learned in one's personal analysis and in supervision in clinical work, if the training and supervising analysts are competent in working with their patients' dreams. It can be learned to a lesser degree in dream seminars and even from books and papers if the writer is a skilful teacher and uses clinical examples from his own experience. Dream interpretation cannot be taught to people who are not at home or are ill at ease with the form and content of unconscious mental activities. Obviously you cannot teach dream interpretation to those who are blind and deaf to the beauty and wit in the blending of dream formation, free association and interpretation.

Working with dreams makes extraordinary demands on the patient and the analyst. In a sense the dream is the most intimate and elusive creation of the patient; it is so easy to forget! The patient is then asked to associate as freely as possible to the different elements of this strange material, in the presence of his psychoanalyst. He will be torn between the desires to reveal and to conceal the hidden contents which have unexpectedly risen to the surface. The analyst must listen with free-floating attention, oscillating between the patient's and his own primary and secondary processes. Eventually, he will have to formulate his ideas in words which are comprehensible, meaningful and alive to the patient. Sometimes he may only be able to say, 'I do not understand the dream – perhaps we shall sometime later.'

Some psychoanalysts deny the exceptional position of the dream because they have a special difficulty in learning the technique of dream interpretation. Others decrease the importance of dream interpretation to enhance certain theoretical convictions or to attack or defend the beliefs of some honored teacher. I believe that the dream is the royal road to a knowledge of unconscious activities for both the patient and the analyst, provided the psychoanalyst is not seduced into narrow bypaths and dead-end streets by technical or theoretical prejudices. My conviction of the exceptional position of the dream has been confirmed by daily work with patients, in particular their clinical responses, both immediate and long-range. This conviction has been substantiated by the results of literally hundreds of analysts whose work on dreams are listed in the texts of Fliess (1953), Altman (1969), the *Annual Survey of Psychoanalysis* (Frosch and Ross 1968), the *Index of Psychoanalytic Writings* (Grinstein 1959), the *Psychoanalytic Quarterly Cumulative Index* (1932–66), and the *Chicago Psychoanalytic Literature Index* (1953–69).

I shall close with two quotations. Kurt Eissler has graciously permitted me to paraphrase from a personal communication:

> With hard work and fortunate circumstances an analysis may stop all neurotic symptomology, all acting out, all neurotic slips and errors, and it may make the former patient the epitome of normalcy. Nevertheless, the person will never stop dreaming irrational, instinct-ridden, bizarre dreams, a perpetual proof of the ceaseless activity of the unconscious mind.

And from Freud, who wrote in 1933,

> Whenever I began to have doubts of the correctness of my wavering conclusions, the successful transformations of a senseless and muddled dream into a logical and intelligible mental process in the dreamer would renew my confidence of being on the right track (Freud 1933: 7).

Notes

1 The A.A. Brill Memorial Lecture, 11 November, 1969. I am indebted to Max Schur, Milton Wexler, Alfred Goldberg and Nathan Kites for many

of the ideas in this paper, a collaboration made possible by the Foundation for Research in Psychoanalysis, Beverly Hills, California. The first English edition of the book was translated by A.A. Brill in 1913.

2 See Berta Bornstein (1949), Loewenstein (1951) and Greenson (1967) for examples of their method of dealing with this delicate problem.

References

Altman, Leon L.: *The Dream in Psychoanalysis.* New York: International Universities Press, Inc., 1969.

Arlow, Jacob A. and Brenner, Charles: *Psychoanalytic Concepts and the Structural Theory.* New York: International Universities Press, Inc., 1964.

Benjamin, John, D.: Prediction and Psychopathological Theory. In: *Dynamic Psychopathology in Childhood.* Edited by Lucie Jessner and Eleanor Pavenstedt. New York: Grune & Stratton, Inc., 1959, pp. 6–77.

Bornstein, Berta: The Analysis of a Phobic Child: Some Problems of Theory and Technique in Child Analysis. In: *The Psychoanalytic Study of the Child, Vol. III–IV.* New York: International Universities Press, Inc., 1949, pp. 181–226.

Chicago Psychoanalytic Literature Index. Chicago Institute of Psychoanalysis, 1953–69.

Dement, William C. and Kleitman, Nathan: *The Relation of Eye Movements during Sleep to Dream Activity: An Objective Method for the Study of Dreaming.* J. Exper. Psychol., LIII, 1957, pp. 339–46.

Eissler, Kurt R.: *The Chicago Institute of Psychoanalysis and the Sixth Period of the Development of Psychoanalytic Technique.* J. Genet, Psychol., XLII, 1950, pp. 103–57.

—— On the Metapsychology of the Preconscious: A Tentative Contribution to Psychoanalytic Morphology. In: *The Psychoanalytic Study of the Child, Vol. XVII.* New York: International Universities Press, Inc., 1962, pp. 9–41.

—— Personal Communication.

Erikson, Erik H.: *The Dream Specimen of Psychoanalysis.* J. Amer. Psa. Assn., II, 1954, pp. 5–56.

Fenichel, Otto: *The Psychoanalytic Theory of Neurosis.* New York: W.W. Norton & Co., Inc., 1945.

Fisher, Charles: Discussion in Panel Report on *The Psychoanalytic Theory of Thinking.* Reported by Jacob A. Arlow, J. Amer. Psa. Assn., VI, 1958, pp. 143–53.

—— *Psychoanalytic Implications of Recent Research on Sleep and Dreaming.* J. Amer. Psa. Assn., XIII, 1965, pp. 197–303.

—— Dreaming and Sexuality. In: *Psychoanalysis – A General Psychology.*

Essays in Honor of Heinz Hartmann. Edited by Rudolph M. Loewenstein,

Lottie M.Newman, Max Schur, and Albert J. Solnit. New York: International Universities Press, Inc., 1966, pp. 537–69.

Fliess, Robert: *The Revival of Interest in the Dream*. New York: International Universities Press, Inc., 1953.

Freud, Anna: *Normality and Pathology in Childhood. Assessments of Development*. New York: International Universities Press, Inc., 1965.

Freud, S.: *The Interpretation of Dreams* (1900–1902). SE IV–V.

—— *Fragment of an Analysis of a Case of Hysteria* (1905 [1901]). SE VII.

—— *The Handling of Dream-Interpretation in Psycho-Analysis* (1911). SE XII.

—— *Introductory Lectures on Psychoanalysis. Part II. Dreams* (1916 [1915–16]). SE XV.

—— *A Metapsychological Supplement to the Theory of Dreams* (1917 [1915]). SE XIV.

—— *Remarks on the Theory and Practice of Dream Interpretation* (1923 [1922]). SE XIX.

—— *Some Additional Notes on Dream-Interpretation as a Whole* (1925). SE XIX.

—— *New Introductory Lectures in Psycho-Analysis* (1933 [1932]). SE XXII.

—— *Constructions in Analysis* (1937). SE XXIII.

Frosch, John and Ross, Nathaniel, Editors: *Annual Survey of Psychoanalysis, Vol. IX*. New York: International Universities Press, Inc., 1968.

Gill, Merton M.: *Topography and Systems in Psychoanalytic Theory. Psychological Issues, Vol. III, No. 2, Monograph 10*. New York: International Universities Press, Inc., 1963.

Greenson, Ralph R.: *Empathy and Its Vicissitudes*. Int. J. Psa., XLI, 1960, pp. 418–24.

—— *That 'Impossible' Profession*. J. Amer. Psa. Assn., XIV, 1966, pp. 9–27.

—— *The Technique and Practice of Psychoanalysis, Vol. I*. New York: International Universities Press, Inc., 1967.

Grinstein, Alexander: *The Index of Psychoanalytic Writings*. New York: International Universities Press, Inc., 1959.

Hartmann, Ernest: *The D-State*. New England J. Med., CCLXXIII, 1965, pp. 30–35, 87–92.

Hartmann, Heinz: *Technical Implications of Ego Psychology*. The Psychoanalytic Quarterly, XX, 1951, pp. 31–43.

Isakower, Otto: *A Contribution to the Pathopsychology of Phenomena Associated with Falling Asleep*. Int. J. Psa., XIX, 1938, pp. 331–345.

—— *Spoken Words in Dreaming. A Preliminary Communication*. The Psychoanalytic Quarterly, XXIII, 1954, pp. 1–6.

Kris, Ernst: *On Some Vicissitudes of Insight in Psycho-Analysis*. Int. J. Psa., XXXVII, 1956a, pp. 445–55.

—— The Recovery of Childhood Memories in Psychoanalysis. In: *The Psychoanalytic Study of the Child, Vol. XI*. New York: International Universities Press, Inc., 1956b, pp. 54–88.

Kubie, Lawrence S.: *A Reconsideration of Thinking, the Dream Process, and*

'*The Dream*'. *The Psychoanalytic Quarterly*, XXXV, 1966, pp. 191–8.

Lewin, Bertram D.: *Reconsideration of the Dream Screen. The Psychoanalytic Quarterly*, XXII, 1953, pp. 174–99.

—— *Dream Psychology and the Analytic Situation. The Psychoanalytic Quarterly*, XXIV, 1955, pp. 169–99.

—— *Dreams and the Uses of Regression*. Freud Anniversary Lecture Series, New York Psychoanalytic Institute. New York: International Universities Press, Inc., 1958.

—— *The Image and the Past*. New York: International Universities Press, Inc., 1968.

Loewald, Hans W.: Review of: *Psychoanalytic Concepts and the Structural Theory*, by Jacob Arlow and Charles Brenner. *The Psychoanalytic Quarterly*, XXXV, 1966, pp. 430–6.

Loewenstein, Rudolph M.: *The Problem of Interpretation. The Psychoanalytic Quarterly*, XX, 1951, pp. 1–14.

—— *Some Remarks on Defences, Autonomous Ego and Psycho-Analytic Technique*. Int. J. Psa., XXXV, 1954, pp. 188–93.

Mahler, Margaret S.: *On Human Symbiosis and the Vicissitudes of Individuation: Volume I, Infantile Psychosis*. New York: International Universities Press, Inc., 1968.

—— *Psychoanalytic Quarterly Cumulative Index, Vols. I–XXXV, 1932–66*. New York: The Psychoanalytic Quarterly, Inc., 1969.

Rapaport, David and Gill, Merton M.: *The Points of View and Assumptions of Metapsychology*. Int. J. Psa., XL, 1959, pp. 153–62.

Schur, Helen: An Observation and Comments on the Development of Memory. In: *The Psychoanalytic Study of the Child, Vol. XXI*. New York: International Universities Press, Inc., 1966, pp. 468–79.

Schur, Max: *The Id and the Regulatory Principles of Mental Functioning*. New York: International Universities Press, Inc., 1966.

Segal, Hanna: *Introduction to the Work of Melanie Klein*. New York: Basic Books, Inc., 1964.

Sharpe, Ella Freeman: *Dream Analysis, A Practical Handbook in Psycho-analysis*. London: Hogarth Press, 1949.

Spitz, René A.: *The First Year of Life*. New York: International Universities Press, Inc., 1965.

Stein, Martin H.: States of Consciousness in the Analytic Situation. In: *Drives, Affects, Behavior, Vol. II*. Edited by Max Schur. New York: International Universities Press, Inc., 1965, pp. 60–86.

Strachey, James: Editor's Introduction: *The Interpretation of Dreams* (1900). Standard Edition, IV, pp. xi–xii.

Thorner, Hans A.: Three Defences against Inner Persecution. In: *New Directions in Psychoanalysis*. Edited by Melanie Klein, Paula Heimann, and Roger E. Money-Kyrle. New York: Basic Books, Inc., 1957, pp. 282–306.

Waelder, Robert: *The Problem of the Genesis of Psychical Conflict in Earliest Infancy.* Int. J. Psa., XVIII, 1937, pp. 406–73.

Waldhorn, Herbert F., Reporter: *Indications for Psychoanalysis: The Place of the Dream in Clinical Psychoanalysis.* (Monograph II of the Kris Study Group of the New York Psychoanalytic Institute.) Edited by Edward D. Joseph. New York: International Universities Press, Inc., 1967.

PART THREE

The dream-space

Every chapter in this part of the book addresses the nature and function of what Masud Khan calls the 'dream-space' as it becomes constituted intrapsychically in the course of development and as it is revealed or gained in the course of a psychoanalysis. Drawing on Winnicott's formulation of transitional phenomena, he 'differentiates a specific intrapsychic structure from the general biological experience of dreaming and from the dream as a symbolic creation'. In two clinical cases he marks the growth in the patients' capacities to use their respective dream lives, having established a restorative 'dream-space' through the work of analysis. In Harold Stewart's examination of a very disturbed woman's analytic progress, he marks the transference evolution alongside the shift in her relation to the dreaming function and her relationship to the dream-space.

Hanna Segal's condensed, historically influential paper recapitulates psychoanalytic contributions to the understanding of symbolic processes, with particular reference to Melanie Klein's contribution to understanding the evolution of symbolic thinking. She offers her own conception of the symbolic equation, which is linked to primitive mental mechanisms, concretization and expulsion. She draws on Bion's useful model of containment, the internalization of an inner space where 'alpha function' or symbolic elaboration can take place. Finally, she shows in clinical material where this function breaks down, where the dream becomes a concrete object to be expelled, not used for the psychoanalytic task of integration.

Pontalis's beautifully evocative 'Dream as object' describes the relationship to the recollected dream of both analyst and patient. He places emphasis on the boundaries and limitations contained by the dream object, the boundaries which mark the separateness of patient and analyst, however much the patient's dream is suffused with the relationship between the two, and however much sleep and dream evoke a state of boundarylessness. His hypothesis is that the 'dream refers to the maternal body in so far as it is an object in the analysis'. This concept adds a specific perspective to understanding the clinical meaning of the dream, the diagnostic potential of dream analysis, and in particular the potentially perverse use of dream interpretation. Anticipating Anzieu, he describes the dream screen not only as a surface for projection but also as a manifestation of Freud's 'protective shield', the ego boundary, again conceptualized as circumscribing a space, a sanctuary, a place of reparation.

James Gammill's chapter traces the constitution of the meaningfully usable dream, linking to Lewin's conceptualization the idea of the internalized container (Bion) or skin (Bick) which holds and transforms projective identifications. In a psychoanalysis the function of 'analytic listening' creates the possibility of establishing this capacity. Its evolution through the analysis of a schizoid patient is described. Developing the links identified in Gammill's chapter, Didier Anzieu's 'The film of the dream', a chapter from his recent (1989) book, *The Skin Ego*, links the dream screen with an internalization of an aspect of the 'skin ego', itself derived from experiences of containment, holding, protection and stimulation. The dream screen here is conceived as a sensitive ephemeral membrane, a visual envelope whose function it is to contain the dream which attempts to repair the damage daily done to the skin ego. Anzieu's synthesis brings together much of the thinking which precedes it, the classical concerns along with the developments evolving out of Winnicott, Klein and Bion.

4

The use and abuse of dream in psychic experience

M. MASUD R. KHAN

The psychoanalytic theory of dream interpretation, or the psychoanalytic theory of dreaming, has been recently discussed by Paul Ricoeur in his monumental book *Freud and Philosophy: an Essay on Interpretation* (1965). Richard M. Jones in his book *The New Psychology of Dreaming* (1970) has carefully discussed the implications of the recent researches in the psychophysiology of sleep and dreaming for the classical dream theory.

Drawing on Freud's correspondence with Fliess I have suggested above (pp. 29–46 [this publication]) that:

> What enabled Freud to transform this heroic subjective experience of self-analysis . . . into a therapeutic procedure was his genius for abstraction, which led him to re-create all the vital elements of the dreamer's situation in the analytic setting, so that in a wakeful conscious state the person in analysis can psychically *re-experience* through transference-neurosis the unconscious psychic disturbances and states of arrest that are distorting his ego-functioning and affective freedom.

I then offered the concept of 'The Good Dream' and detailed what were prerequisites of the sleeper's intrapsychic situation which enabled a 'good dream' to materialize. I shall repeat here only two of the fourteen features I discussed there, because these are relevant to my discussion:

1 Ego's narcissistic capacity for gratification from dream-world in lieu of either the pure narcissism of sleep or the concrete satisfaction of reality. This implies a capacity to tolerate frustration by the ego and accept symbolic satisfactions.
2 A capacity in the ego for symbolization and dream-work, in which sufficient counter-cathexis against primary process is sustained for the dream to become an experience of intrapsychic communication.

My clinical work in the decade since that paper was written has made it necessary to state that for the analytic clinician it is as important to search for the *meaning* of the dreamt and the reported dream, as the patient's *experience* of the dream as a thing in itself. The obverse of 'the good dream' is not a 'bad dream', but a dream that disrupts the intrapsychic actualization of some emergent and on-going process intrapsychically, in life or in the analytic process. Hence I shall present my argument in terms of two categories of dream-experience: one relating to the incapacity to use symbolic processes entailed in dream formation, and the other about the dream-space in which the dream actualizes.

The incapacity to dream

Every analytic clinician relies on dreams for access to the patient's repressed unconscious, and all of us have experienced a *shift* in the quality and usage of the dream by the patient during the course of his analysis: the dreams help us to get in touch with the unconscious fantasies and object relationships as well as reveal to us and the patient the preconscious defence mechanisms of the ego which are not otherwise accessible to observation or through the patient's introspective account. The greater, and one could say subtler use of the transference in contemporary techniques of analytic therapy have somewhat shifted our emphasis on the dream as the prime vehicle of the unconscious material.

The title already indicates that the verb 'use' I am borrowing from Winnicott's theories. Two essays of his have greatly influenced my thinking in this area and have helped me to organize a certain type of clinical experience that had been impressing itself upon my attention for some years now. The two essays by Winnicott are: 'Dreaming, fantasying and living' and 'The use of an object and relating through identifications' (both published in his book *Playing and Reality*, (1971b). I shall very briefly give you the essentials of Winnicott's argument.

In the first paper Winnicott gives the case history of a middle-aged woman whose whole life till then had been disturbed and usurped by fantasying or 'something of the nature of daydreaming'. From his material Winnicott infers:

> Dream fits into object-relating in the real world, and living in the real world fits into the dream-world in ways that are quite familiar, especially to psychoanalysts. By contrast, however, fantasying remains an isolated phenomenon, absorbing energy but not contributing-in either to dreaming or to living. To some extent fantasying has remained static over the whole of this patient's life, that is to say, dating from very

early years, the pattern being established by the time that she was two or three. It was in evidence at an even earlier date, and it probably started with a 'cure' of thumb-sucking.

Another distinguishing feature between these two sets of phenomena is this, that whereas a great deal of dream and of feelings belonging to life are liable to be under repression, this is a different kind of thing from the inaccessibility of the fantasying. Inaccessibility of fantasying is associated with dissociation rather than with repression. Gradually, as this patient begins to become a whole person and begins to lose her rigidly organized dissociations, so she becomes aware of the vital importance that fantasying has always had for her. At the same time the fantasying is changing into imagination related to dream and reality.

In his second paper Winnicott carefully distinguishes between object-relating and use of an object. He sums up his argument as follows:

To use an object the subject must have developed a *capacity* to use objects. This is part of the change to the reality principle.

This capacity cannot be said to be inborn, nor can its development in an individual be taken for granted. The development of a capacity to use an object is another example of the maturational process as something that depends on a facilitating environment.

In the sequence one can say that first there is object–relating, then in the end there is object–use; in between, however, is the most difficult thing, perhaps, in human development; or the most irksome of all the early failures that come for mending. This thing that there is in between relating and use is the subject's placing of the object outside the area of the subject's omnipotent control; that is, the subject's perception of the object as an external phenomenon, not as a projective entity, in fact recognition of it as an entity in its own right.

The more I have thought about these concepts of Winnicott the more convinced I have become that they can be fruitfully used towards a true understanding of a certain type of dreaming in our patients. Dreams which I had so far considered as a sort of intrapsychic defence against painful memories and fantasies or which had struck me as variants of a special type of manic defence now I evaluate in a different way and clinically find this approach helpful.

During the first months of a young male patient's analysis, when the patient was deeply absorbed, both in his recall and in the transference, with traumatic experiences from his childhood, he reported his first dream, a very long and complex one, full of bizarre details. He had taken up most of the session telling it and then had remarked: 'I have been able to tell you only part of the total dream. I was dreaming it all night long and it was very vivid in its details and events.' He paused for some comment from me and all I said to him was: 'I get the impression that you have failed to dream the dream that was emergent from our recent work and instead have been taken over by this absurd *mélange* of images. I wonder whether you have slept at all last night.' He was taken aback by this remark and with embarrassment told me that all his life since puberty he had such dreams and they always left him feeling depersonalized and jaded. He furthermore added that after such dreams he always had the feeling he had not slept at all but had been enmeshed in a macabre world which he compulsively kept spinning into further complexities and episodes, without getting anywhere. That many a time he had wanted to talk about these dreams but then lost contact with them by the time he arrived for his session. It would be equally true to say that had I asked associations to any of the elements of the dream, the patient would have responded with copious material which would lend itself to quite meaningful interpretations. But what had impressed me suddenly was the whole dream as a fatuous psychic event, and how much it had disrupted the on-going process in his analysis at this stage. From here it became possible to discuss and explore a very specific and hidden dissociation in him which he could now talk about as being responsible for what he felt to be his lack of imaginative empathy with what he read or saw on the television or even heard from his friends. He would easily regress into this type of dream-mentation: a rapid conglomerate of bizarre images that scampered through his head while he was reading, listening or watching. He stated that he did not have to be properly asleep to sink into this type of dreaming. It only needed for him to be depersonalized a little from stress or tiredness to be taken over by it. And he had always been conscious of its deleterious effects on his thinking and involvement with persons and real life. What was even more distressing for him was the fact that even in social company he would drift away into this type of dreaming and often his friends had remarked on his falling asleep while listening to them.

What deterred me from interpreting this use of dream as a variant of masturbatory fantasies was the lack of any special sexual elements or excitement in it. It was a thing in its own right, a highly organized intrapsychic structure which usurped the function of real dreaming or fantasy or even creative thinking. It was the exact obverse of what Marion Milner has described as the state of reverie.

As the analysis progressed we were able to see more clearly the genesis of this condition. He began to recall how throughout his childhood he had suffered from horrible nightmares, none of which he could recall. These nightmares had stopped around puberty. When the patient had dreamt and reported that long dream he was just beginning to be able to talk about the horribleness of his childhood. He came from a well-to-do professional family and was an only child. The father, a successful businessman, was an alcoholic and the patient had been witness to endless scenes of alcoholic rage by his father. Quite often during his childhood his mother would escape to his bedroom and sleep there to get away from her husband's alcoholic rantings. The parents had separated when the patient was ten years of age. He had stayed with his mother.

It is not my intention to go into the complexity of determinants that went into his type of dreaming. A few need to be pointed out, however. The acute nature of traumata in his childhood had obviously interfered with the maturational capacity to use dreams for wish fulfilment or preservation of sleep. The two prerequisites that I have mentioned from my earlier paper that facilitate the ability to dream were lacking in him. He could only have nightmares. At puberty when the familial situation had changed he was faced with the new maturational threat of genital sexuality and incest. He had in this climate started to dream these long bizarre dreams which negated both libidinal strivings and wish fulfilment and curtailed imaginative elaboration of instinct which is the function of true fantasy and dream in psychic inner reality.

Instead, a dissociation had established in his personality. He was a highly intelligent boy who became a very successful solicitor. He had sought treatment when his concentration with his clients had begun to sag and he would drowse away into these dreams – though at first he was not aware of the existence of these dreams in his drowsy states. That this dissociation served a defensive function against very painful memories and specially rage became quite obvious as the analysis progressed. What I wish to stress here, however, is an incapacity to use dream as a creative intrapsychic function and structure. The patient could not distance himself from this structure in him. He felt literally possessed by it. He was as much *the dream* itself as the dream was his concoction. It was this which had always made him feel unreal when his colleagues praised his work. He never said: 'I have finished a case' to anyone. His phrase was: 'The case has been finished now.' He could not establish an 'I am' status in his self-experience in what he did because of this dissociation.

The next question that arises is why did he create this complex dream-structure instead of regressive fantasying. In fact he was a very shrewd and logical person. A partial answer lies in his high IQ which had enabled him to study avidly from a very early age and with meticulous objectivity. That was his flight from his familial nightmare. But all the more larval, preconscious, imaginative processes had to split off, until at puberty they were synthesized into these dream-structures that were as unreal as they were compulsive in his psychic reality and experience of himself.

To return to Winnicott's concepts. I wish to suggest that the capacity to *use* the dream-mechanisms and the dream itself as a psychic experience is the result of adequate environmental provisions that facilitate the phase-adequate maturational processes. When this is lacking, hybrid and bizarre intrapsychic structures get organized that negate dreaming and any personal use of it.

Actualization of dream-space

The second argument I suppose is that in the inner psychic reality of any given patient we should distinguish between the process of dreaming and the dream-space in which the dream actualizes. We know from Freud's monumental work that one of the basic functions of dreaming is wish fulfilment. We also know that dreaming is a capacity. And this capacity to dream is dependent upon the inner psychic climate at any given time in a person as well as the availability of certain ego-functions to be able to use that symbolic discourse which is the essence of dream-formation (cf. Part One, this volume and Ricoeur 1965). I shall give a clinical example to explain my argument.

Clinical material

I am reporting from the treatment of a young girl of twenty-three who has been in analysis for some three years. She had to come to analysis because she was apathetic and listless and lived in a state of continuous day-dreaming of a fatuously romantic type where she would one day meet the ideal lover and live happily ever afterwards. This type of continuous day-dreaming consumed all her libido and she had very little energy left for relating to others or doing any executive work by way of learning a skill or education. She is a beautiful and extremely intelligent girl. Apart from this benign state of depersonalized self-engrossment she had no symptoms and she felt normal and at ease with herself. Some eighteen months after starting analysis a ghastly event happened in her life. This girl, who was a virgin, went to a party, got rather drunk, which was unusual for her, and was picked up by a young, rather psychopathic man who escorted her home and seduced her in a very crude and abrupt way. When she reported the experience the next day in her analysis, she had little sense of shame or guilt about it because she had no experience of it as a personal event at all. It had all happened to her, or rather she had let it happen to her, and we could make absolutely no use of it for many months in the analysis. She just put it aside and I let her. I very

96

strongly believe that each patient has a right of privacy to their own experiences, and the fact that something happens to a patient does not give us the complementary right to intrude upon him with what we know clinically and theoretically to be the potential meaning of the behaviour. It was obvious to me that the whole event was a gross and absurd piece of acting out, but I also felt that the patient needed me to contain it, without explanation or interpretation, until she could reach a point in her own psychic development where she could return to it and discover what it meant for her. She relapsed into her withdrawn celibate state.

Some three months ago this girl met a young boy who became very fond of her and gradually she could tolerate an affectionate and emotional relationship to evolve between them. In due course, she allowed him to make love to her, which in this context was quite true to both instinct and affectivity in her experience. The night she had her first intercourse with this youth she dreamt, what she called, a most graphic redramatization of the 'rape scene' (her phrase). I recount the dream as she reported it:

In my dream I am in my room and Peter is fucking me. I realize what is happening and stop it.

I was very impressed by her use of the phrase '*in* my dream' because I felt that she was referring to the dream-space now in distinct contra-distinction to the life-space or the room-space in which the original seduction event had happened. From her association, two things are quite clear: first that the experience of tenderly being made love to had enabled her to get at the rage and anger that had been pent up in her since puberty and which had not allowed her to use her body for instinctual gratification or emotional relating to the heterosexual love object. The threat to her was that if she got at her sexual feelings it would simultaneously release her rage and anger as well. Just as in this dream, the redramatization of the rape scene cancels the tender sensual experience which she had with her boyfriend. She felt very guilty about having dreamt the dream and also very sad for her boyfriend. But as we worked on the dream during the week it became gradually clear that there was a second aspect to it which was more important to her, namely that in her own dream-space she had been able to actualize the experience of her selfhood and instinctuality which some three months earlier had been randomly acted out by her. She felt, and I was in full accord with her, that she had reached a completely new capacity to use her inner world and dream-space to actualize instinctual experiences and object relations which in her life-space would be only destructive and disruptive to her well-being and character.

One of the significant changes in her after having had this dream has been that she can now tolerate being both loving towards her boyfriend as well as aggressive and hostile without feeling that everything thereby is directly jeopardized. The whole stasis of her character has eased and she is very much freer of her fatuous day-dreaming and could even, to use her own phrase, look forward to actualizing new experiences in her dream-space. This has changed the quality of her sleep for her which up to now has been merely a compulsive way of being absent from life and yielded little rest or vigour to her on waking.

Discussion

The concept of dream-space in my thinking, has gradually crystallized from watching and studying Winnicott's therapeutic consultations with children where he uses the Squiggle Game and which he has reported with such veracity and vividness in his book *Therapeutic Consultations in Child Psychiatry* (1971a). I began to discover in my clinical work with adults that they can use the dream-space in exactly the same way as the child uses the transitional space of the paper to doodle on. Furthermore, it was important for me to distinguish between the process of dreaming which articulated unconscious impulses and conflicts from the dream-space in which the dream actualizes this experience. I have also gradually begun to realize that in many patients for a long time the process of dreaming can be available to them but not the dream-space, hence they derive very little satisfaction from their dreams and have a very poor sense of the experiential reality of the dreamt dream. In this context it is advisable to reduce clinically interpretation of the dream content to the minimum, because over-elaboration of the dream process can screen the incapacity in the patient to establish the dream-space. Furthermore, it is my clinical experience that when patients cannot establish a dream-space in their inner reality they tend to exploit their social space and object relations to act out their dreams. I am here proposing that a dream that actualizes *in* the dream-space curtails acting out of dreams in the social-space. The dream that actualizes in the dream-space of a given patient leads to personalization of the dream experience and all that is entailed in it by way of instinct and object-relating.

According to my way of thinking, the dream-process is a biologic given of the human psyche but the dream-space is an achievement of the developmental process in a person, facilitated by infant care and environmental holding. One further suggestion I offer is that the dream-space is the internal psychic equivalent of what Winnicott has conceptualized as the transitional space which a child establishes to discover his self and external reality.

I wish also to distinguish the concept of dream-space from Bertram Lewin's (1946) instructive concept of dream screen. The dream screen is something *onto* which the dream imagery is projected, whereas the dream-space is a psychic area *in* which the dream-process is actualized into experiential reality. The two are distinct psychic structures, though complementary to each other.

It is a generally accepted analytic concept that the incapacity to dream and/or the incapacity to contain the dreamt dream leads to acting out in our patients. I am suggesting that it is the incapacity in a patient to use the dream-space to actualize the experience of the dream-process that leads to acting out of dreams into social space. I am also suggesting that we should consider a patient's compulsive dreaming and reporting them in analysis as a special type of acting out, which screens the patient's lack of dream-space in his inner psychic reality.

The hypothesis of dream-space is offered as a specific intrapsychic structure where a person *actualizes* certain types of experiences. This type of actualization is differentiated from the general biologic experience of dreaming and from the dream as a symbolic mental creation. Clinical material is given to illustrate this hypothesis.

It is further argued that the psychic capacity in a person to *actualize* such experiences in the dream-space enables them to curtail acting out of unconscious internal conflicts.

References

Freud, S. (1900) *The Interpretation of Dreams, Standard Edition of the Complete Psychological Works of Sigmund Freud*, SE 4/5.

Khan, Masud (1962) 'Dream psychology and the evolution of the psychoanalytic situation', *International Journal of Psycho-Analysis* 43: 21–31.

Lewin, Bertram (1946) 'Sleep, the mouth and the dream screen', *The Psychoanalytic Quarterly* 15: 419–34.

Ricoeur, P. (1965) *Freud and Philosophy*, New Haven, CT: Yale University Press (1970).

Winnicott, D.W. (1951) 'Transitional objects and transitional phenomena', in *Playing and Reality*, London: Tavistock (1971).

—— (1971a) *Therapeutic Consultations in Child Psychiatry*, London: Hogarth Press.

—— (1971b) *Playing and Reality*, London: Tavistock Publications.

5

The function of dreams

HANNA SEGAL

Ernest Jones tells us that until the end of his life Freud considered *The Interpretation of Dreams* his most important work. This is not surprising. While his studies on hysteria revealed the meaning of symptoms, it was his work on dreams that opened up for him and us the understanding of the universal dream-world and dream-language. For the structure of the dream reflects the structure of personality. What follows is a brief review of the classical theory of dreams.

Repressed wishes find their fulfillment in the dream by means of indirect representation, displacement and condensation, and by the use of symbols. Freud put these symbols in a slightly different category from other means of indirect presentation. Dream-work is the psychic work put into this process. By means of dream-work a compromise is achieved between the repressing forces and the repressed, and the forbidden wish can find fulfillment without disturbing the repressing agencies. Freud did not revise the theory of dreams in the light of his further work. For instance, he did not tell us how his views on dreams were affected by his formulation of the duality of instincts and the conflict between libidinal and destructive phantasies. He also, at the time of his basic formulations about the dream, did not yet have available to him the concept of working through. I feel rather uneasy about the dream being conceived of as nothing but a compromise: the dream is not just an equivalent of a neurotic symptom. Dream-work is also part of the psychic work of working through. This accounts for the analyst's satisfaction when, in the course of analysis, 'good' dreams appear.

The classical theory of dream function takes for granted an ego capable of adequate repression and of performing the psychic work of dreaming. To my mind this implies that the ego is capable of a certain amount of working through of internal problems. It also takes for granted the capacity for symbolization. Now, when we extend our psychoanalytical research we come across patients in whom these functions, on which dreaming depends, are disturbed or inadequate.

To begin with I shall say a few words about symbolization. Freud took the existence of symbols as given, universal and, I think, unchangeable. This, of course, was particularly so before he broke with Jung and the Swiss school of analysts. In his paper on symbolism, Jones (1916) referred to the main break with the Swiss school. He implied, though he did not explicitly state, that symbolization involves psychic work connected with repression: 'Only the repressed is symbolized – only the repressed needs to be symbolized.' Melanie Klein (1930) made the next big step forward. In her paper on symbol formation she gave an account of the analysis of an autistic little boy who was incapable of forming or using symbols. In her view, symbolization occurs by a repression and displacement of interest in the mother's body so that objects in the external world are endowed with symbolic meaning. In the case of Dick, a phantasied, sadistic and projective attack on his mother's body gave rise to a paralyzing degree of anxiety so that the process of symbolization came to a standstill and no symbol formation occurred. The child did not speak or play or form relationships. I investigated further those phenomena and described the psychic dynamics of the formation of what I call the symbolic equation or the concrete thinking characteristic of psychoses. I also described the symbol proper, which is suitable for purposes of sublimation and communication. Briefly stated, the theory is that when projective identification is in ascendance and the ego is identified and confused with the object, then the symbol, a creation of the ego, becomes identified and confused with the thing symbolized. The symbol and the object symbolized become the same, giving rise to concrete thinking. Only when separation and separateness are accepted and worked through does the symbol become a representation of the object, rather than being equated with the object. This, in my view, implies a full depressive elaboration, the symbol becoming a precipitate of a process of mourning. The disturbance of the relationship between the self and the object is reflected in a disturbance in the relationship between the self, the object symbolized and the symbol. The terms 'symbolic equation' and 'symbol' are discussed more fully in chapter 8 [original publication].

To Jones's 'only what is repressed needs to be symbolized', I add 'only what can be adequately mourned can be adequately symbolized'. Thus, the capacity for non-concrete symbol formation is in itself an achievement of the ego – an achievement necessary for the formation of the kind of dreams covered by Freud's theory.

We know that in the psychotic, the borderline, the psychopathic, dreams do not function in this way. In the acute psychotic there is often no distinction between hallucination and dream. Indeed, there is no clear distinction between states of being asleep or awake. Delusion, hallucination, night-time events, which could go by the name of dreams, often have the same psychic value. In non-acute states, but when psychotic processes are in ascendance, dreams may be experienced as real and concrete events. Bion (1958) has reported a patient who was terrified by the appearance of his analyst in his dream, as he took it as evidence of having actually devoured the analyst. Dreams may be equated with feces and used for purposes of evacuation; or, when minute internal fragmentation occurs, they may be experienced as a stream of urine and the patient may react to having dreams as to incidents of incontinence (Bion 1957). A patient can use dreams for getting rid of, rather than working through, unwanted parts of the self and objects and he can use them in analysis for projective identification. We are all familiar with patients who come and flood us, fill us with dreams in a way disruptive to the relationship and to the analysis.

I had an opportunity of observing this type of functioning of dreams in two borderline psychotic patients, both of whom dreamed profusely, but in whom it was the function rather than the content of the dreams to which attention had to be paid. In these patients, dreams were often experienced as concrete happenings. This was particularly clear with my woman patient. This woman, who was very quarrelsome in a paranoid way, would bring a dream in which she was attacked by X or Y, or sometimes by myself. If I attempted to understand some aspect of the dream, she would say indignantly, 'But it is X or Y or you who have attacked me,' treating the event in the dream as a completely real event. There was apparently no awareness that *she dreamed* the dream. Similarly, an erotic dream in which, say, a man pursued her, was felt as virtual proof of his love. In fact, her dreams, although she called them dreams, were not dreams to her but realities. In this they paralleled another mental phenomenon in her life, in which she used a similarly misleading word. She experienced weird and bizarre sexual phantasies and freely spoke of them as 'phantasies', but if one enquired into them more closely, it became apparent that these were not phantasies but hallucinations. They were felt as real experiences. For instance, she walked very awkwardly because she felt she had a penis stuck in her vagina. When she imagined having a relationship with someone, she used the word 'phantas' but in fact believed and behaved as if it were a reality. For example, she accused me of being jealous of her sexual life, of ruining her relationships, when in fact she had no sexual life or relationships. So what she called 'phantasy' and what she called 'a dream' were in fact experienced as a reality, though she weakly denied it. These so-called dreams constantly invaded the external reality situation. For instance, she would complain about the smell of gas in my room and it would transpire later that she dreamed of bursting a balloon or exploding a bomb. The evacuation that occurred in the dream seemed to invade the perception of the reality.

These concretized dreams lend themselves particularly to purposes of expulsion. This was especially clear in my male patient who used to write his dreams, *in extenso*, in a little notebook. He had volumes and volumes of them. For instance: following his mother's death he had dreams of triumph over her, aggression, guilt and loss, but in his conscious life the mourning for his mother was conspicuous by its absence. Such interpretations as 'You have got rid of your feelings for your mother in your dream' were more effective in bringing about some conscious experience of his affect than was any detailed analysis of the dream. He was using the dream to get rid of that part of his mind which was giving him pain; he discharged it into his notebook. He dealt similarly with insight. An insightful session was often followed by a dream which seemed closely related to it. In other patients this kind of dream is usually a step in the working through. In his case, however, such a dream more often than not meant that he got rid of all feelings about the previous session by making it into a dream and ridding his mind of it.

Similarly, in the woman patient the dream was part of an expulsive process. For instance, when she complained about the smell of gas in my room, she expelled the gas into the room.

The dreams of both patients were characterized by very poor and crude symbolization. I was struck both by the concreteness of the experience and the invasion of reality, as though there was no difference between their mind and the outside world. They had no internal mental sphere in which the dream could be contained. Elaborating on Winnicott's concept of transitional space, Khan (1972) described it in terms of dream-space. In this regard, I found most helpful Bion's model (1963) of mental functioning, particularly his concept of the alpha and beta elements and of a mother capable of containing projective identification.

Bion has distinguished between alpha and beta elements of mental functioning. Beta elements are raw perceptions and emotions suitable only for projective identification. These raw elements of experience are to be gotten rid of. Beta elements are transformed by the alpha function into alpha elements. Those are elements which can be stored in memory, which can be repressed and worked through. They are suitable for symbolization and formation of dream thoughts. It is the beta elements which can become bizarre objects or concrete symbols in my sense of the word. I think they are elements of the psychotic-type dream; alpha elements are the material of the neurotic and normal dream. Alpha function is also linked with mental space. In Bion's model, the infant's first mode of functioning is by projective identification. This is an elaboration on Freud's idea of the original deflection of the death instinct and Klein's concept of projective identification. The infant deals with discomfort and anxiety by projecting it into the mother. This is not only a phantasy operation. A good mother responds to the infant's anxiety. A mother capable of containing projective identifications can transform the projections in her own unconscious and respond appropriately, thereby lessening the anxiety and giving meaning to it. In this situation, the infant introjects the maternal object as a container capable of containing anxiety, conflict, and so on and elaborating it meaningfully. This internalized container provides a mental space and in this space alpha function can be performed. Another way of looking at it would be that it is in this container, in which alpha functioning can occur, that primary processes begin to be elaborated into secondary ones. The failure of the container and alpha functioning results in the inability to perform the dream-work and, therefore, the appearance of psychotic, including concrete, dreams.

I would like to give an example which shows vividly, I think, the function of dreaming and its failure, resulting in concretization. The material comes from an unusually gifted and able man who has a constant struggle with the psychotic parts of his personality. We ended a Friday session with the patient expressing enormous relief and telling me that everything in that session had a good resonance in him. On Monday, he came to his session very disturbed. He said he had a very good afternoon's work on Friday and Saturday morning, but he had a dream on Saturday which had disturbed him very much. In the first part of the dream, he was with Mrs Small. She was in bed and he was either teaching or treating her. There was also a little girl (here he became rather evasive) – well, maybe a young girl. She was very pleasant with him, maybe a little sexy. And then quite suddenly someone removed a food trolley and a big cello from the room. He woke up frightened. He said it was not the first part of the dream that frightened him but the second. He felt it had something to do with a loss of internal structure. On Sunday he could still work, but he felt his work lacked depth and resonance and he felt something was going very wrong. In the middle of Sunday night, he woke up with a dream, but he could not hold onto it and instead became aware of a backache low in his back – maybe the small of his back.

He said the Mrs Small part of the dream did not disturb him because he could quickly see through it. In the past, Mrs Small, whom he does not think much of, represented a belittling of Mrs Klein (klein = small). He understood that and supposed she represented me changed into a patient and also into a sexy little girl. He supposed it was an envious attack, because on Friday he felt so helped by me. He then had some associations to the cello – his niece had one, his admiration for Casals and a few others — which led me to suggest tentatively that it seemed to be a very bisexual instrument. That interpretation fell rather flat. What struck him more, he said, was that it is one of the biggest musical instruments around. he then said that I had a very deep voice, and that another thing that frightened him was that when he woke up from the dream he could not remember what we were talking about in the session.

It seems to me that the whole situation, which in the first night was represented by the dream, in the second night happened concretely. By changing me into Mrs Small he had lost me as the internalized organ with deep resonance. The cello represented the mother with deep resonance, the mother who could contain the patient's projections and give a good resonance; with the loss of this organ, there was an immediate concretization of the situation. In his dream on Saturday night, he belittled me by changing me into Mrs Small. This led to the loss of the cello: 'one of the biggest musical instruments around'. He woke up anxious. The function of the dream to contain and elaborate anxiety began to fail. The next night, instead of a dream, he had a pain in the small of his back. Hypochondriasis, much lessened now, had at one time been a leading psychotic-flavored symptom. The attack on the containing functions of the analyst, represented as the organ with the resonance, resulted in the patient's losing his own resonance (his depth of under-standing) and his memory (he could not remember the session). When this happened, he could only experience concrete physical symptoms. The belittled analyst, who in the dream was represented by Mrs Small, became a concrete pain in the small of his back.

My attention has been drawn recently to a borderline phenomenon exhibited markedly by the two borderline patients mentioned earlier. They both frequently presented what I have come to think of as predictive dreams. That is, their dreams predicted their action, and what had been dreamed had to be acted out. Of course, up to a point, all dreams are acted out, as the dream expresses problems and solutions carried out also by similar means in life, but in these patients the acting out of the dream was extraordinarily literal and carried out in complete detail. For instance, my male patient was often late and, not surprisingly, often dreamed of being late. What drew my attention to the predictive character of his dreams was the extraordinary precision with which a dream predicted his lateness to the minute. He would come two, six or forty-five minutes late and give me a reason plausible to him, but later in the session he would report a dream in which he was late for a meal or a meeting for exactly the number of minutes which he actually was late on that day. I do not think it was a *post hoc* interpretation he put on his dreams since he wrote them down carefully first thing in the morning. I also became aware that a Thursday or Friday dream containing plans for acting out over the weekend was by no means a dream substituting for acting out, but often was carried out in precise detail. This, of course, could have been a failure of my analysis of the dream preceding the weekend. Other patients sometimes bring a similar plan for acting out in order to warn the analyst and get help; effective analysis then obviates the need to act out. But I have a feeling that there was something so powerfully automatic in this patient's compulsion to act out the dream that analysis seldom moved it. Often he would not report the dream until after the weekend.

In the woman patient, these predictive dreams relate particularly to paranoid dramas. There was a kind of row with which I had become familiar. That was characterized by an extraordinary automatic progression, apparently totally unaffected by my response. The session could go something like this: She would say in an accusing voice, 'You frowned at me.' There were any number of responses that I tried at different times. For instance, I could interpret, 'You are afraid that I am frowning at you because you slammed the door yesterday.' Or I could ask, 'What do you think I am frowning about?' Here she might answer, 'You frowned at me because I slammed the door.' Or I could be silent and wait for developments, but my silence would be taken as a confirmation that I was terribly angry with her. Then it would be, 'Not only do you frown, but now you are silent, which is worse.' I never said 'I did not frown,' but I did try pointing out to her that it did not occur to her that she might have been mistaken in her perception. This could only make it worse, because now not only did I frown, but I accused her of being mad. In either case, I had a feeling that my response was completely irrelevant and the quarrel, in which certain roles were assigned me, would continue in a completely automatic fashion. At some point, however, usually when an interpretation touched on some fundamental anxiety, she would tell me a dream. Then it would appear that the row we were supposed to be having in the session was an almost word-for-word repetition of the row she actually had in the dream, either with me or her mother or father or some thinly veiled transference figure, such as a teacher. This response to an interpretation – telling me a dream – only happened, however, when the row had run its course, at least for a time. The other similar interpretation, given earlier in the session, would be ignored or woven into the row. Now, I have come to recognize the particular feeling in the counter-transference. It is like being a puppet caught in someone else's nightmare and totally unable to do anything but play the allotted role, usually that of the persecutor. So later, when the row would begin in this particular way, I would sometimes simply say, 'You have had a quarrel with me or someone like me in the dream', and sometimes this would obviate her need to act out in the session.

It is as if in the predictive dreams of both patients, functioned as what Bion (1963) called a 'definatory hypothesis'. They defined in detail how the session was to unfold.

I was wondering in what ways the predictive dreams differed from the evacuative dreams, whether of the kind I described in my male patient, or the kind that the woman patient experienced, which then spilled over, as it were, into reality. I think they are somewhat different. I think that the evacuating dream actually evacuates something successfully from the patient's inner perception. Thus, after my patient dreamed of mourning his mother, he did not need to mourn her. The predictive dreams, however, seem to be dreams which do not entirely succeed in the evacuation, and they seem to remain in the patient's psyche like a bad object, which the patient then has to dispose of by acting the dream out. The evacuation does not seem to be completed until the dream has been both dreamed *and* acted out. This was very marked with the woman patient. Going through the row, telling me the dream, getting the interpretation gave her enormous relief, but I was seldom convinced that the relief was actually due to an acquired insight. It seemed rather to be due to a feeling of completed evacuation.

In conclusion: we can say that we are far from having exhausted the possibilities of understanding the world of dreams opened up by Freud, but our attention is increasingly drawn to the form and function of dreaming rather than to the dream content. It is the form and the function which reflects and helps illuminate the disturbances in the functioning of the ego.

References

Bion, W.R. (1957). Differentiation of the psychotic from the non-psychotic personalities. *International Journal of Psycho-Analysis* 38: 266–75. In W.R. Bion, *Second Thoughts*. New York: Jason Aronson, 1977.

—— (1958). On hallucination. *International Journal of Psycho-Analysis* 39: 341–9. In W.R. Bion *Second Thoughts*. New York: Jason Aronson, 1977.

—— (1963). *Elements of Psycho-Analysis*, London: Heinemann Medical Books. In W.R. Bion, *Seven Servants*. New York: Jason Aronson, 1977.

Jones, E. (1916). The theory of symbolism. In E. Jones, *Papers on Psycho-Analysis*. 2nd ed. London: Ballière, Tindall and Cox, 1918.

Khan, M. (1972). The use and abuse of dreams. *International Journal of Psychotherapy* 1.

Klein, M. (1930). The importance of symbol formation in the development of the ego. *International Journal of Psycho-Analysis* 11: 24–39. In M. Klein, *Contributions to Psycho-Analysis 1921-1945*, pp. 236–50. London: Hogarth, 1948.

6

Dream as an object[1]

J-B. PONTALIS

Die Traumdeutung (1900): the title itself already links, indeed irrevocably unites, the dream and its interpretation. Freud, at the same time as he totally revises it, places himself in the tradition of the various seers, secular and religious, where the dream is consecrated to its meaning, thus to some extent neglecting the dream as *experience*: the subjective experience of the dreamer dreaming and the intersubjective experience in therapy, when the dream is brought to the analyst, both offered and withheld, speaking yet silent. Perhaps when with Freud the dream travels to its definitive status through interpretation, and the dream *dreamt in images* is converted into the dream *put into words*, something is lost: every victory is paid for by exile and possession by loss.

My intention is to place myself antecedent to *Traumdeutung*, but to recapture that which the Freudian method, in order to exercise its efficiency to the fullest, necessarily put aside. I wish to understand what appears to me to be an opposition between the meaning and the experience, by situating myself in analysis in order to find my guide marks. I feel justified in such an undertaking by some of the post-Freudian works and by a certain reticence on my part in deciphering the contents of a dream in a clinical encounter when I could not perceive what it represented as experience or as a refusal of experiences. As long as one does not appreciate the *function* that the dream fulfils in the analytic process, and as long as the *place* that it fills in the subjective topography remains indeterminate, any interpretation of the *message* of the dream is at best ineffective; at worst it maintains an unending complicity about a specific *object*, which remains an unclarified libidinal cathexis between analyst and patient: it is no longer a language that is circulating; it is a currency.

Certain events have led me to this point of view. An analytic conference was held in October 1971, the subject-matter of which was 'Dreams in therapy'. This was a deliberate reminder of a conference held thirteen years earlier with a far more scientific title: 'The use of oneiric material in adult psychoanalytic therapy'.[2] This change of title, which was more or less deliberate, was not thought up just to avoid repetition. By presupposing an equivalence between 'dream' and 'oneiric material', and, furthermore, by centring the debate on its 'use', there was a risk that the entire discussion could immediately turn to the different techniques of treatment of this material. The foreseeable individual differences of opinion were confined within the bounds of a spectrum which those taking part in the conference had in fact already covered. Broadly speaking, there were two opposing tendencies, often to be found in the same analyst. The first tendency, which one would be mistaken in calling classical, without further examination, maintained that the dream was the 'royal road' and suggested that even, in the attention given to it, it should be understood in therapy as a language apart. The other tendency did not consider the dream as anything different in its nature from the total contents of a session.

The change of the title, if it showed a renewed persistence of interest, also indicated a shift in emphasis, which became more vague and more radical — 'What about the dream in analysis?' One no longer presupposed the *practical* status of the dream in an analytic situation. For its theoretical status, as defined by Freud — the dream is a hallucinatory wish fulfilment — leaves all the questions unanswered, once the organization of wish fulfilments and defences effectively takes its part in the transference ('part' as in a scene in a stage play).

It was foreseeable from the very wording of the title of the conference that the dream did not present itself to analysts in 1971 as it did in 1958, and that our perception of it could well have changed with time. I remember coming out of the meeting, mentally going over a proposition I had made which distinguished between the dream as an object, as a place and as a message. I came to the conclusion, with some nostalgia, that 'The dream is no longer what it used to be!' The next day the following words were spoken from the couch, words that the patient had seen as graffiti on a wall: 'Nostalgia is no longer what it used to be', a proposition which makes one — dream.

So much for the events.

If we consider the dream as an object and as intimately related to the object of nostalgia, which is itself indefinably self-reflecting, then it does not give rise to a single relation, but to a number of 'directions for use', and it does not have the same function for each person. In any case, this function is necessarily different for today's analysts from what it was for Freud. A banal remark, but what are its consequences?

On reading *Traumdeutung* we tend to confuse the *object* of investigation
– the dream – with the *method of interpretation*, and the *theory of the psychic
apparatus* that it has allowed its author to form. However, there is nothing
absolute about the interdependence between these three terms. The
analysis of dreams, and above all of his own dreams, was for Freud the
means of recognizing the function of the primary process, as through
a microscope. But, perhaps in an attempt to challenge any misconception
that books about dreams tend to reinforce, he was quick to dissociate
himself from romanticism, from mysticism of the oneiric, of the idea
that the dream, by the privilege of its birth, is directly related with the
unconscious. I am thinking of one particular sentence, which may seem
surprising at first, in which Freud (1923) quite clearly shows his reservations
– probably in opposition to Jung – about the place of a 'mysterious
unconscious'. Freud added a footnote in 1914 to *Die Traumdeutung* stating
'It has long been the habit to regard dreams as identical with their manifest
content; but we must now beware equally of the mistake of confusing
dreams with latent dream–thoughts.' Freud returns several times, with
much emphasis, to the idea that the dream is nothing more than a 'form
of thinking', a 'thought like any other'. This idea should be compared
with the conviction that, even though a large part of 'dream thoughts'
can be influenced by the analyst, at the very least 'on the mechanism
of the dream-formation itself on the dream-work in the strict sense of
the term one never exercises any influence: of that one may be quite
sure'. Freud's desire to master his dreams led him to analyse their
construction, the way in which they are made, rather than search into the
conditions of their *creation* and of the creative power that they bear
testimony to. The dream-work is what interests him. The *dream-work*,
or in other words the series of transformations that take place from the
initial factors that triggers them off – instinctual impulses and the day's
residues through to the end product: the dream narrated, recorded, put
into words. Whatever may occur from this product once it has come
forth from the dream machine, whatever may be achieved before the
machine is put into motion, is the wish to sleep really reducible to an
assumed primary narcissism?

Freud was certainly aware of the necessity to 'complete' his *Interpretation
of Dreams* by studying the relation between sleep and dreams. But this
'metapsychological supplement to the theory of dreams' does not appear
to have for him any effect on the interpretation of dreams, nor does it
question its function of the 'guardian of sleep'. On the other hand, the
connexion between the desire to sleep, the desire *to dream*, and the desire
of the dream (which is represented in the dream) is not the nodal point
in Freudian thought. It is not only the study of transformations, and of
their mechanisms and laws, that holds Freud's attention: the *before*

110

and *after* seem secondary. However, though this dream-work allows itself to be analysed exemplarily on the dream *model*, it is not reserved for the dream-formation. Freud himself has analysed the dream-work with as much illumination when it is concerned with other formations of the unconscious – forgetfulness, symptoms, the phenomenon of *déjà vu*, and so on. This is a harder task when it is concerned with unconscious fantasy and transference, because the *process* of composition constantly blurs the rigour of the construction.

Once the structural homology has been established between the different formations of the unconscious, all psychoanalytical research aims at specifying these differences. This was the path opened by the *Traumdeutung* which does not represent for us a book of the analysis of dreams, even less a book *of* dreams, but a book which by the mediation of the laws of the *logos* of dreams discovers the laws of all discourse and lays the foundations of psychoanalysis.

One cannot dispute that it is harder to locate the primary process in the transference relation than in the text of the dream: it is no longer a question of a text. But there is no *psychoanalysis* (I do not say analysis) outside of that which moves, which curbs itself yet breaks loose within the transference, in *deed* even if it only manifests itself in *words*. I am not dealing with the question, albeit fundamental, of the legitimacy of placing an equivalence between the 'session' and the dream. This bias can go so far that the whole of the text of a session can be considered as being amenable to interpretation through and through. In principle this is already disputable, in practice it risks instituting a terrorism – persecution and docility – for which the Kleinian school does not always seem to take into account the consequences. Freud had concentrated on the dream itself and neglected the capacity to dream.

The dream does not have to be, as such, an elected object for analysis. We are well aware that more than one cure has progressed without any interpretation or even contribution of dreams, and that it is often the opposite when therapy goes on indefinitely. But for Freud, Freud the man, this was undoubtedly and passionately so. We all know today that Freud accomplished his self-analysis by methodically and continuously decoding his own dreams (cf. Anzieu 1959): for a certain time he liter-ally made appointments with his dreams and, even more astonishingly, his dreams kept the appointments. It would be a distortion and belittling merely to attribute to them the simple function of *mediators*, which allowed Freud 'full recognition of his Oedipal conflict', and so on. It is a different matter altogether: to Freud, the dream was a displaced maternal body. He had committed incest with the *body of his dreams* he penetrated their secret, he wrote the book that made him conqueror and possessor of the *terra incognita*.

The first metamorphosis which commands all the others was accomplished — from the unnameable Medusa's head to the Sphinx that spoke the enigma: all that remains is to decipher the enigma. Freud came out as Oedipus at the end. The affective intensity was such that, after three-quarters of a century, his successors are re-examining the *body* become corpus of his dreams: *take the body literally.*

One does not have to invoke the Oedipus of Freud, or Freud becoming Oedipus, to establish that the dream is an object invested libidinally by the dreamer, and is the bearer of dread and of enjoyment. Daily experience suffices. But psychoanalysts, at least in their written works, seem to have paid little attention to relations with the dream-object. One no longer speaks with precision, but about dreams of compliance or seduction — which is in a way true of all dreams confided to a Freudian ear. Each of us can ascertain that the dream, however misleading the content, is placed between the analyst and the analysand: *a no man's land* that protects the two, though none is certain from what. The introduction of a dream in a session is often experienced as a calm excitement, if one may put it that way; a truce, a lull, *an enraptured complicity.* The complicity arises in part from the fact that one has something in common to analyse, in a sensorial exchange of the visual with hearing. But the lull arises from the fact that something absent becomes sentient on the horizon from our dual stare and listening — becomes present by staying absent. In fact, however, many of the networks established in an associative way are convergent; no matter that the affect cannot be changed, there still remains a divergence between the dream put into images and the dream put into words — one might almost say put to death. I evoked earlier the relationship, which nourishes the romantic tradition, between the dream and the unending object of nostalgia: it is inscribed at least twice in every dream, in its regressive aim and in the divergence itself. The contribution of the dream tends to satisfy in both partners the search for an evanescent object, lost—found, absent—present, never totally reached by the signs that move it away by pointing to it. There is a certain comfort to be found in this. Is not the wildest dream already tamed? The unexpected finds refuge in a place of reserve: walled gardens, towns where architectural styles from different eras are placed side by side, an enclosed stretch of sea . . . . The meaningless has taken form, the discordant multiple finally comes to rest in *one* dream. Its uncertain shape keeps me at an equal distance from my inner objects and the demands of a reality, which is more or less linked in part with the superego — a paradox that sets its own price, especially when I am no longer caught within it but am releasing myself from it by speaking it. It is the nightmare that breaks the dream state — far more than the awakening, which can maintain the sweet, throbbing uncertainty.

This is how I would now interpret Nacht's words: 'A dream is only a dream after all'. The author of these words, however, could not similarly have disputed the transference that actualizes the psychic *reality* as illusion. But the ambiguous nature of the proposal remains, and holds that it can be concerned only with the dream as object: a dream, even if it is caught at the moment it was dreamt, and whatever may be the impact of the day's residues, is certainly never *actual*, but it can *actualize* what is repressed in a resurgence that is often startling. *It is the relation that we maintain with it that commands its effects.* But then every dream partakes of the very aim of the dream: complete satisfaction, without fail, of the wish, its *fulfilment*. And every dream provides a 'true' hallucination, different in this from the genuine hallucination which always remains problematical for the subject. Perhaps the very perception of the dream is the model for all perception: *more perception* than any perception in an awakened state.

Let us consider a current formula; 'I had a dream last night but only scraps of it remain.' One does not pay much attention to that, one waits for what follows. But only if it is repeated with some insistence, and if the ensuing narration of the dream is not particularly noticeable for its gaps, then it can be understood differently: it indicates the relationship that the subject is trying to maintain with dream-object at the moment when he gives it to a third party to look at. The Oedipal reference, which leans on a representation of the analytical situation, is then manifest: 'You have to be aware, in a way that assures me that you are, that I am forever inadequate to this dream, to this body that I'm allowing you to take a glimpse of. The power to interpret it, to penetrate it, is yours. But the exquisite pleasure, never gratified, of which I *have* the experience and you only the glimpse, is mine.' My hypothesis is that every dream refers to the maternal body in so far as it is an object in the analysis. In the example I have given, the analysand forbids himself to *know* it. In other cases the subject uses the '*analytical*' method of decomposition of elements to master the situation, by means of *bits* of the body of the dream, and so on. The pathology itself of the subject is revealed in the 'use' of the dream, not in the content. The dream-object is caught secondarily in an oral, anal, phallic organization, but the dream process is originally linked to the mother: the variation of scripts that are represented in it, and even the range of meanings that he invests in the therapy (faeces, present, work of art, 'imaginary child', hidden treasure, 'interesting' organ, fetish), unfold against the background of this exclusive relationship. Dreaming is above all an effort to maintain the impossible union with the mother, to preserve an undivided totality, *to move in a space prior to time*. This is why certain patients demand implicitly that one must not get too close to their dreams, that one must not touch or masticate the body of the dream, that one must not shift the 'representation of things' to the 'representation of words'.

One of them said to me: 'This dream pleases me more than it interests me. It's like a picture made up of pieces, a collage.'

This analogy with the picture brings us to the question of place. The dream place – space – is not unrelated to what painting attempts to circumscribe, to a painted picture. There has not been enough emphasis on the primary nature of the visible in the dream: the dream makes visible, and gives its visible place to the *déjà vu*, which has become invisible.

The neurophysiological works on the paradoxical phase have now experimentally confirmed this primary nature of the visible. It would seem that the dream corresponds to an awakened phase in contrast to deep sleep, and this is confirmed by rapid eye movements as though the dreamer dreaming was having to see. This is also where the notion of the dream as a film screen is given its full import – even if clinical experiments rarely confront us with 'blank dreams' as Lewin (1953) himself emphasizes. At the very least, Lewin's observations make it manifest – the blank dream being a borderline case – that every dream image is projected onto a screen or, as I would refer to put it, supposes a space in which the representation can effect itself. The main point is not that the dream unreels like a film (a comparison, a slip of tongue even, often made by the dreamer). It can also take the form of a drama, a serial novel or a polyptych. But there can be no film without a screen, no play without a scene, albeit just one imaginary line, no picture without a canvas or a frame. The dream is a rebus, but to be able to inscribe the rebus we ask for something like a sheet of paper, and to reconstruct the puzzle we ask for a thin piece of cardboard. Freud noted that one of the mechanisms undergone by the dream-work was considerations of representability: 'dream-thoughts' can be present in the dream only by changing into visual images. In other words the 'representatives' of wish fulfilment have to be visually representable, or yet again, the unconscious does not demand to be represented. Inversely, it is a demand that is submitted to by the dream. But Freud, to my knowledge, does not attach himself to the effects entailed by such a constricting demand, notably the valorization of the visible–invisible pair and the wish–sight pair. He only examines the modifications that must be undergone by the abstract for it to become concrete.

Let me remark at this point that if it took painters so long to reach the deliberate aim of painting their dreams – an aim that is debatable with regard to the demands of the painting as much as to the unreeling of the dream process – it is because there is a very profound homology between the dream-work and the painter's work.

Speaking of the place of the dream leads one at first to consider the following contradiction. On the one hand, the effects of condensation and displacement, the games of substitution and reversal, the whole mode of the functioning of the primary process are not reserved for the dream-work, and, as Freud (1900) indicates, it is not necessary to 'admit the existence of a special symbolizing activity of the mind'. On the other hand, the dream accomplishes itself in a specific inner space. And we are well aware that there are other places in which the instinct manifests itself, in which the *id* expresses itself, without representing itself: an 'over here' representation — probably the field of the death instinct — when the instinct remains fixed on the 'representatives', which actualize themselves directly in compulsive *acting*, or which are repeated by fate; and an 'over there' representation, which is more problematical, in which instinctual, always present, produces the open space of the work and of the action. The dream still occupies a median situation.

When Freud, on questioning himself on the 'beyond' and the 'further than' of the pleasure principle returns to the question of traumatic dreams, he grants the necessity of conditions previous to the establishment of the dream as wish fulfilment: the capacity to dream demands that it should be 'accomplished before another task'. The whole speculation of *Beyond the Pleasure Principle* (1920), which is so close to the analytical experience in its use of biological metaphor, is ultimately aiming at defining it. For the time being let us just consider the following hypothesis: the dream can only achieve its 'binding' function after a kind of 'pre-binding' has been established. The dream process cannot function according to its own logic unless the dream-space — the 'psychic system' — has been constituted as such.

Just as one can see a claim to maintain a 'reserved sector' away from the field of transference in resorting to reality, so one can consider the valorization, by the analyst and the analysand, of the dream in therapy as a sign of concern to assign limits to the unconscious — as if it could dwell somewhere specific — a concern, effectively answered by the dream, to circumscribe the primary *process* in a *form* (a *Gestalt*).

Dream-object, dream-space: the connexion between these two dimensions of the dream is narrow. In practice, we pass incessantly from one to the other. Schematically I would distinguish two modes of relation to the dream-object which represent two types of specific defence against the virtualities that the opening of the dream-space allows: the manipulation of the dream machine and the reduction of the dream to an inner object. I remain deliberately descriptive.

It is not only in recent times, even if recent times are increasing them, that we meet the analysand—analysing (*analysés–sants*) who are experts at coding and decoding, who are inventive with word games, who are knowledgeable in all kinds of combinations and who are qualified to remonstrate with the most subtle of analysts and on the ability of 'deconstruction'. A resistance, one could say, in which one must see a modern

115

atavar of 'intellectual resistance' that has been known for a long time and which should be situated, under the apparent mentalization which denies the affect, in an aggressive transference. One can see in *mentalization* in contrast to intellectualization, the inverted equivalent of *conversation*: the 'mysterious leap' is effected from the psychic to the mental. It is remarkable that psychoanalysis should have found the leap more easily in the somatic: its aim being to cut short any interpretation of the analyst, to challenge him in advance, or to make him insert himself into the range of possible interpretations. So be it. But resistance to what? To the *meaning*? One could only maintain this by appealing to the very thing that appears to be lacking in such patients: the experience – the *feeling* of the dream. Respect for the text of the dream often leads us to efface the difference between dreams recorded in writing (or remembered before the session) and the dreams which are found again during the session. It is clear that following the patient along the way of an interpretation of the content of his dreams can only maintain a relation of amused competition in intellectual acrobatics. On hearing them one sometimes asks oneself if they have really lived their dreams, or if they have dreamt them directly as dreams, and dreamt them finally in order to tell them.

'The use of dreams in analysis is something very remote from their original aim,' wrote Freud (1923) – an incidental and profound remark which brings to light the 'responsibility' of the analysis in this *perversion* of the dream to which I have just referred. For we are concerned with a perversion: to be master of the dream-object by manipulation and by a seizure that breaks it down into elements, to make the analyst-witness the accomplice of his pleasure – does this not evoke the sexual pervert who treats the bodies of others as machines for desiring his own fantasy? Can the wish find its fulfilment, can an interpretation give satisfaction? This kind of patient will bring *dream after dream*, and relentlessly manipulate images and words. The dream will incessantly move him further away from self-recognition, while he claims to look for it by auto-interpretation. I would say that he *steals* his own dreams from himself. Dreams change with analysis, and with our culture. For example, one only has to read Victor Hugo's few narratives of dreams in *Choses vues*. Although we would say that they were particularly marked by secondary elaboration, they are still, both for him and for us, *events of the night*, in tune with the events of the day. In a way, psychoanalysis is strangling the eloquence of oneiric life.

The use of the dream as an object for manipulation and connivance (a use which is not, of course, the monopoly of the pervert who is recognized as such) is one side of the relation to the dream-object. I have drawn it in bold outlines, almost as a caricature, because I feel it is an area of our practice that receives poor attention. The other side is to be found in dreams in which the narrator seems to want to prolong the pleasure he had, albeit taking little interest in the actual content of the dream. To the extent that the production of dreams and above all the remembrance of them are one of the symptoms (of general observation) of the analysis, we must expect the analysed subject to obtain primary and secondary gains from them. It is important therefore to grasp which aspect of oneiric activity is thus valorized, invested, eroticized even. It could be the dream as such, as a representation of an *elsewhere*, guarantor of a perpetual *double*, or a staging, a 'private theatre' with its permutation of roles that allows one never to assume any of them; or it could be one of the mechanisms of the dream – in which case there would be more sources for interpretation. One can find something useful in the functioning of these mechanisms much as a writer does in his methods of writing: the condensation, which collects in one image the impressions from multiple or contradictory registers, satisfies our desire to deny the radical difference; the compulsion to symbolize, dear to Groddeck, the wish to establish new links indefinitely, and in so doing to lose nothing. The displacement would appear to have a particular value: in fact, it offers the analysand the possibility of never having to remain at a fixed point, but of assigning himself and elusive vanishing point, of being variable from the adopted perspective, always at another place and therefore ready to 'get out of the venture without loss'. The subject identifies himself with the displacement itself, as though with a phallus, which is everywhere and nowhere, *nulliquité* more than ubiquity. This specific relation to the dream-object is often spotted by the analyst in that he feels he has been assigned the position of a spectator (a spectator of dreams that are not his own). The eventual richness of 'ideas that come' in fact aims at excluding him, at reminding him that the dream cannot be *shared*. Thus dream-space is a *territory*, in the sense of animal ethology. The dream is an inner object which the dreamer keeps for himself, as though he were turning the solipsism subjacent to the dreamt dream to his own advantage: it is his own thing, it belongs to him, he places his own little associative pebbles round it, not to show the way, but to encircle his territory, to assure himself that it does belong to him. This is why the interpretation, even if it is sought after, is immediately limited, without any effect of rupture. In the end the dream-process is diverted from its major function – to produce wish fulfilment, or make it rise to the surface – to being taken as an aim in itself. The dreamer attaches himself to his dreams so as not to be cast adrift, and in the constant and stable object that is the analyst he finds the 'moorings' (*corps mort*) as a complement that guarantees to anchor him.

One could rightly say that such an attitude could be readily described in terms of resistance and transference. But something would be lost from the areas of pleasure and fear: libidinal economy, that is jointly perceptible in the dream-work and in the relation to the dream. The interpretation is productive when a wish and a fear, that increase the ones that figured during the course of the dream, actualize themselves in this relation.

By evoking a *perversion* of the dream or its *reduction* to an inner object, one must surely presuppose that there exists a true *nature* of the dream, that it has its own finality and that it holds virtualities, the facilitation of which would be one of the aims of therapy.

On reading Winnicott, one is struck by the way he makes the dream *come* as though he were fishing for it. The phrase is his: 'I now began to fish around for dreams' (Winnicott 1971). This approach is even more significant when one knows of the author's reluctance to offer – for him a euphemism for impose – interpretations that carry symbolic references, with which the patient, who finds in this an opportunity to reinforce his *false self* always risks complying. This reserve is manifest throughout the 'therapeutic consultations'. It goes as far as to hold a mistrust of the 'fantastic', a mistrust which contrasts with the attention and respect given to the 'true' matter of the dream. But it is less the *meaning* of the conflict, which can be disclosed elsewhere – sometimes in the behaviour of the child during the interview – that is sought for in the dream, than the *capacity* to which it bears witness. Winnicott (1971) explicitly states when discussing his squiggle game with children:

> One of the aims of this game is to reach to the child's ease and so to his fantasy and so to his dreams. A dream can be used in therapy since the fact that it *has been dreamed and remembered and reported* indicates that the material of the dream is within the capacity of the child, along with the excitements and anxieties that belong to it.

If we follow the analogy through, it leads us to the hypothesis we started with. How close they are to each other, the child who *must* suck his little piece of blanket to be able to fall asleep (Winnicott 1953), and the adult who must dream to be able to continue sleeping! We are assured that they would both become ill or mad if they were deprived of this almost imperceptible little thing: scraps of wool, scraps of dreams – they cannot bear to be separated from the thing that connects them with the mother by making her absent: deprived of the transitional dream they would fall into the loneliness that hands you over to the other and takes away your capacity to be alone with someone (cf. Winnicott 1958). 'Only scraps of it remain.' But let us recognize the belief behind the complaint: the less there remains, the more the evocative power of the object belongs to me. I've got everything I need because I've got what I'm lacking.

Let us now consider the dream screen. Lewin (1953) connects it with the desire to sleep, the prototype of which is the sleep of the well-fed infant; the blank screen without any visual images is identified with the breast. The visual is provided by other desires, disturbers of sleep; they form the dream.

This distinction between sleeping and dreaming is certainly present in and made use of by Freud, but it does not go so far as to define itself as an *opposition*. We know that this is the case in neurophysiological research; and I believe that Lewin's work leads to the same conclusions, once one has taken into account its equivocal nature which is found in the very ambiguity of the experience of satisfaction — at the same time oral satiety and the appeasement of hunger/thirst, but also the thirst to rediscover not so much the *state* of appeasement of need as the whole of the process. It is this process, which contains anxiety and excitation throughout, that the dreamer searches for, whereas sleep is satisfied with the resolution of tension.

It would appear then that the dream is aiming at a permanence, at the suspension of the wish, not the achieved satisfaction; the object of the wish is the *wish itself*, whereas the object of the wish to sleep is the absolute, the zero point of appeasement.

The dream screen then should not only be understood as a surface for projection, it is also a surface for protection, it forms a screen. The sleeping man finds the thin film in the screen that shelters him from excess of excitation and destructive trauma. Surely this evokes the 'protective shield', that membrane that Freud (1920) hypothesizes in the metaphor of the living cell. But, whereas the protective shield protects one against the outside, the dream screen protects one against the inside. This is where the 'biological' and the 'cultural' blend with each other. The barrier against the death instinct is also a barrier against incest consummated with the mother, incest which combines joy and terror, penetration and the act of devouring, the nascent body and the petrified body.

We can now have a better understanding of why the 'binding' of the dream depends on the representable. That which I can see, which I can represent to myself, is already something that I can hold off: the annihilation, the dissolution of the subject is held aside. The dream is the navel of the 'seeing–visible' (*voyant–visible*; Merleau-Ponty). I can see my dreams and see by means of it. Death, as we all know, is not something to be looked at in the face. The nightmare is a sign of the turning point. Compare this with the lucid confidence of one of Winnicott's (1971) child patients on the subject of one of his 'horrible' dreams about witches: 'Sometimes I would like to go on with it and find out what was horrible, instead of waking.' Then I feel penetrated within my kingdom (incubi).

I am no longer at home anywhere. I am robbed (cheated) to the point of being able to wander in my 'hinterland' — but delivered, bound hand and foot, to powers which *because they are all-powerful* are necessarily maleficent and death-dealing.

There is of course nothing absolute about the opposition between sleeping and dreaming — or, if one prefers, between the Nirvana principle and the pleasure principle: the wish to sleep and the wish to dream are both permeable by each other. Something of the wish to sleep infiltrates into the unravelling of the dream process itself, dedicated in its various forms to regression; and the objects of the former — a return to its origins — tends to absorb the shapes of the latter. Inversely, our dreams colour and modify all our sleep. One could even establish a kind of balance: when the wish to sleep is stronger than the need to sleep, the wish to dream changes into a need to dream. And even more: when the conflict is unceasingly *acted* in the scene of the world, then entry into the scene of the dream is refused us. The 'real' space takes up all the room. Our objects of investment capture the interests of the ego and the sexual instincts by confusing them, thereby mobilizing all our energy. Sleep then is above all a restorer, the expression is used here in the Kleinian sense of restoration of narcissism, the reparation of the inner object that has been cut to pieces by destructive hate. The condition of the dream-work is that the ego be 'repaired'.

One last question: if the dream is in essence maternal, is not its interpretation paternal by position? As we have seen it is often avoided, challenged in advance as though by a 'Be quiet, you'll succeed in making me lose my dream, it'll fade away'. And it is true that all interpretation is a 'symbolic wound', but also that like the wound, it may be wished for: by definition it puts the unnameable at a distance, but at the same time it wipes out the visible — 'my dream will fade away'. It is paternal in that, even if it wants to be allusive, it is a reducing agent of the meaning with regard to the multivalence of the images: it introduces a law *of* and *in* the meaningless; finally, in the sexual sense, the analyst's words penetrate the body of the dream, which is itself penetrating. Therefore the power of the analyst is best located in the field of the interpretation of dreams: the power of speech is an answer to the imaginary power of the dream, and takes its place. One could say it is a murder, for certain a substitution. But this substitution is well on the way long before any verbal interpretation: the dream itself is already an interpretation, a translation, and what it represents is already inscribed, captured.

The illusion given to us by the dreamt dream is that of being able to reach that mythical place where nothing is disjointed: where the real is imaginary and the imaginary real, where the word is a thing, the body a soul, simultaneously body-matrix and body-phallus, where the present is the future, the look a word, where love is food, skin is pulp, depth surface — but all of this in a *narcissistic space*. Surely the wish to penetrate the dream is an answer to the guilty fear of being penetrated by the dream, a defence — which is successful — against the nightmare. But the deep waters of the dream do not penetrate us, they *carry* us. We owe it to the dream to *come to the surface* in the indefinitely renewable cycle — in the interpenetration of day and night: a hole of the shadow in the hollow of the day, luminous beams crossing in the night, intersecting our days and nights until that moment that humanity has always pretended to call the last sleep, when in reality it dreams of the first sleep.

Notes

1 Translated from the French by Carol Martin-Sperry and Masud Khan.
2 The first was a conference organized by the Société psychanalytique de Paris in 1958, whose proceedings were published in *La Revue française de Psychanalyse* (1959, no. 1). The second was held in October 1971 under the joint auspices of L'Association psychanalytique de France and La Société psychanalytique de Paris.

References

Anzieu, D. (1959). *L'auto-analyse*. Paris: Presses Univ. de France.
Freud, S. (1900). The interpretation of dreams. SE 4/5.
—— (1920). Beyond the pleasure principle. SE 18.
—— (1923). Remark on the theory and practice of dream interpretation. SE 19.
Lewin, B.D. (1953). Reconsideration of the dream screen. *Psychoanal. Q.* 22, 174–99.
Winnicott, D.W. (1953) Transitional objects and transitional phenomena. In *Playing and Reality*. London: Tavistock Publications, 1971.
—— (1958). The capacity to be alone. *Int. J. Psycho-Anal.* 39, 416–20.
—— (1971). *Therapeutic Consultations in Child Psychiatry*. London: Hogarth Press.

7

The experiencing of the dream and the transference

HAROLD STEWART

The aspect of the role of dreams in psychoanalysis that I wish to discuss here concerns the dreamer's experience of himself in relationship to the events in the dream, and the possible changes of this experience that can occur during the course of analysis. I am concerned with this one aspect of the manifest content of the dream as reported by the dreamer and its relationship to the state of the transference. This experiential aspect of the dream should not be confused with the various emotions that the dreamer might feel during the course of a dream. Thus a fairly healthy person might experience his dreams as though he were actively involved in the varying events in the dream, or else passively observing them, or perhaps alternating between activity and passivity, but he would not feel that only one sort of experience was, as it were, 'allowed' to him in his dreams to the exclusion of all others. He might experience varying emotions during the course of the dream, such as anger, fear or jealousy, but these are not the same sort of experiences as the former and it is with them that this paper is concerned.

My interest in this topic was first aroused by observations on a patient over the course of her analysis, which lasted about six years. My patient was a young woman who had been confined to a mental hospital for three years before being accepted for analysis, suffering from a border-line schizophrenic psychosis with a severe urinary disturbance. She was depersonalized with almost no sense of self, suffered from derealization and had numerous bizarre conscious fantasies that were almost delusional in quality. A devilish mother-figure who lived in a far-off provincial town persecuted her, and she worshipped a benign father-God up in the heavens. With all this, she remained uncertain during the first two years of her analysis whether she was ill or not. During this period, the transference was characterized by my being experienced as something possibly helpful or harmful, probably unnecessary rather unreal and at a great distance from her. In short, there was little sense of involvement with me in the analysis.

She was a prolific dreamer of long, involved dreams and the interpreting and working with them played an essential part in the progress of the analysis. For most of this early period, she was not quite sure whether she had dreamt her dreams or whether she had actually lived them in reality. It is a common observation that some psychotics do experience their dreams as reality, and this can be theoretically conceptualized on the basis of the use of the process of symbolization. Segal (1957) made the point that psychotics use symbols as substitutes for instinctual activities, whereas neurotics and healthy people use them as representatives of these activities. Since an essential process in dream formation is that of symbolization, this difference will become manifest in the dream. My patient was on the border between substitution and representation and so had difficulty in distinguishing between them. Thus one experience of herself in her dreams was that it was not a dream but a piece of reality. Yet at the same time she also experienced it as a dream and it is to this aspect that I shall now turn.

In her dreams she always felt that it was like being in a cinema or theatre watching activities that were proceeding on the screen or stage but never feeling any sense of participation in these activities, even though in some of these activities that she was watching she herself was participating. Her experience was always that of the passive onlooker and rarely the active participant. Events were always at a distance and it is clear that these events represented the split-off, denied aspects of herself having relationships with others, projected to a distance and passively watched. This mirrored her relationship with me in the transference and the distance from her of her persecutory devil-mother in the provinces and her idealized father-God in the heavens. She was usually able to offer some associative material to the dream, but much interpreting had to be based on direct translations of the symbolic meanings of the manifest content particularly in terms of the transference.

By the end of two years, the situation had altered. She realized that she was very ill and that she really needed me and the analysis if she wanted to recover. We now entered a phase of delusional transference, or transference psychosis, if that term is preferred, where I was experienced not only as the helpful, needed, idealized analyst but also as the persecuting murderous devil-mother or agent of the mother. She was in a state of terror for much of the time. The important point for this paper is that her experience of her dreams changed too. Apart from fully realizing that her dreams were only dreams, she no longer felt as though she were in a cinema or theatre and was no longer the passive onlooker of distant events. Instead she felt involved and almost overwhelmed by events in the dream, often struggling furiously with them. There would still sometimes be two of her, but both were actively involved. At times she had such panic from this experience of being overwhelmed that she would awaken from the dream in an anxiety state. Thus the intrapsychic and interpersonal changes that had occurred in the transference were mirrored by the changes in her experience of her dreams. The split-off denied aspects were no longer projected to a distance but had been accepted back, not completely, but into the transference relationship, and the struggle and anxiety experienced represented her fears of being over-whelmed, particularly by her devilish, murderous impulses. Clinically she was now more involved in working at and using her dreams to gain insight into her condition. Over the course of several months this phase was worked through and we entered the third phase, that of the transference neurosis. By this time she had almost become a whole person with a fairly firm grasp of reality. The bizarre fantasies and the depersonalization had disappeared, she had a good sense of self and was able to tolerate moderately depressing feelings. We were left with the task of resolving her urinary disturbance and sexual inhibitions. Now once more her experiencing of her dreams changed. Instead of the ego–overwhelming of the previous stage, she now had the sort of dream experience that most people have, the type I described at the beginning of the paper. She was either looking, or being battered, or anxious, or experiencing freedom, but not being restricted to any single type of experience. On the whole, her experiencing was of a tolerable, participating kind. Thus her experiencing of her dreams now involved the new integration of her ego with its improved functioning in both the intrapsychic and interpersonal spheres, as seen in the transference.

These observations demonstrated what we already know: that intra-psychic functioning and interpersonal relationships are intimately con-nected. The dreamer's experiencing of his dream, an intrapsychic function, mirrors the state of the transference, an interpersonal function. Interpreta-tion of either has its effect on the other gradually to cause change in both. In terms of clinical practice, these dream-experience changes constitute another indicator of progress in the analysis in terms of the ego's capacity for integration. This would then complement that other dream indicator of change: the observation of symbolic changes in the manifest content of dreams. So far, I have observed the three stages described in two patients. In others, I have seen only the first and third stage; they did not seem to go through the stage of ego-overwhelming. This could mean either that the three stages only occur in certain patients with a particular sort of psychopathology, or that other patients have not told me of this second stage in a way that I could pick up. I have usually found these phenomena in severe hysterical, phobic and borderline schizoid personalities who use the mechanisms of splitting, denial and projection to an excessive degree.

The notion of the dream screen, first proposed by Lewin (1946), clearly fits the dream experiencing of the first phase. He thought that all dreams were projected on to a screen which is occasionally visible, and interpreted the screen to be a symbol of both sleep and the ego's fusion with the breast in a flattened form with which sleep is unconsciously equated. He thought that the visual imagery of the dream represented wishes that would disturb the state of sleep. Rycroft (1951) thought that the dream screen was not present in all dreams but a phenomenon that occurred in the dreams of patients who were entering a manic phase. It symbolized the manic sense of ecstatic fusion with the breast and a denial of hostility towards it. I would agree with Rycroft that the dream screen is not present in all dreams and that it could symbolize fusion with the breast and denial of hostility towards it, but I am not so sure about the manic sense of ecstatic fusion. My patient had been having these dreams long before her analysis started and I could detect no affect that would suggest anything like a sense of ecstasy. I would postulate the notion that in addition to fusion and denial of hostility towards the breast, it also represents the desire for a mother (breast) who can survive, contain and care for the unwanted projected aspects of the self.

As I have previously mentioned, the second phase, in which the experience of the self in the dream was of being almost overwhelmed, would represent the return to the self of these unwanted projected aspects and the upheaval in the self that occurred in the fight for and against the acceptance of them. The struggle is fought in the transference. In the third phase, the self was fairly whole and so the dream experience was that of the fairly whole person; that is, the average healthy or not too neurotic person.

A rather different approach to this phenomenon was that of Sheppard and Saul (1958). They used the manifest content of dreams for the study of ego activities, particularly unconscious activities. They differentiated ten categories of ego-functions and subdivided each category into four subgroups, which list differing degrees of ego awareness in dreams of impulses welling into it. 'Impulses' were defined as urges, drives needs or other motivating forces expressed in the dream scene. The more the dreamer portrayed his impulses as not being part of himself, the more he was said to be putting them at a distance from his ego, giving rise to the concept of 'ego-distancing'. They devised an 'ego rating system' to obtain some sort of quantitative assessment of this aspect of ego-functioning and demonstrated that the ego of psychotic patients showed greater variations in the number of defence mechanisms used in the manifest dreams than did that of the non-psychotic. The greatest degree of 'ego-distancing' was obtained in the dreams of psychotic patients. They were able to examine the dreams of persons unknown to them and predict with a reasonable degree of accuracy whether the person was psychotic or not.

The experience of the dream of my patient in her first phase certainly portrayed very vividly this concept of 'ego-distancing', particularly in the authors' category entitled 'participation'. But the further developments in my patient from 'ego-distancing' to the sense of 'ego-overwhelming' are not described by them.

To conclude this paper, I would only observe that with all the extensions of our knowledge of intrapsychic functioning and object relationships which has so extended the scope of our therapy, the role of the dream is as important today as it was at the turn of the century.

References

Lewin, B.D. (1946). Sleep, the mouth and the dream screen. *Psychoanal. Q.* 15, 419–34.

Rycroft, C. (1951). A contribution to the study of the dream screen. In *Imagination and Reality*. London: Hogarth Press, 1968.

Segal, H. (1957). Notes on symbol formation. *Int. J. Psycho-Anal.* 38, 391–7.

Sheppard, E. and Saul, L.L. (1958). An approach to a systematic study of ego function. *Psychoanal. Q.* 27, 237–45.

8

Some reflections on analytic listening and the dream screen

JAMES GAMMILL

βοῆς δὲ τῆς σῆς ποῖος οὐκ ἔσται λιμήν ποῖος κιθαιρὼν
οὐχὶ σύμφωυος τάχα[1]

Patients who report the impression of not having dreamed for years have interested me for over two decades. This phenomenon can be found in a wide clinical range (characterological, rather than neurotic or psychotic), extending from the schizoid personality to the apparently normal individual, the latter being often extremely efficient in practical life. Marty and de M'Uzan (1963) stress that many of their severe psychosomatic patients either do not dream, or appear incapable of telling their dreams, or if capable, have great difficulty in associating to them. With some chronic depressive patients, this problem often disappears rapidly, even sometimes with the appointment for a consultation, or with the experience of being listened to by someone felt as caring in the initial consultation, or 'being taken into analysis'. For one depressive woman, a 'dead mirror' in her first dream became the reflection of her being held in her mother's arms.

However, the experience with a young man in his mid-twenties, predominantly schizoid in his personality, has been the most helpful to show by its slow development, the constitution during the analytic process of a *meaningfully usable* dream screen. This patient utilized excessively, in a chronically stabilized and 'obsessionalized' way, the mechanism of projective identification, with loss of important parts of his personality and consequent impoverishment of his internal psychic life (Klein, 1946).

Aspects of history and analytic process preceding the first dream

In the consultation visit, Dr B. recounted a lifeless case-history in a colourless and monotonous tone of voice, as though he were presenting the case of someone else. He was referred by the psychiatrist who had treated his surgeon father for recurrent depressive episodes. Dr B. was considering divorce, though feeling paralyzed by indecision and an incapacity to take realistic steps. Also, he could find no energy nor initiative to write the thesis necessary for the official validation of his medical studies. He attributed his lack of affectivity ('mon flegme britannique') to his congenital disposition. However, it became evident to me that the choice of his wife – beautiful, but epileptic, hysterical and impulsive in character – was highly significant. Unconsciously he sought in her the emotions which were lacking in himself. However, this marriage failed, largely because he could not bear her dramatizations, intense longings for affection and need for care.

Although a nice-looking young man, his facial expression was immobile, somehow evoking in me the image of an empty desert, but with probably far away deep psychic earthquakes, with manifestations so faint as to require a seismograph for detection. I had to ask about his mother whom he described as highly obsessional, preoccupied about the cleanliness of her furniture (which should never be moved) and of her children, as well as their good behaviour. He admitted on questioning to having a sister, one year younger, but maintained that she had no importance for him. Months later, he mentioned his sister's severe childhood anorexia with chronic vomiting and danger of dying, which aroused constant parental concern and care.

After I agreed to accept him for analysis, he added that he had great difficulty in a café even to approach the counter and order a drink; also his voice had bcome so weak that his acquaintances no longer paid attention to what he said. During the first months of analysis I had to pull my chair up near the couch, lean forward to hear, and search for points of interest in his humdrum, poorly articulated material.

After about two months of this material, without spontaneity or sign of anxiety, but marked by a somewhat cold and distant politeness, he told me one day with a glacial and mocking hostility, very audibly, that I was exactly like his father, who had many books, just as he had noticed I had all of the *Encyclopaedia Britannica*. With us both, it was utterly impossible to discuss what was important *for him*. He insisted that his father was only interested in Assyrian and Babylonian history and architecture, always ready to give him lectures without any awareness that his son had no interest in these subjects. Suddenly one day, after a short period of this hostile and somewhat paranoid paternal transference, he said he was astonished to have experienced me as like his father, whereas he was amazed to remark that I listened attentively to *all* he said, suggesting an *authentic* interest in him and his difficulties. However, he was quickly frightened by this upsurge of positive feelings, and soon settled back into his lack-lustre self.

Little by little, I began to realize that important parts of his personality were not in him when with me in the sessions. His description of his Deux Chevaux car in bad condition, hardly able to run, made clear that the car contained a depressed part of himself which he did not recognize. He could not pursue necessary steps for the divorce, largely because his wife contained important instinctual parts of himself. On one hand, he wished to be rid of them; on the other, he feared unconsciously to separate vital aspects of his personality from himself. Her epileptic attacks and hysterical crises represented an uncontrollable, feared-as-psychotic part of him; thus his conscious wishes (without guilt) for her death were essentially linked with a desire to kill this part of himself projected into her.

Afterwards he evoked his adolescence. Because of his parents' depressive fear of poverty, his sister and he had to share the same bedroom in winter to economize on heat. He avoided watching her undress and was disturbed by the least sexual sensation or thought. But he often watched a girl in a distant house undress, and wondered why this had been so important to him, since he could see practically nothing. For the first time in analysis his tone of voice suggested a desire to be helped to understand. I suggested that one aspect[2] seemed an effort to maintain alive his sexuality by placing it with its object at great distance; for in the situation of sharing his room with his sister, he felt compelled to extinguish his sexuality – thus extinguishing a vital part of himself. From that moment on, his relation to me and to his analysis became much more alive.

The first dream

Soon afterwards he spoke of a parental visit, always previously presented as tedious and boring. This time he mentioned that his mother brought him a cake baked by her. In the following session, he showed greater joy in life, with some evidence of warmth and gratitude towards his mother. It appeared evident that the gift of the cake, accompanied by the analytic work, had contributed to a good inner experience of a loving mother connected with a good feeding breast. But when I suggested this in an interpretation, he laughed tolerantly and assured me (as a foreigner) that in France it is a ritual without significance that provincial mothers bring cakes, even to their adult children, when they come on visits to Paris. Nevertheless, in the following session, he brought *the first dream of his analysis, dream all the more astonishing to him because it had been many years since he recalled even the impression of having dreamed.*

He was in the foyer of a cinema but hesitated to go in and see the film. While waiting, a young woman approaches him, kneels down, pulls his trousers down, takes his penis into her mouth and sucks it passionately. He has some pleasure but feels mainly amused surprise at the girl's passionate eagerness. The other people notice, but show no particular interest.

First associations dealt with the analysis – his tendency to remain in the analytic foyer, hesitating to go further and see more of the inside film of his life. We came to understand that the girl (representing the analyst, but also his sister) contained his own passionate desires, whereas he possessed their object, the penis-breast. Many implicit associations had already appeared in the transference, and I was struck by the richness of associations in this session and afterwards.

About a third of his analysis could be viewed as related to his dream. However, from this complex material, I will emphasize only one theme – his passive femininity. This required differentiation so that a normal receptivity could replace a passively aggressive, highly controlling aspect which prevented establishment of the normal feminine position (Klein 1932), and its integration into his total personality (Bégoin and Gammill 1975; David 1975). This integration, necessary for a full experience of the earliest, predominantly oral, edition of the Oedipus complex, in both direct and inverted forms, derives from a successful elaboration of the depressive position. The resultant early identification with the paternal penis appears necessary for an adequate functioning of the dream screen, identification seen later in child analysis in the hand that moves the small toys on the playroom table, and the hand that draws on paper in an older child.[3]

Discussion

Lewin's (1946) thesis that the dream screen is linked with the nightly taking-in of the breast on going to sleep, with its transformation from a convex to a flattened surface, was theoretically interesting but raised the question of its clinical significance and usefulness. There was one important hint: 'The sleeper has identified himself with the breast and has eaten and retained all the parts of himself which do not appear outlined or symbolized in the manifest dream content.' Later Lewin (1955) states: 'We know that the dream is a wish fulfilment *and a communication ...*' and, 'the manifest dream text coincides with the manifest analytic material, expressing in processed form, latent thoughts become preconscious. *Dream formation* is to be compared to "analytic-situation formation". ...' Also he suggested that the content of the blank dream signifies 'an *intense, primitive, direct experience of the baby in the nursing situation*, inclusive of sleep at the breast' [my italics].

With respect to the clinical material, I wish to emphasize several points. Very considerable attentiveness was necessary to pick up even the faintest indications of affect and of material linked with the remains of my patient's authentic and personal self. It was essential to receive not only the expression of intense hostility from the patient, but also to be able to contain the projection of the hated father image which had come back to life in the analytic process. Later it became evident that his father, immersed in a narcissistic preoccupation with books, also covered an image of his mother, bulwarked behind her obsessional defences, fearing the communication of his once-violent feelings of love and hatred, and of his states of despair.

But it was equally important to be able to receive the projection of a good, even idealized parent, who contained projected good parts of himself, during this initial phase of the analysis. Klein (1946) emphasized that 'The projection of good feelings and good parts of the self into the mother is essential for the infant's ability to develop good object–relations and to integrate his ego'. A depressive mother or father is prevented through guilt from being capable of adequately receiving this *vital contribution* to the feeling of being a good and loving parent. Obsessional defences also interfere with the capacity to accept and deal with sudden *fluctuations* between intense primitive love, linked with idealized projections, and rage and destructive hate, with persecutory projections.

As the patient gained more confidence in my capacity to contain his projections, not only of his internal parents, but also of important parts of himself, there was less need to keep stifled his internal world and feelings or to project them elsewhere. It was important to help him locate the parts of himself[4] which he had projected into other people or things, such as his wife and his car, and to understand the reasons for these projections. It requires considerable time for these dispersed parts to be gathered into the transference.

Bion (1962, 1963) and others who have developed Klein's work (for example, Segal 1964, with respect to fantasy development) have stressed the importance of normal projective identification as the baby's earliest form of communicative psychical relationship to his mother. It is essential in this view[5] that the mother should be able to receive the projection of his primitive parts, feelings and anxiety situations, contain them in order to understand intuitively, and then to respond appropriately by the care, love and understanding she gives. In normal development the baby gradually identifies with these maternal functions. As one element in this capacity of maternal transformation, Bion (1962) underlines the need for what he calls 'maternal reverie'[6] which can probably be considered analogous to the analyst's 'floating attention' with his patient.

Returning to the clinical material, one notes crucial steps in these sessions preceding the first dream: (1) interpretation of his having placed at a distance the libidinal, vital part of him, which had the effect of the analyst giving it back to him; (2) his mother's arrival, bringing the cake, evidently introjected in its symbolic significance; (3) my interpretation, linking this present–day event, the current transference, and the past. Isaacs Elmhirst (1978) has shown how the usefulness of mutative interpretations can be linked with Bion's and Bick's (1968) work.

In my cases in which I could follow the process step-wise, the first dream appeared after a material indicating the introjection of a good breast, with always an implicit or explicit transference reference. However, the good breast was linked not only with a source of good food, but also with a source of understanding which had given proof of its capacity for containment (the 'toilet breast' described by Meltzer 1967). In earliest life, the mother is largely experienced as the breast, and her understanding is essentially transmitted by her way of feeding, handling and holding her baby (Winnicott 1960).

Although Lewin (1955) only formulated introjective identification with the breast in the creation of the dream screen, he gives evidence for projective identification in evoking 'transference remarks in patients who expressed their pre–Oedipal wish to sleep at the breast by fantasies of occupying the same space as the analyst, as if they could walk right into or through him. This is an unusual mapping of the analyst; it puts him in the place of sleep itself'.

Klein (1946) underlined the importance of the internalized good breast as a 'focal point in the ego . . . and instrumental in building up the ego'. In a major contribution to psychoanalytical dream theory, Fain and David (1963) consider that the capacity for rich elaboration in dream life is a reflection of an 'intimate contact with an object who made itself available to the child, became introduced into his conceptual world . . . transmitting to him the capacity [for elaboration] . . . so ardently desired'. By contrast, in the severe psychosomatic cases, with deficient dream life and fantasy activity, Marty *et al.* (1963) note a 'lack of reference to a living internal object'.

Fain and David (1963) appear to share my point of view regarding the concomitant evolution of the dream life with the analytic process in satisfactory analyses:

Each moment of libidinal evolution is translated by an accentuation of structural analogies between the emotional climate of the session and that which shows itself in the dreams reported in the same

132

sessions. Accordingly, the dream(s) no longer appear as foreign bodies in the session, but, on the contrary, in harmony with it. This state is aided and activated by the constant presence of the psychoanalyst in the conceptual world of the patient.

(p. 249)

Lewin (1946) suggested that the dream screen included a skin contribution, which becomes more significant in relation to an important study by Bick (1968). Also, we know from many authors that during the period of dominance of oral libido, the breast is psychically associated to and even assimilated with several aspects and points of contact in the baby's relation to his mother. The baby comes to see in the facial expression and the eyes[7] of his mother certain indications of the effects of his projections; he can feel how her body and skin relate and react to his own. Thus he is a witness to some of the transformations his mother makes of his primitive communications, as well as the receiver of her responses.

In this light, the internalization of the breast with all it comes to signify of maternal parts and functions is of *primary importance*, since it permits the beginning of an internal 'dialogue' with the baby's first internalized love object. Thus I find myself in full agreement with Kanzer (1955): 'The sleeper therefore is not truly alone, but sleeps with his introjected good object. The "dream screen" is a relic and sign of the dream partner.' He also emphasizes the importance of internal communication in dreaming and the view that object relations are 'the elementary units of the mind structurally, dynamically, and economically'. However, he does not link this internal communication with projective identification as I have earlier suggested (1970).

In the perspective which I have attempted to develop the dreamer would have an internal psychic space, derived from his earliest object relation, into (upon) which he could project in the regressive language of visual images[8] the representations of his desires and conflicts, and hope to have his wishes fulfilled and his anxieties allayed, as in early infancy, by the internalized maternal breast. But this inner situation of gratification is often incomplete, and so there are parts of him which *do* (and must), to repeat Lewin, 'appear outlined or symbolized in the manifest dream content'; and there is always some wish (often submerged by fear, guilt or shame) to tell the remembered dream to another person. Von Hug-Hellmuth (1921) pointed out that, even with the latency child's attitude of distrust, 'the child's first attitude at the beginning of the treatment is generally a strong positive transference, owing to the fact that *the analyst, by sympathetic and dispassionate listening, realizes the secret father- or mother-ideal*' [my italics]. And so in this domain, too, we see the complementarity in the interactions of the internal and external worlds.

Freud (1926) writes: 'the external (real) danger must also have managed to become internalized if it is to be significant for the ego'. It appears to me implicit in Freud's work, and explicit in Klein's, that any emotionally important situation must become internalized, including its representation in the dream life, to become 'significant for the ego'. But significance for the ego also implies a complex development of the capacity for thinking, conceptualized in its origins by Bion as alpha-function, by which events impinging on the personality are transformed into 'dream thoughts', central prerequisites for thinking. Bion (1962) writes: 'If the patient cannot transform his emotional experience into alpha-elements, he cannot dream; Alpha-function transforms sense impressions into alpha-elements which resemble, and may in fact be identical with, the visual images with which we are familiar in dreams.' He also says (1963): 'From the point of view of meaning, thinking depends on the successful introjection of the good breast that is originally responsible for the performance of alpha-function.'

I wish to emphasize that *stabilization* of the good internal breast requires prolonged working through of the depressive position (Meltzer 1967). During the first long summer holiday, my patient regressed to his previous schizoid state, and lost temporarily his capacity for dreaming. Several weeks of analytic work were required to re-establish this function, which afterwards remained intact. Although much work remained for the elaboration of the depressive position, one might say that the good internal breast in its 'dream screen' and interrelated 'alpha function', structural, dynamic and economic roles became well established.[9] Concurrently the patient became much more alive in a meaningful relationship to himself, and his affects became richer and more varied. In addition, his relations to others improved, including in the analytic situation, where a more active fantasy life also facilitated the analytic work.

Summary

Pertinent data are represented from the analysis of a young schizoid patient who had an impression of not having dreamed for many years. The author suggests, in line with Bion's work, that the most basic aspect of analytic listening is analogous to maternal capacity to receive and elaborate early infantile psychic communications, essentially projective identification of anxiety situations, overwhelming feelings (positive and negative), and psychic distress from her baby. At the earliest level, this maternal capacity is represented concretely by the maternal breast and its internal space, soon linked in the baby's mind with the maternal face surface and head (to become mental) space. It is felt that the introjection of the breast in this perspective gives richer and more dynamic meaning to Lewin's concept of the dream screen as representing the internalized breast. Certain areas of agreement between the author's conclusions with this and other patients and the important French work by Fain and David on the functional aspects of dream life, as well as that of Kanzer on the communicative function of dreams, are indicated.

Notes

1 In the sense of 'Οιδίπους, Oedipus, as a 'troubled cry from the depths of the lungs', these lines take on a deeper significance:

> Where will your sorrowful cries for help not go to ask for refuge,
> What Citheron will not echo them back in harmony (symphonos)?

One recalls the Chorus emphasizing Mount Citheron as 'the cradle, the wet nurse, even the mother' of Oedipus, and that 'cithara' means lyre, harp or lute (Gammill 1978).

2 At this point it seemed most pertinent to show him the maintenance of a link with a part of himself and an important object relation projected elsewhere. Later the *content* of his voyeurism and latent exhibitionism became very important in the analysis.

3 In 1972 I had not realized the implications for the dream screen suggested in this paragraph.

4 In the normal dreamer, through the play of identification (both projective and introjective, though Freud does not use these qualifications) the different aspects of the self (called 'ego' then by Freud) are present in the dream text (Freud 1900: 322–3).

5 The interested reader should consult the books published by Bion between 1962 and 1970, or the recent book by Meltzer (1978) on Bion's work, as I can only mention it in a general way here.

6 'reverie is a factor of the mother's alpha-function' (p. 36).

7 At this primitive level, the cheeks and eyes are often equated with the breasts and nipples.

8 Isaacs (1952: 104–5) indicates the evolution of visual images, drawing on the bodily concrete internal objects for their origins, and subsequently being transformed into '"images" in the narrower sense, "representations in the mind" . . .'.

9 It may be of interest to compare views expressed in this paper with those presented at the 1975 London Congress in the Dialogue on 'The Changing Use of Dreams in Psychoanalytic Practice', reported by Curtis and Sachs (1976).

References

Bégoin, J. and Gammill, J. (1975). La bisexualité et le complexe d'Oedipe. *Rev. Franc. Psychoanal.* 39, 943–56.

Bick, E. (1968). The experience of the skin in early object-relations. *Int. J. Psycho-Anal.* 49, 484–6.

Bion, W.R. (1962). *Learning from Experience.* London: Heinemann.

—— (1963). *The Elements of Psycho-Analysis.* London: Heinemann.

Curtis, H.C. and Sachs, D.M. (reporters) (1976). Dialogue on 'The changing use of dreams in psychoanalytic practice'. *Int. J. Psycho-Anal.* 57, 343–54.

David, C. (1975). La bisexualité psychique. Eléments d'une réévaluation. *Rev. Franc. Psychanal.* 39, 713–856.

Fain, M. and David, C. (1963). Aspects fonctionnels de la vie onirique. *Rev. Franc. Psychanal.* Supplement. 27, 241–343.

Freud, S. (1900) The interpretation of dreams. SE 4.

—— (1926). Inhibitions, symptoms and anxiety. SE 20.

Gammill, J. (1970). Commentaire sur *The Psychoanalytical Process* de D. Meltzer. *Rev. Franc. Psychanal.* 34, 168–71.

—— (1978). Les entraves d'Oedipe et de l'oedipe. In H. Sztulman (ed.), *Oedipe et Psychanalyse d'Aujourd hui.* Toulouse: Privat.

Isaacs, S. (1952). The nature and function of phantasy. In J. Riviere (ed.), *Developments in Psycho-Analysis.* London: Hogarth Press.

Isaacs Elmhirst, S. (1978). Time and the pre-verbal transference. *Int. J. Psycho-Anal.* 59, 173–80.

Kanzer, M. (1955). The communicative function of the dream. *Int. J. Psycho-Anal.* 36, 260–6.

Klein, M. (1932). *The Psycho-Analysis of Children.* London: Hogarth Press.

—— (1946). Notes on some schizoid mechanisms. *Int. J. Psycho-Anal.* 27, 99–110.

Lewin, B.D. (1946). Sleep, the mouth, and the dream screen. *Psychoanal. Q.* 15, 419–34.

—— (1955). Dream psychology and the analytic situation. *Psychoanal. Q.* 24, 169–99.

Marty, P. and M'Uzan, M. de (1963). La 'pensee operatoire'. *Rev. Franc. Psychanal.* Supplement. 27, 345–56.

Marty, P., M'Uzan, M. de and David, C. (1963). *L'Investigation Psycho-somatique.* Paris: Presses Univ. France.

Meltzer, D. (1967). *The Psychoanalytical Process.* London: Heinemann.

—— (1978) *The Kleinian Development.* Perthshire: Clunie Press.

Segal, H. (1964). Fantasy and other mental processes. *Int. J. Psycho-Anal.* 45, 191–4.

Von Hug-Hellmuth, H. (1921). On the technique of child-analysis. *Int. J. Psycho-Anal.* 2, 287–305.

Winnicott, D.W. (1960). The relationship of a mother to her baby at the beginning. *In The Family and Individual Development.* London: Tavistock, 1965.

The film of the dream

DIDIER ANZIEU

The dream and its film

In its first sense, the French term '*pellicule*' designates a fine membrane
which protects and envelops certain parts of plant or animal organisms;
by extension, the word denotes a layer, also fine, of a solid matter on
the surface of a liquid or on the outer surface of another solid. In its second
sense, '*pellicule*' means the film used in photography; that is the thin layer
serving as a base for the sensitive coating that is to receive the impression.
A dream is a 'pellicule' in both these senses. It constitutes a protective
shield which envelops the sleeper's psyche and protects it from the latent
activity of the diurnal residues (the unsatisfied desires of the previous day,
combined with the unsatisfied desires of childhood) and from the
excitation of what Jean Guillaumin (1979) has termed the 'nocturnal
residues' (luminous, auditory, thermic, tactile, cenaesthesic sensations,
organic needs, and so on, active during sleep). This protective shield is
a fine membrane which puts external stimuli and internal instinctual
pressures on the same plane, flattening out their differences (it is not,
then, an interface capable of separating inside and outside, as the skin
ego does); it is a fragile membrane, quick to break and be dissipated (hence
anxious awakening), an ephemeral membrane (it lasts only as long as the
dream lasts, though one may suppose that its presence reassures the sleeper
sufficiently that, having unconsciously introjected it, he withdraws into
it, regresses to that state of primary narcissism which is a mixture of bliss,
the reduction of tensions to zero, and death, and sinks into a deep,
dreamless sleep) (cf. Green 1984).
   Moreover, the dream is an impressionable 'pellicule'. It registers mental
images which are usually visual in nature, though they do occasionally
have subtitles or a sound track; sometimes the images are stills, as in

photography, but most often they are strung together in an animated sequence as in cinematography or, to use the most up-to-date comparison, a video film. What is activated here is one of the functions of the skin ego, that of a sensitive surface, capable of registering traces and inscriptions. Otherwise the skin ego, or at least the dematerialized and flattened image of the body, provides the screen against which the figures in the dream which symbolize or personify the psychological forces and agencies in conflict appear. The film may be defective, the reel may get stuck or let in light, and the dream is erased. If everything goes well, we can on waking develop the film, view it, re-edit it or even project it in the form of a narrative told to another person.

The dream presupposes the prior constitution of a skin ego (babies and psychotics do not dream, in the strict sense of the term; they have not acquired a sure distinction between sleeping and waking, between the perception of reality and hallucination). Conversely, the dream has the function, amongst others, of trying to repair the skin ego, not only on account of the danger the latter runs of coming apart during sleep, but principally because it has been to some extent riddled with holes caused by the encroachments upon it during the waking hours. In my opinion, this vital function of the dream — of daily reconstructing the psychical envelope — explains why everyone or almost everyone dreams every night or almost every night. Though necessarily omitted in the first Freudian theory of the psychical apparatus, this function is implicit in the second theory: in what follows, I shall try to render it explicit.

The Freudian theory of dreams revisited

Spurred on by his passionate friendship with Fliess and elated by the discovery of psychoanalysis, between 1895 and 1899 Freud interpreted nocturnal dreams as imaginary wish fulfilments. He dissected the psychical work carried out by the dream at the three levels which then for him constituted the mental apparatus. He concluded that an unconscious activity associates thing-presentations and affects with instinctual impulses, thus rendering those impulses representable. A pre-conscious activity articulates word-presentations, on the one hand, and defence mechanisms, on the other, with those representative and emotional presentations, thus working them up into symbolic figurations and compromise formations. Lastly, the perception-consciousness system, which shifts its operation during sleep from the progredient pole of motor discharge to the retrogredient pole of perception, hallucinates these figurations with a sensory and affective vividness that endows them with an illusory reality. The dream-work succeeds when it crosses the successive barriers of the two censorships, the one between unconscious and preconscious, the other between preconscious and conscious. It is therefore liable to two types of failure. If the disguise under which the forbidden desire hides itself does not deceive the second censorship, one awakes in anxiety. If the unconscious representatives short-circuit the detour through the preconscious and pass directly into consciousness, the result is *pavor nocturnus* or nightmare.

When Freud worked out his second model of the psychical apparatus, he did not have time to re-cast the whole of his theory of dreams from the new point of view and contented himself with revising it only at certain points. These revisions do, however, lead in the direction of a more complete systematization.

The dream realizes the desires of the id, given that these include the whole range of drives – sexual, auto-erotic, aggressive, self-destructive – expanded by Freud at the time of the second model. The dream realizes these desires in conformity with the pleasure princip........... the psychical functioning of the id and which deman.......... unconditional satisfaction of instinctual demands, and .... with the tendency of the repressed to return. The .... dreams of the superego: if certain dreams seem more like wish fulfilments, others are fulfilments of a threat. The dream realizes the desire of the ego, which is to sleep, and it does so as a servant of two masters, by bringing imaginary satisfactions to both the id and the superego at the same time. The dream also realizes the desire, which belongs to what certain of Freud's successors have called their ideal ego, of re-establishing the primitive fusion of ego and object, of recovering the happy state of intra–uterine organic symbiosis the infant enjoys with its mother. Whilst the mental apparatus in the waking state obeys the reality principle, maintaining limits between self and non-self, between body and psyche, accepting the limitation of its possibilities and affirming its claim to individual autonomy, in dreams, by contrast, it lays claim to omnipotence, and expresses boundless aspirations. In one of his short stories, Borges, describing the city of 'The Immortals', shows them spending their time dreaming. To dream is in fact to deny that one is mortal. Without this nocturnal belief in the immortality of at least a part of the self, would our daytime lives be tolerable?

In the post-traumatic dreams discussed by Freud (1920) as an introduction to his second psychical topography, the dreamer repetitively re-lives the circumstances preceding the accident. These are anxiety dreams, but they always stop just short of representing the accident, as if that could be retrospectively deferred and avoided at the last moment. These dreams, as compared with the preceding ones, fulfil four new functions:

139

—— to repair the narcissistic wound inflicted by the fact of having had a traumatic experience;

—— to restore the psychical envelope rent by the traumatic breach;

—— retroactively to control the circumstances which gave rise to the trauma;

—— to re-establish the pleasure principle in the functioning of the psychical apparatus, which has regressed under the impact of the trauma to being subject to a compulsion to repeat [*Wiederholungs-zwang*].

Might not what happens in the dreams of those suffering from traumatic neuroses simply be considered as a special case? Or rather, are we not dealing here – this is at least my personal conviction – with a more general phenomenon, which lies at the root of all dreams and is merely magnified in cases of trauma? The drive as a simple pressure (viewed independently of its aim and object) irrupts into the psychical envelope repeatedly during both waking and sleeping hours. There it produces micro-traumas which, in their qualitative diversity and quantitative accumulation, beyond a certain threshold constitute what Masud Khan (1974a) has termed a 'cumulative trauma'. It becomes necessary for the psychical apparatus to seek on the one hand to evacuate this overload and, on the other, to restore the integrity of the psychical envelope.

Of the range of possible means for doing this, the two most immediate, which are often found in tandem, are the formation of an envelope of anxiety and of a dream-film [*pellicule*]. The psychical apparatus was overwhelmed, when the trauma occurred, by the surge of external excitations which breached the protective shield, not only because they were too strong for it but also, and Freud (1920) emphasizes this point, because of the state of unpreparedness of the psychical apparatus, which was not expecting such a surge. Pain is the sign of this surprise breach. For there to be trauma, there has to be a levelling out of internal and external energy. Now, there are certainly some shocks so great that, whatever the subject's attitude towards them, the organic disorder they create and the rupture of the skin ego are irremediable. Generally, however, the pain caused is less if the breach has not occurred by surprise and if someone can be found as quickly as possible to function, both by the words they speak and the attention they give, as an auxiliary or substitute skin ego for the injured person. (I use 'injury' here to refer equally to a narcissistic wound as to a physical injury.) In *Beyond the Pleasure Principle*, Freud describes this defence against trauma as mobilizing counter-cathexes of energy of a corresponding intensity in order to equalize the internal cathexis of energy and the quantity of external energy introduced by the excitations which have suddenly appeared. This operation involves a number of consequences. The first three, in the list which follows, are economic, of the sort with which Freud primarily concerned himself. The fourth is topological and topographical; Freud merely sensed its significance, which we have now to develop here.

1 These counter-cathexes have as their counterpart an impoverishment of the rest of psychical activity, particularly sexual and/or intellectual life.

2 If, as a result of a physical trauma, there is a lasting lesion, the risk of traumatic neurosis is diminished, because the lesion summons up a narcissistic hyper-cathexis of the damaged organ, which binds the excess excitation.

3 The greater the degree of cathexis and the quantity of bound (i.e. quiescent) energy in a system, the greater its capacity for binding and therefore its capacity to resist trauma; hence the constitution of what I term an anxiety envelope, the last line of defence of the protective shield: anxiety prepares the psyche, by the hyper-cathexis of its receptor systems, to anticipate the possible occurrence of trauma and to mobilize a quantity of internal energy as nearly as possible equal to the external excitation.

4 From a topographical point of view now, encircled and sealed off by a permanent counter-cathexis, the pain of the traumatic breach subsists in the form of unconscious psychical suffering, localized and encysted at the periphery of the self (cf. the phenomenon of the 'crypt' described by Nicolas Abraham 1978, or the Winnicottian notion of a 'hidden self').

The anxiety envelope (a first defence and a defence by means of affect) prepares the ground for the appearance of the dream-film (the second defence, a defence by representation). The holes in the skin ego, whether produced by a serious trauma or by an accumulation of micro-traumas carried over from the day or occurring during sleep, are transposed by the work of representation to locations where the scenarios of the dream may then unfold. The holes are thus plugged by a film of images which are, essentially, visual. The skin ego is, originally, a tactile envelope, lined with sound and gustato-olfactory envelopes. The muscular and visual envelopes develop later. The dream-film represents an attempt to replace the deficient tactile envelope with a visual envelope, both finer and flimsier, but also more sensitive: the protective-shield function is re-established *a minima*; the function of the inscription of traces and their transformation into signs is, by contrast, intensified. Every night, to escape the sexual appetites of her suitors, Penelope unravelled the shroud she had woven by day. The nocturnal dream works in the opposite direction: it re-weaves by night those parts of the skin ego that have become unravelled by day under the impact of exogenous and endogenous stimuli.

My conception of the dream-film ties in with the study published by Sami-Ali (1969), of a case of urticaria: observing in a female patient the alternation of periods of outbreaks of urticaria without dreaming with periods of urticaria-free dreaming, Sami-Ali advances the hypothesis that dreams serve to conceal a disagreeable body image. I would rephrase his intuition as follows: the illusory skin of the dream masks an irritated, raw skin ego.

These considerations prompt me also to reconsider the relations between the latent and manifest content of dreams. As both Nicolas Abraham (1978) and Annie Anzieu (1974) have in their separate ways noted, the physical apparatus is a structure of layers interlocking one within the other. Indeed, for there to be contents, there have to be containers, and what on one level is a container may become a content on another. The latent content of the dream aims at being a container of instinctual pressures by associating them with unconscious thing-presentations. The manifest content seeks to be a visual container of the latent content. The narration of the dream after waking seeks to be a verbal container of the manifest content. The interpretation that may be given by the psychoanalyst of a patient's account of his dream on the one hand takes apart the various layers (as one might strip away the successive skins of an onion) and on the other restores the now split and conscious ego in its function as a container of the representative and affective representations of the instinctual pressures and traumatic breaches.

Case study: Zenobia

I give this patient, an eldest child, deeply affected by the sad loss of her position as an only child, the pseudonym Zenobia, in memory of the splendid queen of ancient Palmyra who was deposed by the Romans.

A first analysis with a colleague seems to have been concerned essentially with Oedipal feelings, their hysterical organization, ensuing complications in her love life and her frigidity, which diminished but none the less did not disappear. She comes to consult me because of a state of quasi-permanent anxiety which, since that first analysis, she has not been able to repress, and secondarily, on account of that persistent frigidity which she seeks both to cure and to deny by throwing herself into ever more complicated liaisons.

The first weeks of her second analysis are dominated by an intense transference love, or, more precisely, by the transference into the cure of her habitual seductive advances towards older men. Though I do not tell her so, I recognize the hysterial ruse underlying this all too obvious attempt at seduction: she is seeking to win the interest and attention of a potential partner by offering him sexual satisfaction, when she really wishes to obtain from him the satisfaction of her ego needs, which were ignored by those in her early environment. Little by little, I show Zenobia that her hysterical defence mechanisms are protecting her — ineffectively — from faults in her basic narcissistic security, faults connected with an intense anxiety that she might lose the love of her mother and with the many early frustrations of her psychical needs. Zenobia remained marked by a quasi-traumatic contrast between these frustrations and the generosity and pleasure with which her mother had satisfied her bodily needs up until the birth of a rival brother.

The seductive transference disappears as soon as Zenobia becomes convinced that the psychoanalyst is prepared to occupy himself with her ego needs without claiming a premium of erotic pleasure in exchange. At the same time, the quality of her anxiety changes: depressive anxiety, connected with the experience or the fear of loss of the mother's love, gives way to a persecution anxiety, even older and more formidable.

In the course of a summer holiday abroad, she has had, so she tells me on her return, the very pleasant experience of living in a larger, lighter and better-situated flat than the one she occupies in Paris. I understand all these details, without telling her so, as reflecting the development of her body image and of her skin ego: she feels more at ease in her skin, and experiences a deep need to communicate, but this skin ego now taking form provides her neither with a sufficient protective shield nor with a filter enabling her to discern the origin and nature of the excitations. In fact, what was by day a dream flat by night became a positive nightmare. Not only did she not dream there, she could not even get to sleep; she imagined that burglars might get in. This anxiety persists after her return to Paris: she has not really begun to sleep properly again.

I interpret her fear of a break-in as having two sides to it: on the one hand, she fears a breach from outside, a breaching by an unknown man of the intimate parts of her body (rape anxiety), but also the psychoanalyst's breaching of the intimate regions of her psyche; on the other hand, she fears a breach from within, by drives of her own of which she has no knowledge, chief among them a violent resentment of the frustrations caused by those around her both now and in the past. I explain to her that the intensity of her anxiety is the cumulative result of a confusion between the external breach and the internal one, as well as between sexual and psychical penetration. This interpretation is aimed at consolidating her skin ego both as an interface separating external from internal excitation and as an inter-locking within a single self of envelopes differentiating the psychical ego from the bodily ego. The effect of this is immediate and quite lasting: she begins to sleep well again. But the anxiety she had until now experienced in her life tends to become transferred into her analysis.

The following sessions are characterized by a mirroring transference. Zenobia repeatedly demands that I speak, that I say what I think, how

I see things, that I provide an echo for what she is saying and that I say what I think of what she has said. My counter-transference is put to the test by this insistent and endlessly renewed pressure which places almost physical constraints upon me and deprives me of my freedom of thought. I can neither keep silent, since she takes this for an aggressive rejection which threatens to destroy her developing skin ego, nor can I enter into her hysterical game of reversing the situation, in which I become the patient and she the analyst. By trial and error, I develop a double-edged interpretative procedure. On the one hand I remind her of – or explain to her – an interpretation I have given previously, which is likely to answer in part to what she is asking of me and which shows her what I as analyst am thinking and how what she says resonates within me. On the other hand, I try to elucidate the meaning of her demand; sometimes I explain to her that checking that what she says is echoed in me is an expression of her need to receive an image of herself from another so that she can produce one of her own; sometimes that knowing what her mother was thinking, what her life with her husband was like, what relations she had with a cousin, her supposed lover, and why she had had other children, had remained for her, Zenobia, a set of painful questions to which she received no answer; and sometimes also that by subjecting me to a hail of questions, she was reproducing, in an attempt to master it, a situation in which she must herself as a very small child have been subjected too early to a hail of stimulations too intense for her to be able to cope with them in her thinking.

Sustained analytic work enables her to extricate herself to some degree from the persecutory position. She rediscovers with me the security of a first relationship with the good maternal breast, a security destroyed by the disillusionment she felt when that breast produced other babies.

The long holidays pass off without difficulty and without any disruptive *passages à l'acte*. Upon resuming our work, she gives herself up to a serious regression. In the three-quarters of an hour of our session, she tests out a state of enormous distress. She relives all the pain of being abandoned by her mother. The amount of detail that she is then able to summon up and to recount regarding the quality of that suffering reveals that her skin ego has made advances: she has acquired an envelope that enables her to contain her psychical states, and the doubling of her conscious ego enables her to observe herself and to symbolize those parts of herself which are ill. She brings out three orders of detail, which I draw together each time in an interpretation. Firstly, I explain to her that she has been hurt by her mother's abandonment, by being deposed from her position as an only child: we already know this intellectually, but it is necessary for her to rediscover the intensely painful affect which she had felt at the time, but brushed aside. Secondly, I advance a hypothesis which had suggested itself to me during the earlier period of mirror transference: even during the phase in which she had been an only child, communication with her mother had been deficient; the mother had lavished food and physical attention upon Zenobia, but had not paid sufficient heed to the baby's inner feelings. In response to this, Zenobia tells me that her mother shouted at the least little thing (I suggest a connection here with her fear of being breached by noise); Zenobia had not been able to distinguish for certain at the time what originated with her mother and what within herself; the noise expressed fury, but she did not know whose. Thirdly, I suggest that this failure to take account of her primary feelings/ affects/phantasies had doubtless also been reinforced by her father, whose jealous, violent character my patient could from that point discuss openly.

This session is one of prolonged emotional intensity. Zenobia sobs and is on the verge of breaking down. I give her advance warning of the end of the session, so that she can prepare herself internally for the interruption. I tell her that I welcome her suffering, that she is in the process of experiencing, perhaps for the first time, an emotion so fearsome that she has not until now allowed herself to feel it and has sealed it off, deported it and encysted it at the periphery of herself. She stops crying, though when leaving she is noticeably unsteady on her feet. Her ego finds in that pain which she has at last made her own an envelope that strengthens her feelings of the unity and continuity of her self.

The following week, Zenobia has reverted to her habitual defence mechanisms: she does not want, she says, to go through such a painful experience again in her analysis. Then she mentions the fact that she has been dreaming a great deal, continuously in fact, every night since returning from holiday. She had not intended to tell me. At the next session, she announces that she has decided to tell me about her dreams, but, as there are too many of them, she has divided them up into three categories: the 'beauty queen' type, the '*boule*' type, and a third category which I forget, not being able to note down everything at the time and finding myself overwhelmed by the copiousness of the material. She spends session upon session reporting her dreams to me in details as they occur to her. I am overwhelmed or rather, abandoning the effort to remember, understand and interpret everything, I let myself be carried along by the flow.

In dreams of the first category, she either is herself or sees in the dream a beautiful girl whom some men are about to strip naked on the pretext of examining her beauty.

The *boules* dreams she herself interprets as related to the breast or the testicles. She returns to them later, concluding that the *boule* is a breast/testicle/head. She also refers here to the slang expression '*perdre la boule*' (for '*perdre la tête*'), meaning 'to go mad'.

Zenobia's dreams were weaving her a new psychical skin to replace her deficient protective shield. She began to reconstitute her skin ego from the moment I interpreted her auditory persecution, emphasizing the confusion she experienced between noise coming from outside and the noise made in her head by her inner rage, split off, fragmented and projected. Her account now made her dreams parade before me without halting over any particular one, and not allowing me either the time or material for a possible interpretation. What she gave was an overview. More precisely, I had the impression that her dreams were flying about somewhere above her, surrounding her with a bower of images. The envelope of suffering gave way to a film of dreams through which her skin ego took on greater consistency. Her mental apparatus was even able to symbolize this renascent activity of symbol-formation through the metaphor of the *boule*. This condensed several representations: that of a psychical envelope in the process of completion and unification; that of the head – that is to use Bion's expression, an apparatus for dealing with one's own thoughts; that of the all-powerful maternal breast, lost inside which she had until now gone on living regressively in phantasy; that of the masculine reproductive organs, the lack of which caused her pain when she had been dislodged, by the birth of a brother, from her place as the privileged object of her mother's love. In this way, the two dimensions of her psychopathology, the narcissistic and the objectal, intersected, prefiguring the intersecting interpretations I was to give her in the following weeks, which would alternate between attention to her pre-genital and Oedipal sexual fantasmatics and concern for the faults and hyper-cathexes (for example, of a seductive nature) of her narcissistic envelope. In effect, for the subject to acquire a sexual identity, two conditions must be fulfilled. One is a necessary condition: he must have a skin of his own, within which he can indeed feel himself to be a subject to contain that identity. The other condition is that he must have sufficient experience, in connection with polymorphous perverse and Oedipal phantasies, of the erogenous zones on that skin and the *jouissances* that may be enjoyed there.

A few sessions later, a dream comes up on which it is at last possible for us to work:

She is leaving home and the pavement has caved in. You can see the foundations of the house. Her brother arrives with his whole family. She is lying on a mattress. Everyone is watching her quite calmly. For her own part, she feels disgusted. She wants to scream. She is being subjected to a horrible ordeal: she has to make love with her brother in front of all the others.

She wakes up feeling exhausted.

Her associations take her back over a recent dream of bestiality which had disturbed her greatly, and lead her to speak of the loathsome character of the sexuality she had experienced, in childhood and in her first heterosexual relationships in adolescence, as a revolting ordeal. 'In their love-making, my parents were like animals . . .' (pause). 'I am particularly afraid that the confidence I have in you may be called into question.'

I: 'That would be the pavement caving in under you, the foundations threatened. You want me to help you contain the excess of sexual excitation which has been inside you since childhood and of which your analysis makes you more and more intensely aware.' The word 'sexuality' has been used for the first time in her analysis, and it is I who use it.

She explains that she had lived her whole childhood and adolescence in an unpleasant state of permanent and confused excitation, which she was unable to get rid of.

I: 'This was sexual excitation, but you couldn't identify it as sexual because no one around you had given you any enlightenment on the subject. Moreover you were not able to identify in what places in your body you felt that excitation, since you did not have a sufficiently clear picture of your feminine anatomy to do that.' She departs in a state of great calm.

At our next session, she goes back to the copious dream material with which she has been inundating me: it has flowed out of her on all sides and she is afraid it will be beyond my capacity to master it.

I: 'You put me in the same situation of being overwhelmed by your dreams as you are in yourself with your sexual excitation.'

Zenobia is able to formulate her question, which she has held back since the beginning of the session: what do I think of her dreams?

I declare myself willing to reply here and now about her dreams, since those around her in her youth had not replied to the questions she had had about sexuality and she has since felt an uncontrollable need to ask others what they felt and what they thought she was feeling. I do however make it clear that I will not pass judgement on either her dreams or her actions. It is not for me to decide, for example, whether incest or bestiality is good or evil. I then communicate two interpretations to her. The first seeks to make a distinction between the object of attachment and the object of seduction. With the dog, which embraces her in the earlier dream, she is experiencing an object with which she communicates at a primitive and essential level, by tactile contact, the softness of fur, body heat, the caress of its licking. These feelings of well-being in which she allows herself to be enveloped enable her to feel well enough in her own body to experience a specifically sexual and feminine, though troubling, desire to be penetrated. With her brother in the latest dream, the sexuality is bestial in a different sense: it is brutal. She has hated him at birth, he will be able to avenge himself by possessing her and this will be to commit a monstrous, animal act of incest with him. He is the doughty lover from whom, as a little girl, she imagined she might receive her sexual initiation.

Secondly, I put the emphasis on the interference, embarrassing for her, between the sexual need of her body, which is not yet completely developed, and her psychical need to be understood. She abandons herself to the brutal sexual desire of the man as a victim who believes that this is required to attract his attention and to obtain, at the price of the physical pleasure she gives him, satisfaction of her ego needs, a satisfaction which is at times hypothetical, at times impossible (this is an allusion to the two types of experience that have succeeded one another in the history of her sexual life). Hence the seductiveness which is so much to the fore in her relations with men, the game in which she ensnares only herself; I remind her that the first months of her analysis with me were devoted to re-playing and to undoing this game.

The psychoanalytic work begun in this series of sessions continued for some months. It brought about some significant changes, through a series of jolts (following the pattern of development through breaks and abrupt reorganizations typical of this patient) in her professional and love life. Only much later did it become possible to analyse the direct leap Zenobia made from orality to genitality and the short-circuiting of anality that characterized her case.

The envelope of excitation, hysterical background to every neurosis

The above sequence illustrates the necessity of acquiring both a skin ego and the attendant feelings of the unity and continuity of the self, not only in order to accede to sexual identity and confront the Oedipal problematic, but in order first of all correctly to identify the site of erogenous excitation. Limits may then be set to that excitation and, at the same time, satisfactory channels of discharge provided, and sexual desire liberated from its role as a counter-cathexis of the early frustrations suffered through the needs of the psychical ego and the attachment drive.

This case study also illustrates the envelope-of-suffering – dream-film – word-skin sequence that is necessary for the construction of a sufficiently containing, filtering and symbolizing skin ego in patients who have suffered past deficiencies in the satisfaction of their ego needs and who, for that reason, display substantial narcissistic faults. We were able to relate Zenobia's unconscious aggressiveness towards men to the successive frustrations suffered at the hands of her mother, father and finally her siblings. With the development of her skin ego into a continuous, flexible, firm interface, the drives (sexual and aggressive) become for her forces she can use, directing them from certain specific bodily zones towards objects that are more adequately selected, and with aims that promise both physical and psychical pleasures.

To be able to be recognized, which means to be represented, the drive must be contained in a three-dimensional psychical space, localized at certain points on the body surface, and must emerge as a figure against the ground provided by the skin ego. It is because the drive is demarcated and circumscribed that the full force of its pressure is felt, a force capable of finding an object and an aim and of issuing in a free and vital satisfaction. Zenobia presents several features of the hysterical personality. Her treatment brings to the fore the 'envelope of excitation', to use an expression coined by Annie Anzieu. Not having been able to constitute a psychical envelope for herself from the sensory signs transmitted to her by her mother (there was, in particular, a serious discordance between the warmth of her mother's tactile contact with her and the brutality of the sounds she emitted), Zenobia has tried to find a substitute skin ego in a permanent envelope of excitation, cathected in a diffuse, general fashion by the aggressive and sexual drives. That envelope results from a process of introjection of the loving, stimulating mother of feeding and nappy-changing time. In this way, Zenobia's self is surrounded by a belt of excitations which perpetuates in her psychical functioning the dual presence of a mother attentive to her bodily needs and a continuous instinctual stimulation that enables Zenobia to feel she enjoys a permanent existence. But the mother, stimulating as far as her child's body is concerned, is doubly disappointing in that she responds inadequately to that child's psychical needs, and puts an abrupt end to the physical excitations she has caused when she feels it is going on too long, or becoming too pleasant, too questionable or simply too much trouble: paradoxically, the mother becomes irritated by what she induces, and for this she punishes her child, who consequently feels full of guilt. The excitement—disappointment sequence plays itself out simultaneously on the level of the drive, which is over-activated without being able to reach a fully satisfying discharge. Annie Anzieu considers that such a psychical envelope of physical excitation not only characterizes the skin ego in hysteria but also constitutes the hysterical background common to every neurosis. Instead of exchanging those signs which constitute the first sensory communication and which are the basis for subsequent mutual understanding, the mother and child exchange only stimulations, in an escalating process which always ends badly. The mother is disappointed that her child does not bring her all the pleasure she was expecting, and the child is doubly disappointed, at being disappointing to the mother and because it continues to carry within it an overload of unsatisfied excitation.

I would add that this hysterical envelope perverts the third function of the skin ego by inverting it. Instead of sheltering narcissistically within a protective-shield envelope, the hysteric lives happily in an envelope of errogenous and aggressive excitation to the point where he himself suffers, blames others for his condition, feels resentment towards them, and seeks to drag them into repeating this circular game in which excitation engenders the disappointment which in turn revives the need for excitation. In his article, 'Grudge and the hysteric', Masud Khan (1974b) gives a fine analysis of this dialectic.

References

Abraham, Nicolas (1978) *L'Ecorce et le noyau*, Paris: Aubier-Montaigne.

Anzieu, Annie (1974) 'Emboîtements', *Nouv. Rev. de Psychanal.*, 9: 57–71.

Freud, S. (1920) *Beyond the Pleasure Principle, Standard Edition of the Complete Psychological Works of Sigmund Freud*, SE 18.

Green, A. (1984) *Narcissism de vie, Narcissism de mort*, Paris: Editions de Minuit.

Guillaumin, J. (1979) *Le Rêve et le moi*, Paris: Presses Universitaires de France.

Khan, Masud (1974a) *The Privacy of the Self*, New York: International Universities Press.

—— (1974b) 'La Rancune de l'hysterique'; *Nouv. Rev. de Psychanal.*, 10: 151–8.

Sami-Ali, M. (1969) 'Etude de l'image du corps dans l'urticaire', *Rev. franc. Psychanal.*

PART FOUR

The adaptive ego and the dream

The chapters in this part of the book are marked by the development of ego psychology as it has evolved and diversified, mostly in America. The adaptive function of the ego, specifically as it is manifest in the dream, is the subject-matter of these essays, whether the adaptation is seen in terms of classical structural conflict and compromise, or in the self psychologist's occupation with the maintenance of self identity.

Spanjaard's essay of 1969 continues a line of thinking opened up by Erikson, examining Freud's contradictory messages regarding the manifest content of the dream, arguing its integral importance from the perspective of the dreamer himself. 'In almost all our patients we encounter dreams', he writes, 'in which the feature of conflict can already be seen to express itself in the manifest content.' Surveying the dreams interpreted by Freud, moreover, he remarks on the constant presence of a relevant ego or self-state feeling, one utilized by Freud in his interpretations. The emphasis on the self state in dreams is later developed by Kohut and his followers, marking a significant separate development in psychoanalysis.

Greenberg and Pearlman, utilizing the sleep laboratory reports of a man in analysis, add weight to the respect for manifest content, finding in dream material relatively undisguised references to emotionaly significant subject-matter, including transference material from the subject's analysis.

Cecily de Monchaux's brilliant and wide-ranging essay, 'Dreaming and the organizing function of the ego', describes dreaming as a temporary dissociation which promotes mastery or re-integration of potentially traumatic or overwhelming emotional experience. Although her conceptualizations are framed in the tradition of ego psychology, the dream of her essay bears some functional resemblance to the 'Dream as object' of Pontalis. Both utilize Winnicott's notion of transitionality, de Monchaux harnessing it deftly to the tradition of ego psychology. Informed by Kris' concept of 'regression in the service of the ego' as well as Hartmann's concern with the ego's organizing function, she finds a range of adaptive possibilities even in omnipotent uses of symbolization.

The last chapter in this section develops from Kohut's conceptualization of 'self-state dreams' in which manifest imagery of the dream is understood to be giving visible shape to and therefore binding unnameable anxiety caused by a threatened breakdown of a cohesive identity. Stolorow and Atwood generalize from Kohut's conceptualization, describing the function of all dreaming to be the maintenance of the structure of the individual's representational world. The dream reinforces this structure specifically through the 'compelling' form of knowing, the hallucinatory vividness of the dream images. The intense dreams identified by Kohut are understood as an intensification of this general process, the concreteness linked, unusually, to the maintenance of organization. Such imagery, they argue, works like perverse enactments to strengthen a conviction of being 'alive and real'. It is also associated, in the case presented, with acute and violent trauma and intolerable aggression.

For Stolorow and Atwood, the act of interpretation is regarded not as a deciphering of latent meaning, but an act of 'restoring dream symbols and metaphors to their formative personal contexts'. This, of course, is not so far from Freud's intention when he insisted over and over again on the importance of attending to the patient's associations. It might also describe the restoration of a dream-space as disclosed in the processes examined in Part Three.

The manifest dream content and its significance for the interpretation of dreams

JACOB SPANJAARD

The manifest dream content remains the stepchild of dream psychology and dream interpretation, despite the fact that there most assuredly is a 'renewed interest in the manifest content of the dream and an effort to exploit it further than Freud did' (Lipton, reported by Babcock, 1965). It is actually somewhat astonishing, considering the increased understanding which psychoanalysis gained for conscious productions through the development of ego psychology, that insight into the manifest dream, and specifically its function in the procedure of interpretation, should have remained limited. The present writer is of the opinion that certain guidelines can be formulated for this purpose, and that by adequately taking into account the manifest dream content one can arrive at a more useful construction of interpretation without neglecting the most important principles given by Freud in *The Interpretation of Dreams* (1900).

Historical review

In the history of the evaluation of the manifest dream we find features which are also common to the historical development of a number of other areas of psychoanalytic interest such as those of ego psychology and the concept of aggression. As regards the earliest period of the development of psychoanalysis, close examination of such a particular aspect would be out of place: the unconscious and sexuality are in the foreground, and rightly so. Often then – as in the case of Adler with regard to the subject of aggression – it is the opening move of a dissident theoretical development which has the effect on Freud and his closest collaborators of evoking resistance rather than enthusiasm towards further investigation in the same direction. Usually, formulations subsequently appear which lead to integration, as we have seen happen in the 1920s with regard to ego psychology and aggression.

Unfortunately, Freud's views on the manifest dream content never underwent a distinct revision. Presumably, the definite tendency of many of those who strayed from the path of psychoanalysis to accept the manifest content of the dream at face value had something to do with this fact; this tendency, by marring Freud's fundamental discovery of a distinction between the manifest and the latent dream, also damages one of the cornerstones of psychoanalysis as the psychology of the unconscious. Silberer (1912) and Maeder (1912, 1913) certainly did nothing to further Freud's interest in the manifest dream, while Jung, Adler and Stekel (1909, 1911) merely served to induce him to adhere all the more closely to the views already laid down in *The Interpretation of Dreams* (1900). One can find interesting remarks on this subject in Freud (1914).

From the very beginning, Freud views the manifest dream as a mere conglomeration (1900: 104, 449, 500), a façade (1915–17: 181; 1925a: 141; 1925c: 44; 1940: 165). In *The Interpretation of Dreams*, his first technical suggestion (1900: 103) is that one should 'cut up the dreams . . . into pieces' which could serve as points of departure for the indispensable associations. In the *Introductory Lectures* (1915–17: 181–82) he states:

> It is natural that we should lose some of our interest in the manifest dream. It is bound to be a matter of indifference to us whether it is well put together, or is broken up into a series of disconnected separate pictures. Even if it has an apparently sensible exterior, we know that this has only come about through dream-distortion and can have as little organic relation to the internal content of the dream as the façade of an Italian church has to its structure and plan.... In general one must avoid seeking to explain one part of the manifest dream by another, as though the dream had been coherently conceived and was a logical arranged narrative. On the contrary, it is as a rule like a piece of breccia, composed of various fragments of rock held together by a binding medium, so that the designs that appear on it do not belong to the original rocks imbedded in it.

Only sometimes may we find an exception in a 'façade' which is analogous to an existing 'fantasy' or 'day-dream' (1900: 491–3).

The structural theory had little effect on Freud's view regarding dreams. In 1923 (1923b) we first see a distinction being made between 'dreams from above and dreams from below' (p. 111), and not until *An Outline of Psychoanalysis* does he state that 'dreams may arise either from the id or from the ego' (1940: 166). Alexander (1925) was early in pointing out the role of the ego and superego in dreaming, but most of the articles on this matter first appear after 1930.

154

As one would expect, interest in the manifest dream begins to increase concurrently. At this point a brief summing up should suffice: later on I shall return to give closer attention to certain particular considerations. The very first is Federn, who as early as 1914 shows interest in the manifest dream, and later delineates the connection with the structural hypothesis (1932, 1933). (Cf. also Fenichel 1935; Alexander and Wilson 1935; but especially Fenichel *et al.* 1936). However, there continues to exist a hesitancy towards accepting the manifest dream as a product fully deserving serious consideration, and Hitschmann (1933–34) even apologizes for having tried to use it as a basis for drawing psychopathological distinctions. It is only after World War II that a great many more articles appear in which the manifest dream is brought into relation to the role of the ego in dreaming: namely, two panel discussions (cf. Rangell 1956; Babcock 1965), the latter of which was devoted wholly to the manifest dream, and further numerous articles, from amongst which I merely wish to mention those of Miller (1948), Mittelmann (1949), Blitzsten *et al.* (1950), Harris (1951), Katan (1960), Loewenstein (1961), Ward (1961), Peck (1961), Khan (1962), Pollock and Muslin (1962), Richardson and Moore (1963), Mack (1965), Frosch (1967), Klauber (1967), Stewart (1967) and Levitan (1967). In connection with the present subject there are several important publications, first of all those of Saul (cf. Rangell 1956; Saul 1953, 1966; Sheppard and Saul 1958; Saul and Fleming 1959; Saul and Curtis 1967). In these articles the manifest dream is examined for its applicability in evaluating the activity of the ego. Fliess (1953), however, warns against confusing the latent with the manifest dream content: use of the manifest dream concept can tempt the analyst to introduce his own subjective interpretations, and to resort to metaphor and allegory while neglecting the associations of the dreamer himself. Finally, in Arlow and Brenner (1964), dream theory is revised to bring it in line with the structural theory, and the manifest dream is also viewed more as a product fully worthy of analytic interest (pp. 136–40).

The question of how far one is justified in attributing a function to the phenomenon of the manifest dream still remains a compelling one. On this subject Freud's expressed views are not free of contradictions.

The manifest dream is viewed as an affair of the system Cs, which itself is passive, although Freud also points out that there are people who 'seem to possess the faculty of consciously directing their dreams' (1900: 571 ff.; cf. also Ferenczi 1911). The peculiar character of the manifest dream in traumatic neuroses evokes problems (Freud 1920: 32) and is viewed as an attempt 'to master the stimulus retrospectively', by way of which Freud arrives at the concept of 'the compulsion to repeat'. Loewenstein (1949), Stein (1965) and Stewart (1967) present considerations concerning this mastery of traumatic stimuli. Ferenczi (1934)

155

speaks of a traumatolytic function of the dream. Eissler (1966) clearly shows respect for the manifest dream content, which in his view reveals a background of creativity (cf. Lewin 1964), and which thus could be expected to be not only anti-traumatic but also traumatogenic. Eissler is also inclined to take seriously the dreamer's reaction in the manifest dream (1966: 18, n. 2) e.g. of surprise, and the well-known assessment: 'after all, it is only a dream' (cf. Also Arlow and Brenner 1964: 136). He believes that such matters remain as yet insufficiently understood. His hint that a connection can be established with Freud's considerations regarding negation (1925b) strikes me as of great importance. In Levitan (1967) the actual role of the manifest dream content is also given emphasis. In this connection, Lewin's views (1946–64) are important.

However, we find ourselves here approaching a tendency which admonishes us to exercise caution. Freud viewed dreaming as essentially nothing more 'than a particular *form* of thinking' (1900: 506, n. 2; 1914: 65; 1922: 229, 1923b: 112) and held that 'it is the *dream work* which creates that form, and it alone is the essence of dreaming' (1900: 506, n. 2). As soon as one tends to view this dream-work as a form of adaptation, of problem-solving — let alone as a rational or mystical activity — one begins to take leave of psychoanalytic insights in the proper sense. It is misleading to say that dreams are concerned with the tasks of life before us or to seek to find a solution for the problems of our daily work (1925a: 127).

The opinions of Maeder (1912, 1913), and in more recent times those of Bonime (1962) — cf. Levine's criticism (1967) — and Hadfield (1954) must be viewed in this light. The most interesting and valuable representative of this trend, Thomas French, will be discussed separately below. In the present survey I shall omit those techniques of dream interpretation which have a predominantly arbitrary character, such as that of Stekel (1909, 1911) and, more recently, that of Gutheil (1951).

The manifest dream content

In the course of the years the manifest dream content has become for us such a firmly established concept that we now scarcely perceive the problems inherent in it. The problems, however, are there, even in the phenomenon of the manifest dream itself. What the patient tells us may range from a vague remnant to boundless excursions far afield, particularly when we are dealing with resistances (cf. Freud 1923b: 110).

Lewin (1948) describes experiences during sleep which are virtually devoid of content, and terms these 'blank dreams'. Erikson (1954) scrutinizes the manifest dream very closely, and elevates it to the level of a subtle and differentiated piece of information in its own right. In his view, the transition to the latent content is a gradual one. Miller (1964), in connection with the appearance of colour in dreams, shows how lapidary human beings in fact are in their reproduction of perceptions in general, and thus also in respect of dreams in particular.

But it has been especially the experience gleaned from dream research in recent years with simultaneous registration of the EEG and eye-movements, which has shown us that we dream a great deal more than we thought we did, and also that our dreams tend to last a good deal longer than was formerly believed (cf. Dement and Wolpert 1958; Rechtschaffen *et al.* 1963; Fisher 1965). Our knowledge of what a person experiences during sleep thus proves to be extremely fragmentary.

Perhaps this may help explain why so many different aspects of the manifest dream may in turn be taken to serve as points of departure for contemplation (cf. Alexander and Wilson 1935; Erikson 1954, 1964; Federn 1914; French 1937a, b; Harris 1951, 1962; Hitschmann 1933–34; Levitan 1967; Lewin 1946–64; M.L. Miller 1948; S.C. Miller 1964; Blum 1964; Richardson and Moore 1963; Saul 1953, 1966; Saul and Curtis 1967; Stewart 1967).

To all these aspects I should like to add still another, or at least to isolate it from the composite which is the manifest dream. It is a familiar aspect, one which virtually fully corresponds to that pointed out by Freud in 'counter-wish' dreams (1900: 146–59), and it is this: I believe that if we closely observe the manifest dream content, we will find that in almost all our patients we encounter dreams in which the feature of conflict can already be seen to express itself in the manifest content. The dreamer is always present himself; he may appear as a mere shadowy observer; more often, however, in the narration of the dream his involvement and especially his intentions are revealed through the often bizarre events in the dream. In this respect I am at variance with Freud, who holds the view that the ego may not appear in the manifest dream and, when present, is without remarkable significance (1900: 322–3). In going over the ninety extensive accounts of dreams which appear in *The Interpretation of Dreams*, I thus found *not a single one* in which the self (the 'I') did not appear in the narrative! In only thirteen instances were there no indications that not *all* was going as the dreamer should have wished. One almost always encounters something in the nature of, for example: 'I was alarmed', 'I arrived too late', 'I felt impatient', 'an uncomfortable feeling', 'I was surprised', 'we were frightened', 'I could not find', 'I could not go'.

The associated affect may have such intensity that one may assume that it is this which awakens the dreamer (cf. Freud 1900: 267; Levitan 1967). Originally Freud regarded these affects and thoughts mainly as elements belonging to the latent dream content. However, his extensive discussion of the Uncle dream shows that for Freud, too, this matter presented not inconsiderable problems (cf. below, p. 164).

Federn (1932) and Grotjahn (1942) have pointed out that the dreamer experiences himself in continuity with his waking existence. Sheppard and Saul (1958) devised an interesting quantifying investigation with an ego-rating system, based on the distance of the 'ego' from the motivating forces experienced in the manifest dream content.

It seems to me that nowadays we have no qualms about equating the manifest dream with a neurotic symptom. In the 'Fliess Papers' (1892–99: 258, 276, 336) Freud clearly draws the analogy between dream and neurosis (cf. also Lewin 1955), but in *The Interpretation of Dreams* Freud only hesitantly makes such a comparison and links the compromise quality mainly to the ego's tendency to preserve the state of sleep. Later on he nevertheless calls it a compromise-formation, presumably following Ferenczi's (1911) example (cf. Freud 1900; 572, 579). In the *Introductory Lectures* (1915–17: 411) he again draws the analogy between the content of a phobia and the façade of the manifest dream (cf. also 1909: 229) and still later (1923a: 242) we find: 'a *compromise-formation* (the dream or the symptom) . . .'

My thesis is that the manifest dream content usually has a subjectively conflictual aspect, and that this aspect offers us the opportunity to evaluate the most superficial layer of the conflict and thus to arrive at a construction of the potentially most useful interpretation.

What does Freud himself actually do, warning as he does in all his publications that the manifest dream content must not be taken seriously? In fact, he often trespasses against this very rule. This begins already in the case of the 'Irma' dream. He includes the reproaches which he directs at Irma in the manifest content as a very essential element in his interpretation, and even feels embarrassment of having 'invented such a severe illness for Irma simply in order to clear' himself (1900: 114).

A few other examples: in the dream in which a lady wants to give a supper party (1900: 147) she is unable to obtain all the necessary items, although she tries her best to do so. Viewed from the vantage point of the manifest content, she is clearly blameless, Freud is able to interpret this dream in the sense: 'What the dream was saying to you was that you were unable to give supper parties, and it was thus fulfilling your *wish* [italics, J.S.] not to help your friend to grow plumper.' The reason is jealousy because her husband admires a plumper figure (1900: 148). When Freud (1900: 469) wonders why he did not feel disgust during a dream in which he was micturating on the seat of something like an open-air closet, covered with small heaps of faeces, he likewise betrays respect for the manifest dream content as information which is by no means negligible. Still more remarkable is the discussion of typical dreams of 'the death of loved relatives' (1900: 266), in which he expresses surprise at the fact 'that the dream thought formed by a repressed wish [is] entirely eluding censorship and passing into the dream without modification'. In the case of these typical dreams, the exhibitionistic and death-wish dreams, he has directed his attention precisely towards the manifest content, and has taken precisely the affect, embarrassment or grief, as a prerequisite for the established latent significance of the dream.

What exactly does Freud mean by the phrase 'the dream thought formed by a repressed wish'? Actually in chapter VII and elsewhere, he clearly separates the wish from the rest of the latent content. If he means here that the latent dream thought is the death-wish, then we must observe that this wish is in fact very obviously distorted. If, on the other hand, he means merely the thought, 'The relative is dead', then this is indeed expressed directly, eluding censorship, but the linking of the dreamer of this thought with a wish is not thus self-evidently established, as Freud indeed further states: 'there is no wish that seems more remote from us than this one . . .'. Naturally we must assume that the latent dream content is indeed the death-wish, and then when we examine the manifest dream content we see precisely the defence against the latent content with a particular clearness. In the first place it *happens* without the participation of the dreamer, and furthermore there is so much grief that the dreamer does not dream that he wishes his relative dead, but exactly the opposite (cf. Van der Sterren 1964). Every connection with the wish has been concealed: the censorship is evident.

In addition, I only wish to mention Freud's discussions in connection with the first dream from 'A case of hysteria' (1905a: 64ff.). Employing the manifest dream content, he finally states (1905a: 85): 'The intention might have been consciously expressed in some such words as these: "I must fly from this house, for I see that my virginity is threatened here; I shall go away with my father, and shall take precautions not to be surprised while I am dressing in the morning."' He further discloses the infantile material as a background, but the interpretation of the superficial and contemporary conflict is identical with the manifest dream content.

There is one class of dreams regarding which Freud never denied the direct significance and interpretability of the manifest dream. These are the 'undisguised wishful dreams' (1901: 655), which were first extensively discussed in chaper III of *The Interpretation of Dreams*; they are the dreams of convenience, dreams of children and of persons suffering privation. Quite remarkably, in the theoretical chapter (1900: 509) Freud takes as his point of departure a fragment viewed as belonging to such an 'undisguised wishful dream', a state of affairs which gives rise to a number of confusing deliberations such as the original rejection of the compromise character of the dream mentioned above. However, in the undisguised wishful dreams there is no need at all to camouflage the wish fulfilment, for these wishes are not involved in an intrapsychic conflict, at most in a conflict with the wish of sleep. Rather, it is the impossibility of their fulfilment in reality which provides the stimulus for illusory fulfilment in a dream. It is self-evident that such dreams can be anticipated in children: after all, they are able to achieve so little in reality; furthermore, so many things are forbidden to them from without. I have the impression that such undistorted wishful dream contents also repeatedly occur in conflictual dreams, and that they often constitute nuclei to which repressed dream-wishes are anchored. The dream of an unmarried homosexual woman may serve as an example: her wish for a penis was strongly denied, but she was able consciously to accept her wish for a child. After a day during which she sat for hours with her sister's baby on her lap, she dreamt that she had borne a child, but that despite her attempts to do so she could not sever the connection with her baby formed by the umbilical cord.

The conclusion is thus justified that Freud did indeed pay attention to the content and form of the manifest dream; certainly – in fact, as a matter of definition – in the case of the undisguised wishful dreams, but also in the conflictual dreams of his patients. He did so despite his warnings – correct as they are in themselves – against taking the manifest dream at face-value against metaphorical or allegorical approaches to interpretation, and against taking 'The dream as a whole' as one's point of departure (1900: 103). These are warnings which have had to be repeated again and again (Fliess 1953; Waldhorn 1967), a fact which might very well signify that there are reasons other than those of resistance for the tendency that analysts have to see more than a mere façade, a conglomeration with a bit of secondary revision, in the manifest dream content.

The technique of interpretation and the latent dream content

Manifest and latent dream content are concepts which reciprocally determine each other's meaning. In the process of dreaming it is the dream-work which leads from the latent to the manifest content, and in interpretation we carry out an action 'in a direction opposite to [that of] the dream work' (Freud 1940: 169), with which the circle is completed, and whereby the question of how we actually interpret is simultaneously bound up with the theory of dream psychology. When we pause to consider what the essence of the procedure on interpretation is, we are immediately confronted with all sorts of questions.

In the very first place: what exactly is *the latent dream content* itself? On this point misunderstandings prove to exist, for which imprecise formulations of Freud himself are partially responsible.

In chapter II of *The Interpretation of Dreams*, we first read of this matter. Having extensively summed up his associations to the 'Irma' dream, Freud says: 'I have now completed the interpretation of the dream' (1900: 118). Partly owing to other statements of a similar nature (1900: 279; 1915–17: 226), this seems to have contributed to a conception that the essence of the latent dream content, also called the 'dream thought', would consist of the totality of the associations to the manifest dream. One can deduce this from the fact that in his *New Introductory Lectures* (1933: 12) Freud is compelled to say: 'Let there be no misunderstanding, however. The associations to the dream are not yet the latent dream thoughts.' But what then is? The matter is not so simple as it is customarily suggested to be. One repeatedly comes across the notion that the latent dream thoughts are to be equated with id content (cf., for example, A. Freud 1936: 16; Stewart 1967). Freud himself most certainly did not mean to say this. In almost all his publications dealing with the dream we meet with a formulation which first appears in *The Interpretation of Dreams* (1900: 506): 'The dream thoughts are entirely rational and are constructed with an expenditure of all psychical energy of which we are capable. They have their place among thought-processes that have not become conscious—processes from which, after some modification, our conscious thoughts, too, arise.' And elsewhere (1905 b: 28): 'the latent, but perfectly logical, dream thoughts from which the dream is derived'. Later on (1933: 18), he states more clearly that the dreamer 'refuses to accept' a portion of these latent dream thoughts: 'it is strange to him, or perhaps even repellent'. And then he goes on to work out how the latent dream thought in part represents preconscious thoughts, and in part unconscious. Only as regards the latter may we say that id content might be involved.

The final result of the *interpretation* of a dream is identical with the latent dream thought (1933: 10) — but how precisely do we go about the interpretation? Remarkably enough, I have nowhere in Freud's writings been able to find an exact formulation of this procedure!

Alexander (1949: 62) is of the opinion that 'no general rules can be given', any more than they can 'for solving a crossword puzzle'. Naturally, one sees the procedure implicitly in the many works on the subject of dream interpretation which Freud wrote, but the first place in which he is more explicit is in the *New Introductory Lectures* where he says, referring to the dream thoughts (1933: 12):

The latter are contained in the associations like an alkali in the mother-liquor, but yet not quite completely contained in them. On the one hand, the associations give us far more than we need for formulating the latent dream thoughts – namely all the explanations, transitions, and connections which the patient's intellect is bound to produce in the course of his approach to the dream thoughts. On the other hand, an association often comes to stop precisely before the genuine dream thought: it has only come near to it and has only had contact with it through allusions. At that point we intervene on our own; we fill in the hints, draw undeniable conclusions, and give explicit utterance to what the patient has only touched in his associations. This sounds as though we allowed our ingenuity and caprice to play with the material . . . Nor is it easy to show the legitimacy of our procedure in an abstract description of it. But you have only to carry out a dream analysis yourselves or study a good account of one in our literature and you will be convinced of the cogent manner in which interpretative work like this proceeds.

In the *Outline* (1940: 168), we read: 'the dreamer's associations bring to light intermediate links which we can insert in the gap between the two [between the manifest and latent content] and by aid of which we can reinstate the latent content of the dream and "interpret" it'.

Freud himself admits that he is unable to lay down exact rules, and in his description he has to resort to imprecise terms such as 'mother liquor' and 'intermediate links'.

Another source of difficulty is that we always tend to view the latent dream thought as a wish, which somehow or other, for better or worse, strives for fulfilment in the manifest dream. Did Freud in fact intend to convey this idea? In *The Interpretation of Dreams*, wish and dream thought are repeatedly distinguished from each other, even though a continuity may exist between them.

In 'Two encyclopaedia articles' (1923: 241), we find:

If we disregard the unconscious contribution to the formation of the dream and limit the dream to its latent thoughts, it can represent anything with which waking life has been concerned – a reflection, a warning, an invention, a preparation for the immediate future, or, once again, the satisfaction of an unfulfilled wish.

The remarkable thing is that the manner in which psychoanalysts interpret dreams differs from that of non-analysts precisely in regard to the formulation of a wishful character for the latent dream content. We are not content with an interpretation of the dream as a mere replica of daily life, such as 'Your dream tells us how unhappy you feel', and so on; instead, we always try to formulate both the wish and the counter-force; that is, to formulate the conflict (Arlow and Brenner 1964: 141)

162

centring round the 'attempt at the fulfilment of a wish' (Freud 1933: 29) which we find in the dream. The wish-fulfilment hypothesis – or, methodologically speaking, perhaps better termed: wish-fulfilment model of interpretation (De Groot 1961) – is the cornerstone of psychoanalytic dream psychology, and thus also of the technique of interpretation. Freud repeatedly avers that this principle applies only to the unconscious infantile wish in the dream, which sometimes coincides with the day residue or even may constitute the least accessible portion of the latent dream thought. As early as his letters to Fliess (1892–9: 274) he formulates this, and in *The Interpretation of Dreams* he draws the distinction between 'the capitalist' and 'the entrepreneur' (1900: 561). Does the wish-fulfilling nature of the dream apply only to the capitalist, that is, the unconscious infantile wish, or to other disturbing dream stimuli as well, such as the day residues, of which Freud says (1900: 564): 'There can be no doubt that is they that are the true disturbers of the sleep'? Freud is continually in doubt on that question (1900: 606): 'I have already gone a step beyond what can be demonstrated in assuming that dream-wishes are invariably derived from the unconscious.'

It is in the *Outline* (1940: 169) that we first find a formulation which is congruent with the usual interpretation technique:

> With the help of the unconscious, every dream that is in process of formation makes a demand upon the ego – for the satisfaction of an instinct, if the dream originates from the id; for the solution of a conflict, the removal of a doubt or the forming of an intention, if the dream originates from a residue of preconscious activity in waking life. The sleeping ego, however, is focused on the wish to maintain sleep; it feels this demand as a disturbance and seeks to get rid of the disturbance. The ego succeeds in doing this by what appears to be an act of compliance: it meets the demand with what is in the circumstances a harmless *fulfilment of a wish* [Freud's italics] and so gets rid of it. This replacement of the demand by the fulfilment of a wish remains the essential function of the dream work.

Of course, this is in agreement with the examples from *The Interpretation of Dreams*, such as the 'Irma' dream, the well-known dreams of convenience, and the dreams instigated by bodily needs, in which the infantile wish is no longer so readily apparent.

To what extent the question of wish fulfilment remains a problematical area may be seen from the deliberations in *Beyond the Pleasure Principle* (1920), as well as from Jones (1965), for example, who points out how seldom in fact the infantile wish is interpreted; and furthermore Weiss (1949), Erikson (1964: 195, 198), Stein (1965), Eissler (1966) and Stewart (1967).

Even if one continues to use the attempt at wish fulfilment as one's point of departure, one cannot escape the difficulty of deciding what should be interpreted as wish fulfilment, and what as a defence. However, this is actually a problem which pervades the analysis as a whole (cf. Waelder 1936). Originally the concept of 'censorship' was proposed, as one of the main sources of the dream distortion which results in the differences between latent and manifest dream content, and thus the question seemed to have been settled in a simple and lucid manner. However, Freud himself points the way to the inherent difficulties in this position of his discussion of the 'Uncle' dream (1900: 141), where he states that: 'The affection in the dream did not belong to the latent content . . .; it stood in contradiction to [the latent dream thought] and was to conceal the true interpretation of the dream.' Freud later returns to these friendly feelings, placing them after all − I think properly so − mainly in the latent dream thoughts and saying that they 'probably arose from an infantile source' (p. 472), so that there, too, we catch a glimpse of the gratification of an infantile wish. One finds a still nicer illustration in 'A case of hysteria', where Freud presents a synthesis of the manifest dream following the analysis. He points out there (1905: 88) how the patient was 'summoning up her infantile love for her father as a protection against the present temptation'. Here we see, then, an Oedipal desire being used defensively, while it is noteworthy that it appears rather undistinguished in the manifest dream content!

In my opinion it would be most in keeping with the general nature of the psychoanalytic process of interpretation, were one to drop the distinction between wish and defence with regard to the latent content of the dream. Moreover, I doubt very much whether anyone in actual practice can successfully maintain this dichotomy. Since the introduction of the structural hypothesis and the development of ego psychology, we have become amply aware that precisely the defences also have a latent and unconscious character, so that we have come to interpret dreams − the latent dream thought − not solely as expression of wishes, but as the expressions of *conflicts* (cf. Arlow and Brenner 1964).

With this, dream interpretation delivers us in the midst of the dynamics which we know so well from our analytic work. Defences appear as 'wishful activity that inherently provides libidinal and aggressive gratifications or leads to it, or both, at the same time as it serves counterdynamic purposes' (Schafer 1968). Multiple functioning and hierarchic layering of the psychic apparatus are prevailing. We are dealing with conflict between aspects of the total personality, with a splitting of the ego − in neuroses, too (Le Coultre 1967).

It is striking how many analysts will interpret a dream directly from the manifest content and without associations, especially when they know the patient well. Lorand (Rangell 1956) and Kligerman (Babcock 1965) point out that under certain circumstances this may be necessary, or on the other hand show how useful a dream may even be without the associations. Saul (Rangell 1956) tries to show in particular how one can draw prognostic conclusions from the manifest dream, even simply from the way in which 'the ego accepts and acts upon in the dream'. He advises us to take the manifest dream well into account, with regard to the nature of the communication, 'the level', 'the headlines', 'the current'; to 'distinguish the dynamics from the content', to evaluate in terms of 'fight or flight', and so on.

Finally, we can say that the value of the manifest dream is already acknowledged implicitly in the wish-fulfilment hypothesis (or, if one wishes, in the traumatolytic aspect). One must not lose sight of the fact that when we refer to the dream as an attempt at wish fulfilment, we always mean by this the manifest dream. Though the dreamer sleeps, and however absurd and confused a production the dream frequently may be, our analytic thinking has assigned the dream this function, thereby giving it special stature!

Illustrations and considerations

An unmarried woman of about forty, living with her mother, with whom she has an ambivalent relationship, dreams that she takes her mother to the train. Standing on the platform the two converse. The patient urges her mother to get on board because the train is about to leave and, moreover, the mother is not too steady on her feet. The mother, however, thinks that there is enough time and keeps on talking. The dreamer then repeatedly urges her mother to make haste, and at the very moment when the old lady is about to climb on board the train begins to move, so that she falls between the train and the platform!

I shall not attempt a complete interpretation of the dream – here, too, there are various strata superimposed upon one another – but, as could be expected, the ambivalence is striking. I point out to the patient how *she* arranges for mother, to fall under the train, whereupon she retorts – and this is the point I wish to make here: 'Whatever do you mean! It was her own fault. She was dawdling, and I tried my best to make her get in on time!' This amusing experience is of a kind that every analyst encounters again and again. It is a hint towards the meaning of the dream function. In *The Interpretation of Dreams* Freud formulates the situation as follows (1900: 534): 'Here we have the most general and the most striking psychological characteristic of the process of dreaming: a thought, and as a rule a thought of something that is wished, is objectified in the dream, is represented as a scene, or, as it seems to us, is experienced.' And 'dreams make use of the present tense . . . in which wishes are presented as fulfilled' (1900: 535).

There is most certainly a weakening of the reality principle here, as explained by Freud in his 'metapsychological supplement to the theory of dreams' (cf. also Arlow and Brenner 1964), *but* (Freud 1917: 229): 'The dream-wish, as we say, is hallucinated and as a hallucination, meets with belief in the reality of its fulfilment'; and (1917: 230): 'So hallucination brings belief in reality with it'. A certain appreciation of reality, joined to a feeling of continuity of the self – however different and regressed this may be compared with the waking self (cf. Federn 1932; Grotjahn 1942) – has thus been preserved. Freud states that to dream is, in fact, to be partly awake (1900: 575): 'It must therefore be admitted that every dream has an *arousing* effect'; and in the *Outline* (1940: 167) he says:

> The ego organisation is not yet paralysed, and its influence is to be seen in the distortion imposed on the unconscious material and in what are often very ineffective attempts at giving the total result a form not too unacceptable to the ego (secondary revision).

The metapsychological problem connected with this is clearly presented in 'A metapsychological supplement to the theory of dreams' (1917: 234, n. 2).

One must view the dream (1917: 223) 'among other things [as] a *projection* [Freud's italics], an externalization of an internal process'. As early as 1894 Freud (1892–9: 209), in discussing paranoia, speaks of the abuse of the mechanism of projection for purpose of defence'! But in the same text one also finds projection referred to as a psychical mechanism very commonly employed in normal life. 'Whenever an internal change occurs, we have the choice of assuming either an internal or an external cause.' During sleep apparently there is nothing which deters us from creating our own external world, with its causes, by resorting to the mechanism of projection. So we see how our dreamer referred to above could have a feeling of complete innocence.

I believe that such aspects can almost always be found in the dreams of neurotics or, rather, in the *conflictual dreams*, which in fact occupy every individual every night. One can only assume that they may be expected to be lacking in the undisguised, simple dreams, in so far as the latter do in fact occur in pure form. But when impulses, feelings or motives are to be expressed which simultaneously must be warded off, and concerning which one could say that they could not occur even in one's wildest dreams, then indeed the best method of achieving this is to let things *happen* outside the (passive) self. As Freud wrote as early as 1894, this can be done very easily, and one can assume that we are taught from earliest childhood that our own role in a given event determines to what extent we can be held responsible for it. Thus the position, the action and reaction of the dreamer during the dream – which, let us emphasize, is a production in which he himself largely has the power to determine what happens – clearly delineate his own connection with it. One can compare this situation with the structure of Greek tragedy, as discussed by Van der Sterren (1952: 344): 'There is also the idea that the impulse to commit these terrible deeds came from without: that the gods had decreed and the oracle [had] prophesied them'; and 'the Greek word *chrao* means "to desire", "to crave" and "to consult an oracle".' In other words, the tendency to project one's wish is clear here, too.

I should now like to give an illustration from an analysis at greater length, with the associations.

A man of about fifty has difficulties with his passive wishes, and a pronounced tendency to promiscuity, in which his exhibitionistic defensive position is recognizable. The extramarital relationships which he creates to this end, however, are usually ephemeral. During one such relationship, while lodging with his mistress, he dreams:

then I started to fly in a demonstrative way, rather showing off. I wanted to show that I could do it, but I could not get enough altitude and I found myself flying right past the masts of ships . . . the plane was a DC4.

His associations reveal that the DC4, in addition to designating a type of plane, is also a kind of pump, with which the patient is acquainted through his work. It is a marvellous device which by means of corkscrew-like movements sucks up suspensions of solid substances, a trick which the designers copied from certain snakes, which are able to obtain water in the desert in this fashion. The masts of the ships: he has had his sailing boat put in order lately with the aim of using it soon for a vacation with his mistress. He views this as a risky business *vis-à-vis* his wife. Concerning his mistress, he says: 'I cohabited marvellously with her, three times in succession. The last two times were especially wonderful. She simply charms it right out of your penis!' He then tells about an event from his youth, a canoe trip which was actually a feat of daring: he turned over and was saved, after almost having drowned. Let us now have a look at what happens in the manifest dream from the point of view of the dreamer. He wishes to achieve a feat of daring, to fly a plane with dash, to ascend, but he encounters difficulties and almost crashes into the masts of ships. In the face of this threatening accident he himself clearly has the feeling that it is happening to him against his wishes. The associations to the boats in the dream lead to his risky plan to take a sailing vacation with his mistress, and to a former feat of daring in which he almost perished. The aeroplane, which we need not hesitate to

167

interpret as a symbol for the penis, is a DC4 and at the same time stands for the pump which is able to charm water out of the desert; namely, his mistress. The passivity is clearly visible through his boastfulness.

Consciously, expressed is the idea: 'I want to be able to' (cf. Federn 1914, 1932; Saul and Fleming 1959). The 'gods', however, warn: 'Look out, you cannot succeed!' — in other words, he unconsciously no longer wishes to go through with the undertaking because it makes him too anxious. Shortly after having reported this dream he involves his friends in his situation, the consequence of which is, as usual, that he allows himself to be sent back to his wife. In his real life, he acts out the very situation which in his dream he presents as an objective event occurring without his active participation (cf. Roth 1958). An explicit interpretation of this dream would have to go something like this: 'You would like so much to be a he-man and take off with your mistress. However, your anxiety proves to be stronger than the wish, and your longing for safety and protection, greater.' I wish to point out now, here again, a wish is employed to ward off another wish!

Another example:

The patient, a bachelor who is no longer young, is walking with a girl through St Paul's Seminary. They are being led by a guide, but the patient loses contact with the guide. This makes him very uneasy, and he finally remains behind in a little room.

The associations show that there was in fact a seminary of this name close to patient's birthplace; however, he himself is also named Paul. To the little room he immediately associates that it resembled the little bedroom where he used to lie in bed with his sister. When we examine the dream in the light of the insight which is here taking shape, we must conclude that he *wishes* to elude the guide, but not consciously so. We can assume that this saintly Paul, who had been brought up in very pious surroundings, would prefer to conceal certain things associated with his contact with his sister. When I confront him with this suggestion, it proves that he wishes to withhold masturbation fantasies. His uneasiness in the manifest dream must express his conflict with the positive transference in connection with the obligation to report this forbidden material: he wishes to satisfy a guilt-laden sexual fantasy, but at the same time he wards off the secrecy *vis-à-vis* the analyst-father — which for him is a prerequisite for gratification of the sexual wish — by presenting it in the form of an unwished-for disappearance of the guide.

I could amplify these illustrations with numerous others. One is struck repeatedly by the way in which the dreamer, in one fashion or another, in his narrative dissociates himself from the events. A few brief examples will suffice: a patient's brother calls his attention to the fact that he, the patient, has an interest in sexually exciting matters which is atypical for the family. This observation clearly has the effect of increasing his anxiety, and he dreams that he is performing all kinds of activities in a very awkward and childish manner, which he experiences as a great nuisance. In other words, against his will he gives in to his brother. This patient's castration anxiety is especially marked.

A woman patient, who as a child of her parents' middle age, with only much older siblings, has had a great difficulty in growing up, dreams that I put her up with my children, and is furious at me for this. Interpretation: she does not wish to see that she actually would like to remain a child.

Among the dreams described by Freud we need merely point out the typical exhibitionistic and death-wish dreams, the first dream of Dora (1905a) and the dream of the supper party in order to see illustrated the role of this aspect of the manifest dream.

The mechanism of reversal, which Freud views as a routine primary-process portion of the dream-work, and which he suggests applying as a technical device for occasions where a clear interpretation refuses to take shape (1900: 327), is no mere random procedure of the dream distortion, but rather a mode of defence which is always potentially meaningful, just as for example the presence of a great many people in the analyst's consulting room in a dream indicates the wish to conceal a secret, and tends to appear especially when sexual wishes directed towards the analyst evoke anxiety. Moreover, it is striking how often in the course of an analysis, all sorts of undesirable entanglements with the analyst are portrayed in dreams, in disguised or undisguised form (cf. also Harris 1962). These are most certainly products of the transference neurosis.

Views of certain other authors on the significance
of the manifest dream interpretation

Federn (1914, 1932, 1933, 1934) studies dreams closely with regard to the ego feelings manifestly appearing in them, distinguishing between bodily and mental ego feelings, and considering especially the former to be of importance. Later on, when he expresses himself in accordance with the distinctions arising from the structural theory, his views gain in clarity, but at the same time it becomes evident that his ideas regarding the ego are rather deviant and more or less phenomenologically rooted (Jacobson 1954; Fliess 1953; Kohut 1966). In any event, he establishes the role of the manifest dream in the process of interpretation, and it is precisely the experience of the ego (we can preferably call it 'the feeling of self'; Fliess 1953) to which he assigns a very essential function of the manifest dream. He sees it as indicating the 'modality', that is, the position taken by the ego, as expressed in such auxiliary verbs as 'to be able', 'to be allowed', 'to want', and so on. In my opinion this is absolutely correct, and yet to take only the mental or bodily ego feelings into account would seem to be imposing an unnecessary limitation: other aspects of the dreamer's role in the dream should also be potential sources of conclusions concerning the content.

French (1937a, b, 1952; French and Fromm 1964; cf. also the views of Kanzer 1954; Joffe 1965; Noble 1965) in his writings shows a striking evolution of ideas, in which the development of his position regarding dream interpretation can serve as a guideline. In his earliest articles he still adheres firmly to the usual psychoanalytic views, although he does show great interest in the manifest dream, and illustrates how the images appearing in it reveal the way in which the dreamer relates to the problems which are expressed. He sees the alterations in the representation of a key figure in the course of an analysis as indicators of the process of cure, for example when such a figure is at first represented in a dream by a lifeless object, and later on appears as the person himself. In French's subsequent development, however, he strays ever farther away from the usual psychoanalytic views. Most prominent is his idea that the dream-work must be understood as a form of problem solving, a view entirely different from Freud's formulation (1925a: 127).

The dream-work is said to embody a kind of 'practical and empathic thinking', which we must not confuse with verbal thinking. French (1964: 163 ff.) considers the free associations to be 'disintegration products of the dreamer's verbal thinking'. He believes that he is able to grasp the meaning of a dream with another kind of thinking: intuition, common sense and empathy. Joffe (1965), commenting on French and Fromm (1964), correctly points out that 'the reader may forget that the dream is essentially a perceptual phenomenon . . . also a hallucination occurring during sleep'. French attempts to reduce all the phenomena to rational terms (that is, terms understandable in the language of everyday thinking), to a 'cognitive structure'; in so doing he neglects the primitive and bizarre characteristics which Freud has shown us. The arbitrary, whimsical nature of the manifest dream, which is in part determined by the day residues which happen to be available (cf. also Fisher 1957; Fisher and Paul 1959; Kubie 1966) is lost to view.

Although French's approach includes many elements with which I find myself in agreement – including his view regarding the role of the commitment of the dreamer in the dream (1964: 38 ff.) – in my opinion he needlessly abandons too many of the guidelines and insights of Freud's dream psychology, and reduces interpretation to a function of empathy, intuition and common sense. It is also striking that in both cases which he presents (French 1952, 1953; French and Fromm 1964) rather coarse personalities are involved. However, it must be admitted that he went to great pains to validate his method of interpretation (French and Fromm 1964).

Although Saul (1953, 1966; Saul and Curtis 1967; Saul and Fleming 1959; Sheppard and Saul 1958) has made a very astute study of the manifest dream content, calling our attention to the bearing of the role of the self in the dream on the ego-functions (including the defences) — namely, how this role reflects the patient's personality structure — one does not get the impression that his observations have been used to formulate *rules* for the technique of *interpretation*.

However, the word of all these three authors — especially Federn, but also French and Saul — can be said to show a strong kinship with the aims which I have set myself here.

The secondary revision

When we turn our attention to the structure and narrative of the dream we find ourselves dealing with what Freud termed the 'sekundäre Bearbeitung'. This is an aspect of the dream-work which in fact tends to be regarded as a somewhat second-rate function. Freud expresses himself ambiguously on this matter, a fact which is noticeable in the English translations.

Originally (Brill 1913), the term 'secondary elaboration' was employed; later on (Strachey) this became 'secondary revision', an expression which could lend strength to the impression that one was dealing with a function which came into operation only after completion of the dream. To cite a few of Freud's statements: 'Only a single portion of the dream work, and one which operates to an irregular degree, the working over of the material by partly aroused waking thought . . .' (1900: 507); and 'We must assume rather that from the very first [of the dream-work] the demands of this second factor constitute one of the conditions which the dream must satisfy and that this condition, like those laid down by condensation, the censorship imposed by resistance, and representability, operates simultaneously in a conductive and selective sense upon the mass of material present in the dream thoughts' (1900: 499). But, again: 'for the purpose of *our* [Freud's emphasis] interpretation it remains an essential rule invariably to leave out of account the ostensible continuity of a dream as being of suspect origin' (1900: 500). The only case in which Freud accepts the fluency of the manifest dream as significant is where 'wishful phantasies which are present in the dream thoughts in a preconstructed form . . . are used' (1901: 667; cf. 1900: 491–3). In the *New Introductory Lectures* (1933: 21) we find: 'secondary revision . . . after the dream has been presented before consciousness as an object of perception'. In the *Outline* the connection of this function with the not yet paralyzed ego organization is established, so that all things considered, I have the impression that 'elaboration' renders a more faithful translation after all than 'revision'.

Arlow and Brenner (1964: 133 ff.) make the point that in the framework of the structural theory the activity of this ego-function as a component of the dream-work need present no problem. Lincke (1960) and Loewenstein (1961) emphasize the interpretable potential of this façade.

However, it has furthermore been revealed by the most recent dream research (Dement and Wolpert 1958), in which eye-movements and vegetative reactions have been registered, that we most probably dream in the form of long stories, in which the structure is present immediately. Thus we must assume that secondary revision is a factor which is operative in dream formation right from the very beginning.

It seems to me that in the light of present theoretical developments we no longer need hesitate to accord this factor a status in no way inferior to that of the other components of the dream-work. We are then confronted with the curious state of affairs that we have here an aspect of the dream which indeed can be judged on its merits by the application of common sense, inasmuch as its mechanism is identical with that of our waking thought and activity. (Freud 1900: 499: 'highly probably . . . to be identified with the activity of our waking thought'.)

Arlow and Brenner, however, are inclined only to accept at face-value the thought 'This is only a dream', which they view as an exception (1964: 136, 139 n. 10). I see no reason to maintain this limitation.

In the present discussion I shall avoid going into another problematical aspect of the dream; namely its sleep-preserving function – however closely related this may be to the nature of the manifest dream (cf. Jekels 1945; Weiss 1949; Voth 1961; Pacella 1962). Even more enigmatic, and of greater importance for its bearing on the present thesis, is the fact that tendencies regarding which we must assume that they are warded off with maximum strength often are dreamt of openly and with unequivocal sensual involvement. As early as 1900 (p. 264), Freud writes that 'many men dream of having sexual relations with their mothers'. The present author agrees that such incestuous dreams are not so rare as to be considered exceptional, but a convincing explanation for these apparent outlaws of psychoanalytic views on the dream has so far eluded him (cf. Freud 1925a: 132; Frosch 1967; Stewart 1967). Now and again one gets the impression that in such dreams a more acute and present danger is being warded off (cf. Freud 1905a).

Formulation and discussion of the technique of interpretation

To all that has been written on the subject of dream interpretation by Freud and other analysts, I should like to add a sole piece of advice.

When one takes all the *associations* — which one has, indeed, obtained starting from individual elements of the dream, *while ignoring the totality of the manifest dream content* — together with all else that one knows, by virtue of the analysis, concerning the content of the patient's dream, and when one then *views all the foregoing against the background of the manifest dream*, one is in a position to interpret the dream, or, rather, to construct one's interpretation. In doing thus one must take the position of the dreamer himself in the dream narrative as one's starting-point.

This feature indicates his relationship at the moment to the environment and the events which he creates in the dream, while the associations have shown what the elements of the dream stand for.

The question which one always can ask is: Why did the patient act, think and feel as he did in the dream? This is an aspect which issues from the 'not yet paralysed ego organization', and as such can, indeed, be interpreted on the basis of empathy or common sense. Remarkably enough, one repeatedly encounters instances where this technique is used — without its being explicitly delineated (cf. for example, Fenichel 1935). As already stated, the self never fails to appear in a dream.

Of course, one may wonder, in view of the wish-fulfilment hypothesis, why the dreamer does not always succeed in hallucinating something which he experiences as pleasant (cf. Fliess 1953: 78 ff.). One might assert, as Eissler does (1966), that 'for the dreamer adequate escape routes [are] on hand'. However, one must not lose sight of several factors which tend to act in an opposite direction, so as to limit our freedom in dreaming.

First of all, the dream is in general an expression of a conflict. Gratification of the forbidden striving usually meets with failure — even in disguised form — and one sees repeatedly how in the course of a single night there may be a series of dreams (Freud 1900: 333–4) dealing with the same matter, each succeeding dream less distorted and timid than the ones preceding it, until the series often ends with an anxiety dream which awakens the subject. Furthermore, as Freud incontrovertibly was able to show, the material available for expressive use in a dream is largely restricted by the current day residues, so that the dreamer apparently cannot choose to hallucinate whatever he likes.

In addition, there is the question to what extent dreaming may serve towards the mastery of traumata (cf. Freud 1920; Weiss 1949; Loewenstein 1949; Stein 1965; Eissler 1966; Stewart 1967), so that repeated exposure to a traumatic experience might have a function.

Finally, the over-determination and displacement which receive most emphasis in *The Interpretation of Dreams* influence the effect, judgement and secondary revision and with it the elements making up the position of the self in the manifest dream content. Thus they are themselves phenomena which according to Freud (1900: chapter VI, G, H, I), simultaneously reflect the unconscious and warded-off content. Again and again one is struck by the entanglement and over-determination of all component factors.

By taking as a starting-point the most superficial aspect of the dream, that aspect with which, one could say, the dreamer himself is in wholehearted agreement, even in the dream, one best adheres to the 'jeweilige psychische Oberfläche' which Freud recommends as a guideline in 'the handling of dream interpretation in psycho-analysis' (1911: 92): 'the analyst should always be aware of the surface of the patient at any given moment' (cf. also Kemper 1958). In this way one can best recognize the current conflict in the patient, with its forces and counter-forces.

In the course of an analysis it is especially important that one closely follows the vicissitudes of the transference neurosis. And then one may well ask oneself why it is that the patient so often dreams that the analytic session is interrupted, that 'curiously' the analytic situation is other than it actually is: for example, the furnishings of the analyst's consultation room are different, the patient arrives late, he cannot find the analyst's house, to his surprise the analyst somehow looks different, the analyst was angry, and so on. Those cases in which the transference is manifested indirectly are naturally more numerous. 'It became so hot, I was afraid I would burn.' 'Although it was explained to me clearly, I could not make any sense of it at all.' 'Everything was extremely confused.' 'Of course, it was ridiculous that I should have to tell such an expert how he should do it.'

But apart from the transference situation, as I have already shown, one can effect the most convincing interpretation of a dream with a bearing on other current problems of the dreamer, by proceeding from the point in the manifest dream which has been indicated here. One might say that every dream is simultaneously one 'from above' and also 'from below'.

Another pressing question is the extent to which we are in fact able to interpret a dream from 'a single remaining fragment' (Freud 1900: 517). It is certainly true that one is often able to fit in such a fragment, and the associations to it, in the totality of information which one has received or is receiving in the course of the analysis. If we are fortunate, the patient may recall a larger portion of the dream, tending to confirm our interpretation. However, I cannot escape the impression that what we do is often in fact most akin to gambling, when we are totally unaware of the dreamer's role in the dream.

Speaking more theoretically, one can say that this point of departure in the manifest dream is that where the defences are most superficial, most accessible to consciousness (cf. Federn 1932). The point which we choose most closely approximates that where we find negation, as elucidated by Freud (1925b: 235): 'Thus the content of a repressed image or idea can make its way into consciousness, on condition that it is *negated*' (Freud's emphasis).

One can view the dissociated stance of the dreamer's self in the dream as the equivalent of negation in waking life (cf. Eissler 1966): the last bulwark of defence against that which must be warded off. In this situation, an empathic evaluation is appropriate.

Summary

Despite his often having shown consideration for the manifest dream, Freud warned in all his publications against taking the connections and logical elements (secondary revision) which appear in it seriously.

Federn was the first to devote attention to the role taken by the dreamer himself in the manifest dream, while for a number of other authors increasing attention to the manifest dream was one symptom of a departure from psychoanalytic ideas in the strict sense. Parallel with the development of ego psychology, interest in the manifest dream content increased markedly. The present author is of the opinion that the role of the dreamer in the manifest dream is particularly important as a guide for the construction of one's interpretation; namely, in relation to the current conflict.

In most dreams by far, the dreamer – who is always present – appears as dissociating himself in any of a number of various ways from some of the events and images which are hallucinated. First one employs all the associations to the elements of the dream in the usual fashion, and all the knowledge which one has of the dreamer. This material is set against the manifest dream content and, making use of the already manifest dynamic aspects mentioned above, one can then attempt to interpret the dream – particularly in the light of the current *conflict*. In this fashion one can localize the most superficial wish and defence, the latter being comparable with the mechanism of negation.

The author believes that adherence to this principle will enable the analyst at any given point in the course of an analytic treatment to offer an interpretation which satisfies as closely as possible the well-known rule: always be aware of the surface of the patient at any given moment.

References

Alexander, F. (1925). Über Traumpaare und Traumreihen. *Int. Z. Psychoanal.* 11, 80–5.

—— (1949) The psychology of dreaming. In H. Herma and G.M. Kurth (eds.), *Fundamentals of Psychoanalysis.* New York: World Publ. Co., 1950.

Alexander, F. and Wilson, G.W. (1935). Quantitative dream studies: a methodological attempt at a quantitative evaluation of psychosomatic material. *Psychoanal. Q.* 4, 371–407.

Arlow, J.A. and Brenner, C. (1964) *Psychoanalytic Concepts and the Structural Theory.* New York: Int. Univ. Press.

Babcock, C.G. (1965). Panel report: The manifest content of the dream. *J. Am. psychoanal. Ass.* 14, 154–71.

Blitzsten, L.N., Eissler, R.S. and Eissler, K.R. (1950). Emergence of hidden ego tendencies during dream analysis. *Int. J. Psycho-Anal.* 31, 12–17.

Blum, H.P. (1964). Colour in dreams. *Int. J. Psycho-Anal.* 45, 519–30.

Bonime, W. (1962). *The Clinical Use of Dreams.* New York: Basic Books.

Brill, A.A. (1913). The interpretation of dreams. *The Basic Writings of Sigmund Freud.* New York: Random House, 1938.

Dement, W.C. and Wolpert, E.A. (1958). The relation of eye movements, etc. to dream content. *J. Exp. Psychol.* 55, 543.

Eissler, K.R. (1966). A note on trauma, dream, anxiety and schizophrenia. *Psychoanal. Study Child* 21.

Erikson, E.H. (1954). The dream specimen of psychoanalysis. *J. Am. psychoanal. Ass.* 2, 5–56.

—— (1964). *Insight and Responsibility.* New York: Norton.

Federn, P. (1914). Über zwei typische Traumsenstationen. *Jb. Psychoanal. psychopathol. Forsch.* 6.

—— (1932). Ego-feeling in dreams. *Psychoanal. Q* 1, 511–42.

—— (1933). Die Ichbesetzung bei den Fehlleistungen. *Imago* 19, 312–38; 433–53.

—— (1934). The awakening of the ego in dreams. *Int. J. Psycho-Anal.* 15, 296–301.

Fenichel, O. (1935). Zur Tehorie der psychoanalytischen Technik. *Int. Z. Psychoanal.* 21, 78–95.

Fenichel, O., Alexander, F. and Wilson, G.W. (1936). Quantitative dream studies. *Int. Z. Psychoanal.* 22, 419–20.

Ferenczi, S. (1911). *Dirigible Dreams: Final Contributions to the Problems and Methods of Psychoanalysis.* New York: Basic Books, 1955.

—— (1934). Gedanken über das Trauma. *Int. Z. Psychoanal.* 20, 5–12.

Fisher, C. (1957). A study of the preliminary stages of the construction of dreams and images. *J. Am. psychoanal. Ass.* 5, 5–60.

—— (1965). Psychoanalytic implications of recent research on sleep and dreaming. *J. Am. psychoanal. Ass.* 13, 197–303.

Fisher, C. and Paul, I.H. (1959). The effect of subliminal visual stimulation on images and dreams: a validation study. *J. Am. psychoanal. Ass.* 7 35–83.

Fliess, O. (1953). *The Revival of the Interest in the Dream*. New York: Int. Univ. Press.

French, T.M. (1937a). Klinische Untersuchungen über das Lernen im Verlauf einer psychoanalytischen Behandlung. *Int. Z. Psychoanal.* 23, 96–132.

—— (1937b). Reality testing in dreams. *Psychoanal. Q.* 6, 62–77.

—— (1952). *The Integration of Behavior*, vol. 1: *Basic Postulates*. Chicago: Univ. of Chicago Press, 1956.

—— (1953). *Idem*, vol. 2: *The Integrative Process in Dreams*. Chicago: Univ. of Chicago Press, 1956.

French, T.M. and Fromm, E. (1964). *Dream Interpretation*. New York: Basic Books.

Freud, A. (1936). *The Ego and Mechanisms of Defence*. London: Hogarth Press, 1954.

Freud, S. (1892–9). Extracts from the Fliess papers. SE 1.

—— (1900). The interpretation of dreams. SE 4–5.

—— (1901). On dreams. SE 5.

—— (1905a). Fragment of an analysis of a case of hysteria. SE 7.

—— (1905b). Jokes and their relation to the unconscious. SE 8.

—— (1909). Some general remarks on hysterical attacks. SE 9.

—— (1911). The handling of dream interpretation in psycho-analysis. SE 12.

—— (1914). On the history of the psychoanalytic movement. SE 14.

—— (1915–17). Introductory lectures on psycho-analysis. SE 15–16.

—— (1917). A metapsychological supplement to the theory of dreams. SE 14.

—— (1920). Beyond the pleasure principle. SE 18.

—— (1922). Some neurotic mechanisms in jealousy and homosexuality. SE 18.

—— (1923a). Two encyclopaedia articles. SE 18.

—— (1923b). Remarks on the theory and praxis of dream interpretation. SE 19.

—— (1925a). Some additional notes on dream interpretation as a whole. SE 19.

—— (1925b). Negation SE 19.

—— (1925c). An autobiographical study. SE 20.

—— (1933). New introductory lectures on psycho-analysis. SE 22.

—— (1940). An outline of psycho-analysis. SE 23.

Frosch, J. (1967). Severe regressive states during analysis. *J. Am. psychoanal. Ass.* 15, 491–507.

Groot, A.D. De (1961). *Methodology*. The Hague: Mouton, 1968.

Grotjahn, M. (1942). The process of awakening. *Psychoanal. Rev.* 29, 1–19.

Gutheil, E.A. (1951). *The Handbook of Dream Analysis*. New York: Grove Press, 1960.

Hadfield, J.A. (1954). *Dreams and Nightmares*. Harmondsworth, Middx.: Penguin.

Harris, I.D. (1951). Characterological significance of the typical anxiety dreams. *Psychiatry* 14, 279–94.

—— (1962). Dreams about the analyst. *Int. J. Psycho-Anal.* 43, 151–8.

Hitschmann, E. (1933—4). Beiträge zu einer Psychopathologie des Traumes. *Int. Z. Psychoanal.* 20, 459—76; 21, 430—44.

Jacobson, E. (1954). Contribution to the metapsychology of psychotic identifications. *J. Am. psychoanal. Ass.* 2, 239—62.

Jekels, L. (1945). A bioanalytical contribution to the problem of sleep and wakefulness. *Psychoanal. Q.* 14, 169—89.

Joffe, W.G. (1965). Review of *Dream Interpretation* by French & Fromm. *Int. J. Psycho-Anal.* 46, 532—3.

Jones, R.M. (1965). Dream interpretation and the psychology of dreaming. *J. Am. psychoanal. Ass.* 13, 304—19.

Kanzer, M. (1954). A field theory perspective of psychoanalysis. *J. Am. psychoanal. Ass.* 2, 526—34.

Katan, M. (1960). Dreams and psychosis. *Int. J. Psycho-Anal.* 41, 341—51.

Kemper, W. (1958). The manifold possibilities of therapeutic evaluation of dreams. *Int. J. Psycho-Anal.* 29, 125—8.

Khan, M.M.R. (1962). Dream psychology and the psychoanalytic situation. *Int. J. Psycho-Anal.* 43, 21—31.

Klauber, J. (1967). On the significance of reporting dreams in psychoanalysis. *Int. J. Psycho-Anal.* 48, 424—33.

Kohut, H. (1966). Forms and transformations of narcissism. *J. Am. psychoanal. Ass.* 14, 243—71.

Kubie, L. (1966). A reconsideration of thinking, the dream process and the dream. *Psychoanal. Q.* 35, 191—8.

Le Coultre, R. (1967). Splijting van het Ik als centraal neuroseverschijnsel. In P.J. van der Leeuw *et al.* (eds.), *Hoofdstukken uit de hedendaagse psychoanalyse.* Arnhem: van Loghum Slaterus.

Levine, J.M. (1967). Through the looking-glass. *J. Am. psychoanal. Ass.* 15, 166—212.

Levitan, H.L. (1967). Depersonalization and the dream. *Psychoanal. Q.* 36, 157—72.

Lewin, B.D. (1946). Sleep, the mouth and the dream screen. *Psychoanal. Q.* 15, 419—34.

—— (1948). Inferences from the dream screen. *Int. J. Psycho-Anal.* 29, 224—31.

—— (1952). Phobic symptoms and dream interpretation. *Psychoanal. Q.* 21, 295—322.

—— (1953). Reconsideration of the dream screen. *Psychoanal. Q.* 22, 174—99.

—— (1955). Dream psychology and the analytic situation. *Psychoanal. Q.* 24, 169—99.

—— (1964) Knowledge and dreams. *Psychoanal. Q.* 33, 148—51.

Lincke, H. (1960). Zur Traumbildung. *J. Psycho-Anal.* 1.

Loewenstein, R.M. (1949). A posttraumatic dream. *Psychoanal. Q.* 18, 449—54.

—— (1961). Contribution to the study of the manifest dream. *Psychoanal. Q.* 30, 464—6.

Mack, J.E. (1965). Nightmares, conflict and ego development in childhood. *Int. J. Psycho-Anal.* 46, 403–28.

Maeder, A. (1912). Über die Funktion des Traumes. *Jb. Psychoanal. psychopathol. Forsch.* 4.

—— (1913). Über das Traumproblem. *Jb. Psychoanal. psychopathol. Forsch.* 5.

Miller, M.L. (1948). Ego functioning in two types of dreams. *Psychoanal. Q.* 17, 346–55.

Miller, S.C. (1964). The manifest dream and the appearance of colour in dreams. *Int. J. Psycho-Anal.* 45, 512–18.

Mittelman, B. (1949). Ego functioning and dreams. *Psychoanal. Q.* 18, 434–48.

Noble, D. (1965). Review of *Dream Interpretation* by French and Fromm. *Psychoanal. Q.* 34, 282–6.

Pacella, B. (1962). The dream process. *Psychoanal. Q.* 31, 597–600.

Peck, J.S. (1961). Dreams and interruptions in the treatment. *Psychoanal. Q.* 30, 209–20.

Pollock, G.H. & Muslin, H.L. (1962). Dreams during surgical procedures. *Psychoanal. Q.* 31, 175–202.

Rangell, L. (1956). Panel report: the dream in the practice of psychoanalysis. *J. Am. psychoanal. Ass.* 4, 122–37.

Rechtschaffen, A., Vogel, G. and Shaikun, G. (1963). Interrelatedness of mental activity during sleep. *Archs gen. Psychiat.* 9, 536–47.

Richardson, G.A. and Moore, R.A. (1963). On the manifest dream in schizophrenia. *J. Am. psychoanal. Ass.* 11, 281–302.

Roth, N. (1958). Manifest dream content and acting out. *Psychoanal. Q.* 27, 547–54.

Saul, L.J. (1953). The ego in a dream. *Psychoanal. Q.* 22, 257–8.

—— (1966). Embarrassment dreams of nakedness. *Int. J. Psycho-Anal.* 47, 552–8.

Saul, L.J. and Curtis, G.C. (1967). Dream form and strength of impulse in dreams of falling and other dreams of descent. *Int. J. Psycho-Anal.* 48, 281–7.

Saul, L.J. and Fleming, B.A. (1959). A clinical note on the ego meaning of certain dreams of flying. *Psychoanal. Q.* 28, 501–4.

Schafer, R. (1968). The mechanisms of defence. *Int. J. Psycho-Anal.* 49, 49–62.

Sheppard, E. and Saul, L.J. (1958). An approach to a systematic study of ego functioning. *Psychoanal. Q.* 27, 237–45.

Silberer, H. (1912). Zur Symbolbildung. *Jb. Psychoanal. psychopathol. Forsch.* 4.

Stein, M.H. (1965). States of consciousness in the analytic situation, including a note on the traumatic dream. In M. Schur (ed.), *Drives, Affects, Behavior*, vol. 2. New York: Int. Univ. Press.

Stekel, W. (1909). Beiträge zur Traumdeutung. *Jb. Psychoanal. psychopathol. Forsch.* 1.

—— (1911). *Die Sprache des Traumes*, 2nd ed. Bergmann, 1922.

Sterren, H.A., van der (1952). The King Oedipus of Sophoklos. *Int. J. Psycho-Anal.* 33, 343–50.

—— (1964). Zur psychoanalytischen Technik. *Jb. Psychoanal.* 3.

Stewart, W.E. (1967). Comment on certain types of unusual dreams. *Psychoanal. Q.* 36, 329–41.

Voth, H.M. (1961). A note on the function of dreaming. *Bull. Menninger Clin.* 25, 33–8.

Waelder, R. (1936). The principle of multiple function. *Psychoanal Q.* 5, 45–62.

Waldhorn, H.F. (1967). The place of the dream in clinical psychoanalysis. *Monograph Series of the Kris Study Group*, II. New York: Int. Univ. Press.

Ward, C.H. (1961). Some further remarks on the examination dreams. *Psychiatry* 24, 324–36.

Weiss, E. (1949). Some dynamic aspects of dreams. *Ybk. Psychoanal.* 5.

11

A psychoanalytic-dream continuum: the source and function of dreams

R. GREENBERG AND C. PEARLMAN

Introduction

The discovery of physiologic correlates of dreaming – the phenomena of REM (Rapid Eye Movement) sleep – has stimulated re-examination of psychoanalytic theories of dreaming. There have been interpretations both in terms of drive discharge theory (Fisher 1965) and of a more ego-orientated, adaptive conceptualization (Hawkins 1966; R. Jones 1970). A series of experiments in our laboratory has led to the conclusion that REM sleep is involved in information processing in the service of emotional adaptation. Freud's metaphor of the 'mystic writing pad' served as a springboard for both Hawkins (1966) and our group (Greenberg and Leiderman 1966). From our studies of dream deprivation, we have arrived at the following formulation: *emotionally* significant waking experiences touch on conflictual material from the past, arousing *affects* which require either defensive operations or an adaptive shift in response. Dreaming (REM sleep) provides an opportunity for integrating the recent experiences with the past, with a concomitant institution of characteristic defences or a new resolution of the conflict. We have found that REM deprivation impairs this process (Greenberg *et al.* 1970; Greenberg *et al.* 1972a).

In a study of patients with traumatic war neuroses, we found that the greater the subject's awareness of aroused conflictual material before sleep, the greater was the pressure to dream, as reflected by REM latency (time between sleep onset and first REM period. We were able to predict shorter or longer REM latencies on the basis of the psychologic state of the subject prior to sleep (Greenberg *et al.* 1972b). For a more thorough exploration of this area we felt that a study of sleep and dreaming in a patient in psychoanalysis would be fruitful. We expected the analytic material

181

to indicate what was emotionally meaningful to the patient and the analytic situation to stir up conflicts requiring adaptive effort. The sleep laboratory data could then be correlated with the analytic material. In the first part of the study, we made predictions about REM latency and REM time (amount of dreaming per night) from the material in the analytic hours just before and just after each night in the sleep laboratory (Greenberg and Pearlman 1975a). In this paper we present our examination of the dream content, collected in the sleep laboratory.

Before we proceed, however, we should discuss some psychoanalytic concepts which are needed in order to examine the material from the sleep laboratory. The dream process has been an important part of the development of psychoanalysis as a theoretical and clinical body of knowledge. Freud's study of dreams (1900) led him to a number of hypotheses about mental function. This work also led to an emphasis on dream analysis in clinical work. With the passage of years and the development of ego psychology, some psychoanalysts have tended to diminish the importance of dream analysis (Brenner 1969). Greenson discussed this problem in his paper, 'The exceptional position of the dream in psychoanalysis' (1970). He provided excellent examples of how, when the importance of a dream is recognized, its analysis can lead to a breakthrough in clinical understanding. French and Fromm (1964) re-traced Freud's path from theoretical questions to clinical implications of dreaming. They concluded that the dream reflected a process of adaptation, an attempt to resolve current conflicts. In a recent reconsideration of the relationship of the day residue to the dream, Langs (1971) echoed this formulation. He noted Freud's emphasis upon the analytic experience as a highly significant aspect of current reality which often enters directly into the process of dream formation. Most experienced therapists have encountered manifest dreams which are consistent with this observation and which characterize precisely a patient's current emotional state — especially his efforts to deal with transference issues. The crucial question is whether such dreams are fortuitous creations with no significance beyond their current dynamic meaning, or whether they exemplify a more fundamental biological process of adaptation. If the dreams do reflect such an adaptive process, then they deserve careful attention both as indicators of the current state of the analysis and as indications of the need for a re-formulation of theories of the function of dreaming. (These ideas have been extensively discussed and formulated by Whitman *et al.* 1967).

Study

Laboratory methods for studying sleep by EEG recordings permit more detailed investigation of dream material than is possible in the clinical situation alone. Ordinarily, most dreams are forgotten within a few minutes after the end of a REM period. Awakening at the end of a REM period results in more extensive dream recall for most persons (Whitman *et al.* 1963). With few exceptions (such as the just cited work of Whitman and colleagues), however, dreams collected in sleep laboratories have only been examined descriptively without relation to a psychodynamic understanding of the dreamer. The present study was designed to investigate the relationship between the dream and the dreamer with the hope that this information would permit a clearer formulation of the function of dreaming and of the place of the dream in clinical psychoanalysis.

The subject was a patient in psychoanalysis. A brief description of his history and principal fantasy systems appears in a paper by Knapp (1969). Over a period of one and a half years he was studied in a sleep laboratory on twenty-four nights, grouped once a week for four weeks, with intervals of approximately one month between groups. On twelve of the twenty-four nights in the laboratory the patient was awakened at the end of each REM period and asked for dream recall. His dream reports were tape-recorded. The patient's analytic hours on the evening before and morning after each sleep laboratory session were also tape-recorded. All the taped interviews and dream reports were transcribed to provide the basic data for this study.

In a prior paper (Greenberg and Pearlman 1975b) we have described how the scoring of the psychoanalytic material for a variable we called 'defensive strain' enabled us to predict variation in the physiologic parameters of REM latency and REM time. That study demonstrated a clear relationship between aspects of the psychologic situation involving dysphoric affect, types of defences and threatening nature of conflict (all part of the defensive strain core) and aspects of the physiologic situation involving the pressure for REM sleep (REM latency) and the amount of REM sleep. In the present study, we have dealt with the dream content and its relationship to the analytic material. We investigated the source of manifest dream content with specific emphasis on the analytic hour as a significant event in the residue of daily experience. We also questioned whether the organization of the dreams in relation to the issues emerging in analysis might illuminate the possible adaptive function of dreams.

Results

In order to delineate the scope of the data, we will begin with some quantitative aspects of dream recall and reporting. The patient was awakened from two to four times each night (at the end of a REM period) with a total of thirty-eight awakenings during twelve nights. On these awakenings he gave twenty-one detailed dream reports, two fragments, and five reports involving details of the laboratory procedure where the patient was uncertain whether he had been asleep or awake and thinking. On the other ten awakenings the patient usually said he had been dreaming but was unable to recall the content. This frequency of dream reports was high for this patient, since he had considerable difficulty in recalling dreams during analytic sessions unrelated to the sleep laboratory nights when he was awakened. The report that he had dreamed but was unable to recall the content occurred also frequently during these unrelated sessions. All of the dreams reported in detail in the laboratory were reported during the next analytic hour. Only three dreams were reported in a post-laboratory hour that had not been reported in the laboratory.

We now turn to the dream content, to our questions about the analytic hour as day residue and to the organization of dream material as an indication of problems and attempts at solution. As will be seen, these aspects are interrelated.

While we expected to find incorporation of material from the analytic hour (day residue) in the manifest dream, we were surprised to see how much of the manifest content was derived directly from the analytic hour preceding the dream. These residues were obvious and required no interpretation. With the slightest bit of psychoanalytic sophistication, the amount of demonstrable incorporation increased greatly. The assessment of day residue was done separately by each of the authors. In most cases our lists were similar. When only one of us had listed a residue, our discussion about whether to include it was usually based on the question of whether identifying the residue required interpretative effort or whether it would be apparent to a naive observer.

We found three principal groups of day residues. These were: (1) material particular to the analytic hour prior to dreaming, (2) material related to taking part in the sleep laboratory study, and (3) recurrent material that wove through the whole analysis. Every dream had at least one clear residue from the analytic hour (range 1–12). More than half of the dreams had at least seven residues. An obvious question arose concerning these residues. Were they principally derived from indifferent material or did they reflect central issues of the analytic hour? Two different approaches led to the conclusion that the day residues represented the patient's central concerns. The first was inspection of the residues within the context of our understanding of the patient. Some examples will clarify this conclusion.

One night the patient reported the following dream:

Funny sort of dream — *on some kind of raft or sailboat* — on raft were *two workers from factory — A.K. was one - myself and I don't recall the other —* have picture of raft with sail — were on the water — what we were doing there and looking for was waves — all *of a sudden we found ourselves away out* . . . boats and the bigger boats possibly the bigger the waves — I am questioning whether we should go in as Harold . . . I don't question whether we should go swimming or not . . . and said no, don't go — it is cold and *it might be very dangerous - so don't go.* At the end after . . . we start to head for land. That is the end of the dream. We were in the sailboat in the water — *these three people* with our feet dangling — funny kind of sailboat — *all in the same boat* — that is the end.

Residues from the previous hour were: (1) Talk in the hour about a fear that something is lurking there, a threat, concern about being candid and being recorded. (2) In discussing being open and being recorded, he interrupted his talking with the analyst and said (to the tape-recorder) 'Dr Greenberg — you hear that?' the analyst's response was — 'You mean, there are three of us in the room right now?' (3) He referred during the hour to his drifting off — falling asleep — a funny fantasy.

Later during the study he reported the following dream:

I dreamt about throwing *a huge party* in *(?) San Hong Tau* for all my friends. what the occasion was I don't know, but I had as a waiter Dick — all dressed up in white, and another fellow. *My mother was there. It was a mixed party as far as age goes.* It was an *elaborate detail as to what food, hors d'oeuvres, etc.*, and I remember lots of *fish and cheese and sausage. I was walking around making sure everybody got enough food.* They were on small black squares of bread. Quite elaborate — *tons and tons of food.* And walking around, Dick decided he was getting tired. He was going to quit. *I could just as well do his job standing where he was.* This party was for *some person who had not yet arrived* and I don't know who the person was. *The food was quite good and a very big success.* I was about to say just before I was awakened, I said to myself I did not quite guess which type of food I liked best before I started to be awakened. Otherwise, I thought I was dreaming but I was not sure.

The residues from the preceding analytic hour were as follows: (1) He had reported a dream about a lot of people around a dinner table. It was a holiday. His family, including dead members, was there. He was preparing a present for grandfather who is dead and 'who we never had any contact with'. (2) He had talked during the hour about being independent and picking who he wishes to give to. (3) He described his girlfriend Sonia, with whom he was breaking up, waiting on him, giving him an Icelandic breakfast. (4) He referred several times to plans to take Sonia to dinner to a Chinese restaurant or to a smorgasbord. (5) He was thinking about dinner and feeding his stomach. (6) He referred to bringing back packages of candy for his friends. (7) He talked about feeling free, not needing anyone. (8) In reference to changes in business, he said he wants people to look up to him, to think he's a big success. (9) He can do his brother-in-law's job and will impress people with his efficiency. (10) He talked about breaking up with Sonia and doing without her.

In both of these examples, study of the analytic hours prior to the dreams showed clear residues which appeared in the pictorial language of the dream with very little transformation. In our opinion these residues were not indifferent perceptions, exploited by the unconscious. They provided a good sample of emotionally important material with which the patient was dealing. In the first dream this focused on his concern about the dangers of involvement in analysis and in the second on the longings aroused by separation and the need to be assured of supplies and self-sufficiency. Examination of the residues in the other dreams we collected left little doubt in our minds as to their central significance, especially with regard to transference issues.

The other approach to the residues was based on our method of scoring 'defensive strain'. As mentioned earlier, we had already used 'defensive strain' scores of the analytic hours to predict REM latency and REM time. These scores had demonstrated the co-variance of this aspect of the analytic material with the physiologic parameters of the dream-process. Therefore, if the residues from the hour reflected central concerns, one would expect that a score of 'defensive strain' based solely on the material contained in the residues would be very similar to the 'defensive strain' score of the entire pre-sleep hour. If, however, the residue represented indifferent material, there would be no such correlation. Accordingly, we scored, for defensive strain (Knapp *et al.* 1975), all the residues from the hours preceding each laboratory night. We found that these scores were indeed similar to the scores for the whole hour from which the residues were derived. This finding suggested that those factors from the hour which influenced the 'defensive strain' and thereby the pressure to dream (REM latency) were also shaping the selection of content appearing in the dreams. Thus the manifest content of the dream was a sample of current emotionally important material. We shall deal with this issue in greater detail in the discussion.

Our next investigation involved the organization of the dreams, the handling of various issues in successive dreams throughout the night and the relationship of the dreams to the analytic material. The kinds of questions we asked were: Does the organization of the manifest dream show how the patient is dealing with active issues in the analysis? Does the sequence of dreams during the night indicate how the patient will present himself in the next analytic hour? That is, does the sequence show evidence of adaptive work, institution of defensive operations or over-whelming of defences? Could we predict on the basis of the dream activity, the nature of the morning hour or the level of defensive strain of the morning hour?

Some examples will illustrate our approach to these questions. In one evening analytic hour, the patient seemed to be struggling with his concern about getting involved in analysis. He attempted to deal with his concern by displacement to a girlfriend. Even there, his fear about getting involved was apparent and he even had fantasies of getting rid of the anxiety-provoking object by a plane crash. He also resorted to grandiose fantasies to handle his concerns about being passive and helpless. His first dream of the night was as follows:

This dream is driving up a steep hill in my car and there is a lot of ice on the road and I guess I am going up a very difficult street that I shouldn't – it is always at a 45-degree angle. I go up this hill and I get to the top, I turn to the left and I am just barely making it – there is ice – and the car finally does make it and I get to the top. It seems to be on top of a hill and gypsies live around there – I think they are gypsies anyway and a funny thing about it – the car starts to slide backwards and is ready to topple over the side of the hill, but I put my foot out and by that way I can sort of manoeuvre the car forward by taking the wheel and steering and pushing with my left foot. At the top of the hill these gypsies are watching me and finally they take some sympathy – there is some kind of animal like a donkey – I think it is a donkey –but it has a long neck – and they allow me to hitch the donkey to my car and by doing that I can start pulling the car and they are sort of watching me – and I am able to start proceeding – I guess I started proceeding out of the area too quickly and they got very suspicious and they go get another animal which is a more conventional animal . . . a donkey but it was a camel – a camel. They brought this donkey and with this donkey I could hitch up the donkey to my car and go away. I think the top of the hill reminded me of San Francisco, and the ice was definitely ice left by an ice storm, and there was grass on top of the hill – a combination of grass and ice. I think of, of yes, the gypsies were Italians – they were watching me try to save my life and finally when I did open the door, I did push the car away and then they came to my aid after I had succeeded in preventing the car from going over all by myself. So it was a case of stopping the car all by myself before anyone would help me.

This is a long and complicated dream with much symbolism which could probably evoke many associations. From the context of the preceding analytic hour, however, it was quite clear that this man was struggling, in the dream, with the dangers (as he saw them) of the regressive pull of analysis, the problem of how to get help without feeling weak and helpless. In this dream, he arrived at a solution: first help yourself and then you can let others help you, but even then don't move too fast. The defensive strain of the pre-sleep hour was high and a relatively short latency reflected the pressure to deal with these issues. This dream lasted twenty-four minutes, which is rather long for a first REM period. Later dreams of the night showed marked repression. The only content concerned the sleep laboratory or 'dreaming about dreams'. Our assessment of the dreams on this night was that the patient had worked out a solution for the disturbing feelings about submitting and becoming dependent. Thus, the later dreams reflected only his customary use of repression and focusing on external reality. We predicted that he would be less anxious during the morning hour, would use repression, show an improved alliance and perhaps focus on external reality. The morning hour did indeed show a marked fall in defensive strain. He discussed the dream extensively but without much involvement or affect. His concern about revealing himself was displaced to the sleep laboratory and he saw himself as easily able to leave the laboratory if he wished. The hour might be summarized by the idea – 'don't stick your neck out, be a donkey and go forward, but not too quickly'. Thus, in this sample the inter-relationship between the analytic material and the dream content is readily seen. The succession of dreams suggested effective institution of defences and the following hour confirmed this assessment.

Another series of dreams further elaborates these themes. In the pre-sleep analytic hour the patient was struggling with his fears of loving the analyst and his father. He was aware of and disturbed by his inability to let go. By a variety of defences such as: repression, denial, intellectualization, displacement and projection, he attempted to deal with this conflict.

The first dream was as follows:

I think I was one of three and they were in charge of a refrigerator which I had to move – part of the stuff which I had to move belonged to my father and I had to move that out of the refrigerator and it was a big problem – how it would go and where it was going – and against my will and against my timing they took his things out. Then I guess they had me locked up somewhere and finally forced me to cooperate, and I ended up on a three-man line. We were taking things like Coca-Cola out of the bottom shelf of the refrigerator and passing them up lickety split and efficiently as possible into the other refrigerator or into another receptacle. I was sort of working efficiently and putting in ice – there was not a bit of waste motion – it was a beautiful operation in symmetry and moves in the dream. I am not sure I can remember them. I am backing off. Just before that I was also in a bar, I think, and I was waiting for change and there was two dollars, and I got two bills that looked like Worcester certificates. There was some kind of hassle and finally the guy gave me two dollar bills – one was torn and taped up. And passing these back and forth. Finally the guy gave me some correct change and took the two Worcester bills and said he would get change of some sort – I was kind of confused because these were my bills. I shrugged it off and said 'Oh – what the Hell, he is going through all the trouble of changing these Mickey Mouse type of dollar bills.' And I sort of walked off. Back to the refrigerator – there were so many objects – I think there was an old hat of some sort, also objects of his clothes and my clothes – refrigerator and clothes – two other people – I think they were two brothers.

Again, viewing the dream in the context of the preceding hour, one can see the patient struggling with the 'material' related to his dead father – and how to deal with the man who is making change for him (the analyst). He is forced to submit and cooperate – can he carry it off in the cold and efficient manner which he idealized?

The second dream of that night was as follows:

Well, another tough dream to pull out – it is fragments – I dreamed about a police officer named Larry – a school bus – dreamed about running a ranch and Miss Iceland – a beauty queen – and the rancher – his name was King, I guess. The King Ranch. And he married Miss Iceland and I asked him how he met her and he said his cousin fixed him up in Iceland. And about the police officer – I guess he was collecting furniture or something – furniture? – as I talk about this dream of a security number, mentioning furniture – I see an image of an open casket.

In this dream, with obvious heterosexual beginnings, the theme again returns to collecting things and to a casket – death. The patient had frequently used sexual material and grandiose fantasies as a defence against more passive longings for father. Our assessment of the two dreams was that the patient was unable to get away from father's death. We thought the next hour would again deal with the issue of getting involved in analysis – opening up – submitting. He might attempt to cool things but would not succeed.

The succeeding hour did show a higher defensive strain. The material brought out concerns about being a little boy looking for love. Early defensive efforts in the hour did not hold up.

Discussion

By combining data from psychoanalytic sessions with dreams collected in a sleep laboratory, we have attempted to determine the source of the manifest content of dreams and to see if this information helped us to

189

understand the function of dreaming. We found that the manifest content contained many meaningful residues from the pre-sleep analytic hours. This finding is consistent with the work of Witkin (1969: 285–359), Breger *et al.* (1971) and Whitman (1973), who have found direct incorporation of emotionally stimulating pre-sleep experiences into manifest dreams. Since analysis stirs up emotional conflicts it is hardly surprising that material from analytic hours appeared in the patients' dreams. More important, however, was our finding that these residues regularly involved emotionally meaningful material rather than indifferent content. The residues gave a clear picture of the central issues with which the patient was struggling and of his efforts to handle them. This finding confirms the comments by Freud (1923) and Sharpe (1937) and, more recently, Langs (1971) that discovery of 'the day residue' usually leads to immediate understanding of the dream.

Furthermore, examination of the sequence of dreams during the night allowed us to assess the degree of the patient's success in coping with the disturbing material. The different sequences of dreaming (showing conflict resolution or remaining stuck on the same problem) are similar to those described by Offenkrantz and Rechtschaffen (1963). Our defensive strain scores for the analytic hour following each set of dreams indicated the validity of viewing the dream as a mechanism of adaptation, sometimes successful and sometimes not. The fact that both dream content and the physiologic measures of dreaming (REM latency and REM time) reflected these issues further confirmed the interrelationship between the psychological and physiological aspects of dreaming.

These findings shed light on the theories of dream function. What, then, are the implications for the clinical use of dreams? The clear relationship between important waking experiences and the manifest content brings the dream back to centre stage. By looking at the dream from this viewpoint we should be able to formulate a relatively clear picture of the critical psychological issues with which a patient is involved. Of course, it should be noted that not all people are in analysis or undergoing some psychologically stressful experience. Thus, we cannot expect that psychodynamic conflicts will be equally apparent for all dreams. What we are saying is that the REM and dreaming mechanisms appear to be available for use when needed. Perhaps in the non-patient population this mechanism is available for assimilating new experiences in a personally meaningful manner.

Our statement that the manifest dream contains undistorted important day residues did not imply that there is no change at all. Clearly, there is a change in subjective representation or inner language. French and Fromm describe this process as a shift from purely logical thinking to a concrete, practical language, more like that of childhood. Whether this change in language serves a primary purpose of distortion and defence or merely represents the particular, unfamiliar language of the system being used is an old debate (Piaget 1951; E. Jones 1916: 87–144). Baynes (cited by Faraday 1972, p. 121) compared Freud's argument about the disguise function of dreams to the story of the English visitor to Paris who assumed that the Parisians were talking gibberish (French) in order to make a fool of him. Thus, in the dream in which 'three people in a room' was represented as 'three men – all in the same boat', the language of the dream, rather than disguising, actually provided a graphic portrayal of the patient's feelings and wishful thinking about the situation. The language of the dream can then be described as metaphorical and at times sophisticated and different from but not necessarily inferior to waking language.

Thus, the principal defensive use of distortion may occur in the secondary revision as the person attempts to make sense of his dream. Apparent distortion may actually be due to lack of information about the day residue. An historic example of the latter possibility was Freud's 'Irma' dream. Using this dream, Freud demonstrated many of the mechanisms that seemed to be active in the formation of dreams. Through his associations Freud formulated the latent content of the dream and demonstrated the kinds of distortions of that content which occurred in the development of the manifest dream. What Freud did not include in this discussion were the important 'day residues' which have been described by Schur (1966: 45–85). The relatively undistorted incorporation of these affect-laden events into the manifest dream is impressive. With this additional information provided by Schur, we can now see that Freud's formulation of latent content was related to feelings he was struggling with in his relationship to Fliess but because he was apparently unaware of the *important* day residue of the 'Irma' dream, his formulation was only an approximation of the central issues described in Schur's paper. The dream, however, did lead him in the right direction. From this example we can better appreciate the thinking of such dream theorists as Stekel (1943), Jung (1934: 139–62), Adler (1936) and Bonime (1962), who differed with Freud about the extent of disguise occurring in dreams. The concept of disguise was necessary if dreaming served to discharge sleep-threatening repressed wishes (R. Jones 1965). Freud also warned against taking the manifest dream at face-value to avoid the dangers of undisciplined, metaphorical or allegorical approaches to dream interpretation. As discussed by Spanjaard (1969), however, Freud tended to disregard his own warning. He and many other theorists have often focused more on the personal meaning of the manifest dream. Associations to a dream then become, sometimes unbeknownst to the dreamer, associations to emotionally important events (the day residues incorporated in the dream).

When the day residue is discovered by these associations, the meaning of the dream is often quite clear. However, even if the day residue is not discovered, the focus on the dream means that the patient is looking at material of central importance to him, material which it was necessary for him to try to integrate in the dream.

In summary, this study has demonstrated the continuity of mental life in waking and sleeping (dreaming) states. The view of REM sleep (dreaming) as an adaptive mechanism helped to organize our examination of dream material collected during an ongoing psychoanalysis. The results led to some suggestions concerning the clinical analysis of dreams. We have found it important to learn the patient's dream language as shown by his manifest dreams. The manifest dream then provides a vivid subjective view of the patient's current adaptive tasks – an indication of what is active in the analysis.

Our concept of adaptation is similar to that described by Joffe and Sandler (1968), in which the ego attempts to create new organizations of the ideal state of self in order to preserve a feeling of safety and to avoid the experience of being traumatically overwhelmed. Successful adaptation involves a relinquishing of ideals (wishes) which are no longer appropriate to present reality. That these previous ideal states are not always so easily abandoned contributes to the appearance of infantile wishes and the wish-fulfilment aspect of dreaming. We are suggesting that dreams portray the struggle, inherent in the interaction between the wishes of the past and the needs of the present, and reflect the process of integration which appears to take place in REM sleep (Greenberg and Pearlman 1975b).

References

Adler, A. (1936). On the interpretation of dreams. *Int. J. indiv. Psychol.* 2, 3–16.

Bonime, W. (1962). *The Clinical Use of Dreams.* New York: Basic Books.

Breger, L., Hunter, I. and Lane, R. (1971). *The Effect of Stress on Dreams.* New York: Int. Univ. Press.

Brenner, C. (1969). Dreams in clinical psycho-analytic practice. *J. nerv. ment. Dis.* 149, 122–32.

Faraday, A. (1972). *Dream Power.* New York: Coward, McCann, and Geoghegan.

Fisher, C. (1965). Psychoanalytic implications of recent research on sleep and dreaming. *J. Am. psychoanal. Ass.* 13, 197–303.

French, T. and Fromm, E. (1964). *Dream Interpretation: A New Approach.* New York: Basic Books.

Freud, S. (1900). The interpretation of dreams. SE 4–5.

—— (1923). The ego and the id. SE 19.

Greenberg, R. and Leiderman, P.H. (1966). Perceptions, the dream process and memory: an up-to-date version of 'Notes on a Mystic Writing Pad'. *Compr. Psychiat.* 7, 517–23.

Greenberg, R., Pearlman, C., Fingar, R., Kantrowitz, J. and Kawliche, S. (1970). The effects of dream deprivation: implications for a theory of the psychological function of dreaming. *Brit. J. med. Psychol.* 43, 1–11.

Greenberg, R., Pillard, R. and Pearlman, C. (1972a). The effect of dream (stage REM) deprivation on adaptation to stress. *Psychsom. Med.* 34, 257–62.

Greenberg, R., Pearlman, C. and Gampel, D. (1972b). War neuroses and the adaptive function of REM sleep. *Br. J. med. Psychol.* 45, 27–33.

Greenberg, R. and Pearlman, C. (1975a). REM sleep and the analytic process: a psychophysiologic bridge. *Psychoanal. Q.* (in press).

Greenberg, R. and Pearlman, C. (1975b). Cutting the REM nerve: an approach to the adaptive function of REM sleep. *Persp. Biol. Med.* (in press).

Greenson, R. (1970). The exceptional position of the dream in psychoanalytic practice. *Psychoanal. Q.* 39, 519–49.

Hawkins, D.R. (1966). A review of psychoanalytic dream theory in the light of recent psychophysiological studies of sleep and dreaming. *Br. J. med. Psychol.* 39, 85–104.

Joffe, W.G. and Sandler, J. (1968). Comments on the psychoanalytic psychology of adaptation. *Int. J. Psycho-Anal.* 49, 445–54.

Jones, E. (1916). The theory of symbolism. In *Papers on Psycho-Analysis*, 5th edn. London: Bailliere, Tindall, 1950.

Jones, R. (1965). Dream interpretation and the psychology of dreaming. *J. Am. psychoanal. Ass.* 13, 304–19.

—— (1970). *The New Psychology of Dreaming.* New York: Grune & Stratton.

Jung, C.G. (1934). The practical use of dream analysis. In *The Collected Works of C.G. Jung.* vol. 16. New York: Pantheon, 1954.

Knapp, P. (1969). Image, symbol and person; the strategy of psychological defence. *Archs gen. Psychiat.* 21, 392–407.

Knapp, P., Greenberg, R., Pearlman, C., Cohen, M., Kantrowitz, J. and Sashin, J. (1975). Clinical measurement in psychoanalysis: an approach. *Psychoanal. Q.* (in press).

Langs, R. (1971). Day residues, recall residues, and dreams: reality and the psyche. *J. Am. psychoanal. Ass.* 19, 499–523.

Offenkrantz, W. and Rechtschaffen, A. (1963). Clinical studies of sequential dreams. *Archs. gen. Psychiat.* 8, 497–508.

Piaget, J. (1951). *Play, Dreams and Imitation in Childhood.* New York: Norton, 1962.

Schur, M. (1966). Some additional 'day residues' of 'the specimen dream of psychoanalysis'. In R. Loewenstein *et al.* (eds.), *Psychoanalysis – A General Psychology.* New York: Int. Univ. Press.

Sharpe, E. (1937). *Dream Analysis.* London: Hogarth Press.

Spanjaard, J. (1969). The manifest dream content and its significance for the interpretation of dreams. *Int. J. Psycho-Anal.* 50, 221–35.

Stekel, W. (1943). *The Interpretation of Dreams: New Developments and Technique.* New York: Liveright.

Whitman, R., Kramer, M. and Baldridge, B. (1963). Which dream does the patient tell? *Archs. gen. Psychiat.* 8, 277–82.

Whitman, R., Kramer, M., Ornstein, P. and Baldridge, B. (1967). The physiology, psychology and utilization of dreams. *Am. J. Psychiat.* 124, 287–302.

Whitman, R. (1973). Dreams about the group: An approach to the problem of group psychology. *Int. J. Grp Psychother.* 23, 408–20.

Witkin, A. (1969). Influencing dream content. In M. Kramer (ed.), *Dream Psychology and the New Biology of Dreaming.* Springfield: Thomas.

12

Dreaming and the organizing function of the ego

CECILY DE MONCHAUX

In this paper I am going to be concerned with the role of dreaming, not for the sleeper, but for the wide-awake person who reports the dream to the analyst. If I confine the setting to that of the analytic treatment, it is because, as Freud (1923: 117) put it, 'the employment of dreams in analysis is something very remote from their original purpose'. These limitations do not by any means rule out considerations of dream content – indeed, one of my aims in this paper is the clarification of some relations between the form and content of dreams. But I am choosing to tackle the problem here not from the point of view of the relation between content and form *within* the dream, as Erikson (1954), for instance, has done so imaginatively; rather, I want to examine the relation *between* dreaming and other modes of action in analysis.

In the development of psychoanalysis subsequent to the publication of *The Interpretation of Dreams* (Freud 1900), dream theory provided generously for all areas of the growing discipline. Paradigmatically, the neurotic symptom was conceived as a long-term waking dream, its latent content sustained in disguise by defence mechanisms; the concept of topographical regression in the developmental model of the dream was generalized to be applied in the concept of the life history of the dreamer; and most significant of all, the transference phenomenon was understood in dream terms as the expression of an ever-present if latent set of wishes both freed and stimulated by certain features of the analytic situation, as the dream thoughts were both freed and stimulated by the sleep state.

But although dream theory was a bountiful mother to her conceptual offspring, it looked for some time as if she was unlikely to receive a great deal in return. Freud (1933: 8) deplored the thinning out of analytic publications on the dream: 'The analysts', he said, 'behave as though they had no more to say about dreams, as though there was nothing more to be added to the theory of dreams'; none the less, he himself had contributed to this tendency by his later writings on dreams. For instance, in 1923 we find him deprecating an exaggerated respect for the 'mysterious unconscious'; 'it is only too easy', he says, 'to forget that a dream is as a rule merely a thought like any other' (p. 112).

And it was precisely because it was treated as a thought like any other that the dream shared in the profits of what many would claim to be the most significant contribution psychoanalysis has been able to make to the general psychological theory of cognition. I refer here to the discovery that mental functions are modulated by the meaning which we attribute to them. Thus, thinking came to be conceptualized in psychoanalysis, not only as a source of thematic content, as a provider of textual elements to be deciphered, but also as a symbolic version of other psychological processes which were not primarily cognitive in their manifestations – processes which found their place in the psychoanalytic catalogue, not under the heading of 'ego function' but rather under that of 'instinct'.

By virtue of the unconscious attribution of infantile fantasy meanings to cognitive processes, the mode of function of those processes was shown to be dramatically transformed. This transformation is effected by the principle which in learning theory is termed 'generalization'. Generalization may pertain to either or both the response and stimulus components of the process modified.[1] And this is evident in thinking generally and in dreaming specifically.

For instance, the response generalization from defecation to cognition may render thinking expulsive rather than creative, and locate the communication of ideas within the sociometry of the potting couple. From the aspect of stimulus generalization, the products of thinking, thoughts, may become faecal horrors, and in the exercise of this fantasy equation, it is little wonder that they must often be kept secretively hidden away for fear of polluting the intellectual environment. Our understanding of dreaming gains immeasurably from the realization that the person's image of his mind has a powerful effect on the working of his mind. Thus it can be shown that the dream is not only a source and container of fantasy content, but also a unit of fantasy employed by the patient in the enactment of his transference relationship. In his cognitive regression to concretization and animism, the patient can be shown to conceptualize his dreams, along with other mental products, as tangible or living entities. Thus a dream can symbolize a body part frankly exposed or shamefully screened from view, a gift or a weapon, a good internal imago or a bad.

Important as these developments have been for understanding the role of dreams in analysis, and for dealing with them technically,[2] the

196

emphasis has been heavily on the similarity of dreaming to other mental functions. Even Lewin's (1946) brilliant contribution to the understanding of oral fantasy components in dreaming leaned in the same direction. He argued that dreaming was a mentally dramatized form of the feeding cycle of succour and repose, but he did not raise the complementary issue of the extent to which dreaming was *not* an analogue of feeding and sleeping at the breast.

Indeed, so widespread is this emphasis on similarities, that one has cause to wonder that patients still insist on reporting dreams, when other aspects of the subtly analysed transference provide such excellent play and battlegrounds for fantasy and resistance alike. Shall we blame the greed of the unconscious, seeking hungrily to exploit every possible channel of communication? Or is it the cunning twist of a resistance, denying in one channel what is affirmed in another, so that day and night thinking (to use Lewin's 1968 phrase) set up a complex counterpoint to dazzle and confuse the analyst? Or is it that the dream is far from being only a thought like any other, and that the telling of a dream has aspects that are unique and distinctively different from other psychological actions? Can certain intimate and unconscious messages be communicated in no other way than through the action of reporting a dream?

Before I proceed to develop my argument in the attempt to answer these questions, let me clarify my use of the term 'dream'. I mean the action described as the telling of a dream.[3] The telling may be to oneself or to another. We can dicover no way of distinguishing between a dream and the telling of a dream. It was Wittgenstein who pointed out that we do not question whether a person really has a dream or if it merely seems to him that he did (Malcolm 1964).[4]

I am assuming Freud's distinction between manifest and latent content, though I should prefer to characterize this distinction in terms of 'restricted' and 'elaborated' content, rather than as a metaphoric contrast between 'revealed' and 'hidden'. For if we ask what operations are needed to 'reveal' the latent content of a dream, we must answer that they involve the comparison between the 'restricted' dream and the free associations given in the context of the transference relationship. This is all reflected upon by the listening analyst in the context of his knowledge and recall of the patient's life story as told within the same context (and sometimes, though this procedure is doubtful, even drawn from outside it, for example, from 'case material'). Then this is all set within the even more conceptually extended context of the reciprocating listener's interpretive remarks, and his observations as to how the patient reacts on hearing these. It is by this embedding of the raw dream in successively more complex data contexts as the analysis proceeds, that we reach further and further elaborated versions of the dream as first told (for completeness, one should also include that first operation Freud recommended – have the patient repeat his dream and compare the two versions).

There is a snag with the metaphor 'latent' applied to content, despite its yeoman metapsychological service and useful as it has been in the phenomenological account of how patients and analysts feel as the elaborations of the dream telling surprise them; the idea of the 'latent' forecloses upon the question of how the new meanings of the dream become available. The temptation to yield to the simplistic idea that the latent content is waiting like 'Sleeping Beauty' for the prince's interpretive kiss to release her from the curse of resistance blocks the way to scientific curiosity about the progressive and active process of transmutation of meaning which we observe in the course of dream interpretation. When it happens that we re-examine the same dream reports at successive phases of an analysis, we are left in little doubt that there is no final latent content buried at the end of the rainbow.

I have now set the conceptual stage on which I shall argue that dream telling has unique advantages in the achievement of what H. Hartmann (1947, 1950) called 'the organizing function of the ego' – that super-ordinate function which includes differentiation as well as synthesis and integration. By approaching some questions about dreaming from the standpoint of ego psychology, I am to extend the principle that the person's unconscious image of his mind has powerful effects on the working of his mind. I want to advance the thesis that this reflexive principle plays an important part in determining not only the content and form of an ego activity, in this instance, dream telling, but even the very choice of the given medium over other media. Does dream telling have a different unconscious significance and function than other psychoanalytic media such as fantasy recounting and acting out?

On a first hearing, it may be difficult to be certain that the form and content of dream texts differ from the form and content of other psychological texts, such as introspective reports and fantasies. Thanks to Freud, however, we have a set of operations which, when carefully performed to provide the extended and elaborated meaning contexts described earlier, enable us to arrive time and again at the *differentia* he established of primary- and secondary-process thinking. By scrutinizing the transformations he called 'dream work' we are also able to recognize the unique balance between these two types of thinking.

In considering the unconscious significance of dream telling, we must first remind ourselves of the phenomenal features of this activity. In the relatively sane person, the most obvious feature is dissociation from other psychological acts. This is manifest in a number of ways, including that of the conventional form in which the utterance is cast, even on the first telling to oneself. The tense is always past, and the verb 'to have' is usually employed, rather than forms of the verb 'to be' which is commonly used, at least in English, of descriptions of experiences. The telling of the dream entails the reporting of a scenario, usually though not exclusively or always in visual terms, a scenario in which the dream teller is an onlooker or a listener, even though he may also be depicted as a character in the dream text (variations in the distancing of the teller from the story told provide important clues to the ego capacity for differentiation, a point I shall take up later in this paper when discussing some special features of dreaming in schizoid patients). Motivationally, the dream teller disclaims intentionality and instrumentality so far as the production of his dream is concerned. He accepts no responsibility for the occurrence of the event or ordinarily for its content. In terms of Schafer's (1976) action language, the dream teller disclaims agency, acting as if he were reporting a happening, not an action.[5]

There are three aspects of dream telling on which I shall focus in developing my argument: (1) the advantages of exploiting a variety of media of communication; (2) the way in which dream telling achieves a sense of mastery together with the implications of this achievement for the theory of post-traumatic dreams; and (3) the notion that dream telling achieves ego mastery by a process I shall call 'reduction of dimensions', of which symbolization is a special case.

Exploitation of variety of media

It is a metapsychological truism that the ego's capacity to achieve qualitative differentiation rests on a long history of complex interactions. These are interactions between constitution, maturing autonomous functions and learning, and they result in differentiated cognitive structures which gradually secure the binding of impulses and consequently ensure the reduction of anxiety. These differentiated structures may be regarded as instances of benign dissociation between different forms of thought and between thinking and other psychological acts. The sheer number of different types of psychological acts available for anxiety control is an important factor in the reduction of anxiety. In our concentration on the more complex issues of quality of control and defence, I think that we have underestimated the importance of variety of media. If we are to examine the role of dream telling in anxiety control, then perhaps we should begin by acknowledging its basic contribution to the repertoire of media available to us for unconscious exploitation in the interest of keeping our anxiety level within tolerable limits.

This exploitation of the factor of variety of media was very striking in the case of a patient who appeared to have little capacity to defend herself from becoming aware of her sadistic fantasies. The thinly disguised and scarcely elaborate content of these fantasies was expressed in synchronized versions in words, in acting out and in telling dreams; to use the economic metaphor, her manifest anxiety was thereby more attenuated by virtue of the *number* of channels employed than when the full force of her impulses charged through but one channel. With only one channel open, she was completely overwhelmed by what she saw in herself, and would collapse. She came to hope consciously for dreams to take, as she put it, 'some of the load'.

This patient was very concerned with the differences between different forms of thinking and between covert thinking and overt motor action, and was very concerned to keep them apart. She was for a long time preoccupied with the idea that I could not see what to her were dream images, that my experience of them could therefore only be second-hand, faded and 'merely' verbal, compared with the full sensory vividness of her own. It seemed to me that she assigned to me her childhood role as the 'mere' listener to adult emotional scenes which had excited her but whose full quality had eluded her. So long as there was an assumed difference in modality, and she could think that she could *see* but that I could only *hear* her dreams, she had the fantasy of control over the dangers of her participation in the parental relationship. She depicted distressing events but these dreams lacked affect so long as she could reassure herself that, though we were both involved in the same experience, one of us did the seeing, the other the hearing. Her anxiety later began to manifest itself in her waking to nightmares with auditory but no visual content. She would awake terrified to find herself actually making the grunting noises which she also referred to in her non-visual dream report. It was only after achieving these dream accounts that she was able to give me a visual share in her dreaming. She spontaneously had the idea of drawing versions of dreams for me to see. Interestingly, she had always been inhibited in drawing up to this point in her life. And this sharing of private and secret actions with me not only signified that it was becoming safe to be present at a family emotional scene which was no longer fantasied so sadistically, but also marked a change in her attitudes towards her parents' marriage; she began to permit two people to do something good together.

Sense of mastery

No matter how terrifying or chaotic a dream text may be, the person who tells it nevertheless feels it to be *subordinate* to him. In the act of telling a dream, there is a sense of mastery. In this regard, dream reporting can be described in Ernst Kris's phrase (1952) as 'regression in the service of the ego'. So long as the waking person can still say, 'I *had* a dream,' and not something of the order, 'the dream *has* me' – we cannot say that the unconscious has overwhelmed the ego. This characteristic of dream telling as a part-function of the ego predominates in attempts at omnipotent control when the person, in danger of being overwhelmed by fantasy, achieves barely disguised dream texts of impending catastrophe. These are often understood as a breakthrough (the weakened ego of the sleep state failing to maintain defences), but I think the containment of psychic catastrophe within a dream text requires us to be aware also of the attempt at scaling down of the internal world and its imagos to part-object status by confining their expression to a subfunction of the ego.

This claim that dreaming is a form of ego control has implications for the theory of post-traumatic dreams. We can now dispute the conceptual austerity of Freud's theory of these dreams if we look at them from the stance I have been taking in this paper; namely, that dreaming exemplifies superordinate ego-functioning (H. Hartmann 1947, 1950).

On the question of why post-traumatic dreams are repeated, we find Freud's explanation formulated primarily in terms of the economic concepts; this type of dream is said to be repeated in a belated attempt to respond to the excessive arousal stimulated by the traumatic event. To elaborate the economic metaphor further, it is as if by temporal redistribution, the density of excitement per time unit of repeated response can be adjusted, and tension be reduced piecemeal. The ego psychologist has to ask, however, whether any cognitive aspects of action are also implicated in this process of extinction. I think there are two senses in which we must answer 'Yes'. The first is located in the notion of a comprehensive re-enactment of trauma which is implied in Freud's (1920) theory when he speaks of these dreams as 'endeavouring to master the stimulus retrospectively (p. 32). For this formulation to make sense, couched as it is in the language of personal action, intentional cognitive attitudes must be invoked, whether conscious or not. All that the economic model can predicate are content-free discharge phenomena, such as blind panic attacks.[6] The economic model provides no constructs which can be coordinated with the content of the post-traumatic dream text.

According to the cognitive model, the person in shock is making a belated attempt at mastery by imaginatively giving himself another chance – a chance to achieve an outcome different from that which life burdened him with – the real, unwanted event in question. To give himself this second 'go' to achieve a more desirable outcome, to undo the unwanted, he must needs, however, return imaginatively to the opening chapter of his troubled story, to the scene of the crime, as it were. Surely such purposive re-enactment, despite its inevitable partial failure, demands a dream theory which includes in addition to discharge concepts, those of wish fulfilment and of ego control?

A second sense in which I think we can take a stand for the ego in explaining post-traumatic dream repetition has to do with the synthetic function, or integration. An unwanted event occurs — we wish it had not happened. Not only is the content of the event highly aversive, but secondly, the sense of 'unwantedness' is itself aversive. This secondary aversiveness derives from our defensive attempts at denial and dissociation. 'It *has not* happened to me' wars with 'alas, it *has* happened to me'. To maintain at least partial wishfulfilling unreality, we sacrifice personal unity in the deep discomforts of ego splitting.

For the relatively healthy ego, the aversiveness of splitting gradually exceeds that of recalling and re-experiencing the original trauma in memory. Better to be in one piece though crushed, than like the autonomous lizard, shed the injured part. The re-living of trauma, by whatever means, has the result of reducing the split in the ego. Gradually the shocked person is able to include the unwanted event within the context of his idea of himself, however regretfully, sadly and bitterly. If he is to regain a *whole* self, it is under the condition that a *changed* self be accepted. Without this acceptance, he is an incomplete person. I said just now 're-living by whatever means' and I want to ask whether dreaming may not be a specially suitable means of achieving reintegration after stress induced dissociation. *That* it is, and *how* is a means of so doing, we have much analytic clinical evidence for. Further, we have the systematic studies of Breger *et al.* (1971) and of Greenberg *et al.* (1972), who have documented sequences of dreams following traumatic experiences. These show, as do Parkes's (1972) records of dreaming in bereavement, that over time, both in manifest content and in associations, there is a progressive decrease in the frequency of references to the recent trauma and an increase in associatively relevant themes pertaining to the past: the recent trauma memories being gradually linked up and integrated with childhood trauma memories. As Breger *et al.* (1971) say in the conclusion to their study: 'this assimilative process . . . facilitates the integration of strongly felt information into the solutions made available by the dream or primary-process programs'.

But are there certain characteristics of dreaming which make it uniquely suitable to fulfil both the abreactive and integrative functions we discern in the dream following stress?

The classical answer would be that the lowering of defences (vigilance) in sleep enables ego contact with repressed ideas and thereby the undoing of splitting and the promoting of integration. Night and day thinking are conjoined in the compromise which is told as a dream.

But dream telling is a dissociated action itself, and the content of what is told is experienced as such by the teller – as different from the content of day thinking, and in sanity, not to be confused with it. It is not paradoxical, therefore, to propose that a split-off function should be especially appropriate to serve the end of reintegration? Yet it may be precisely because of its dissociative characteristics that the dream becomes the vehicle, the container, of split-off elements. Since the dreamer has the illusion that he is not responsible for his dream, it is safe to put unwanted thoughts into it. It functions as a place of asylum, in which split-off elements can be kept alive until conditions are propitious for their integration with consciously acceptable elements. Dissociation with no access to consciousness, as in the numbing or freezing stages of the primary stress response, gives way to dissociation with partial access to consciousness via night thinking, and this provides a trial ground, a way station on the road to integration. In this respect dreaming functions in a way analogous to that of negation in Freud's (1925) account.

Freud argued that post-traumatic dreams were exceptions[7] to the rule of wish fulfilment: 'the function of the dream has failed' (1933: 29). True, it has failed from the point of view of the sleeping ego, since the sleeper awakens, but how superbly it has succeeded from the point of view of the waking ego – to dream of a traumatic experience with little or no distortion of content or affect is to achieve the ultimate gratification of the wish that what was real was after all only a dream, as Stein (1965) has noted. For instance, in one case, a patient's dreams of someone's dying came to be understood in their elaborate context as exercises in the conversion of real loss into a mere 'dreamed of' loss. He came to call these dreams, 'death disguised as death' dreams. It is perhaps worth noting that this patient admitted great enjoyment of his dreams and of analysis, despite considerable suffering: for him, the fluidity of the analytic process, with its demonstration of the changing and over-determined meanings of his reactions, signified that it was all a dream, in which he could escape the dreadful finality and irreversibility of reality.

Reduction of dimensions

Let us proceed to explore the idea that unless dreaming is a subordinate function, it ceases to be any use to the ego. One way of putting this would be to say that 'the dream must have fewer dimensions than waking experience, rather as a drawing, a sculpture, a poem or a film must have fewer dimensions than the natural event to which it bears some relation in its creator's life. Of course, perception itself is an abstracting activity, and any individual act of perception involves a reductive selection from among the many possible dimensions which in theory specify the given event.

In psychosis and sometimes during analysis, however, the sense of mastery is lost, and then patients feel that their dreams threaten to take over the ego. A patient with intense fears of being engulfed by projected bad imagos showed the underlying fantasy dilemma of the person whose part functions threaten to equal the whole. She began to feel her dreams were as big as she was – that it was like being someone who had swallowed their twin, or like forcing an object into a polythene bag which was the exact size of the object (she made at this time a significant slip of the tongue, in which container and contained were reversed: she spoke of a 'bloodful of lavatory'). There was no room for a remainder of self, and there was danger that she, the container, would split down the middle. This concrete fantasy of being taken over and destroyed by her dreams was lightly hinted at during an earlier defended phase of her analysis when she hummed the tune of a song called 'I Thought I Saw a Dream Walking and Talking'. (This patient's fantasies and dreams had been enormously inflated by unconscious contributions from a mother who, imaginatively inhibited herself, had rarely told dreams, and whose projected aggression was guiltily and collusively received by her daughter to camouflage her own.

What dimensions of experience are surrendered to make the dream a good and comfortable fit for the dreamer? First comes the *temporal dimension*. For the waking ego the dream is *always* in the past tense. As a past event, the dream shares a sanctuary with history, in that it can never be changed. It may be forgotten, it may be shown to be subject to different interpretations than the teller at first realized, but as an existentially past event reported in the present, it has peculiar advantages from the patient's point of view. I was struck by the gains of temporal displacement in dream reporting in the case of a patient with severe persecutory anxieties, a prolific dreamer for whom dreaming meant the relegation of current transference traumata to the past. Dream reports which at first appeared to be confirmatory of themes also apparent in other areas in the analysis were essentially attempts to push the latent content into the past, even if only the past of 'last night'. It was significant for this patient's analysis when she began to report dreams from the broken sleep of the morning of the day on which sessions took place. For a long time she was only able to achieve self-observation in her dream telling; as soon as she was exposed to direct present-tense transference involvement, she acted out her impulses in overt physical behaviour in the session, becoming increasingly frantic when I failed to enact the superego role she sought to project into me in order to fight with it outside, and not inside herself. But in reporting a dream, no matter how destructive its content, she felt secure; she was alive enough inside to produce it, and since it was now felt to be in the past protected by time, neither she nor I could touch it. The resistance cries out loud here, but what I want to extract from the example is the measure of safety for a threatened ego that dream telling afforded the patient. Unable to maintain a structural segregation of superego and ego-functions because of her fear of internal conflict, she projected the superego and so lost control of what remained. Without projection she feared that I would invade her and gang up with her hated internal imagos against her. The only place in which this could not happen was in her dream reports, since by the time she told me of them, she felt they had already been experienced. And, moreover, they had been experienced away from me. Nor did it afford her sufficient control over her degree of anxiety to keep the analysis one day stale as some patients do, being unable to analyse a transference reaction until the session after that in which it occurs. For this patient, a spatial dissociation was also necessary; she had to remind herself that dreams not only occurred away from me, but often that the locale of the manifest content was a distant one. She often told dreams of maps, saw maps in cracks on the wall, and watched carefully to be sure that my chair was never by chance moved closer than usual to the couch. Many sessions took place with her crouching down on the floor in the farthermost corner of the room, or alternatively, standing close to my chair, but behind me in space, as her dreams were behind me in time. You will not be surprised to learn that her strongest conscious fear was of falling asleep and dreaming on the couch.

This patient also provides us with a good example of the way in which dreaming effects another reduction in dimensions – in the number of classes of psychological objects which are dealt with. I refer particularly to the triad of self, internal imagos and external objects, each fantasized as an autonomous being, and each subject to re-location through intro-jection and projection. So long as she was dealing with internal imagos alone, on first waking, she could just be safe. But in the rest of her waking life, the management of this triad proved too difficult for her. Either she feared that she would lose her internal imagos to the external objects, who like the Pied Piper might prove too attractive for them to resist, and so leave her self deserted and depleted; or there was the danger of internal imagos and external objects forming a coalition to attack her self. By maintaining her distance in the transference, both spatially and emotionally, she prevented the first possibility – that I and her internal imagos might get on well together and desert her. Acting out to project her internal objects into me was intended to avoid the second hazard – of the battle being fought within her; better to be intact even if empty. The only time when something safe could happen between her and her internal imagos, without an imbalance caused by external objects, was in telling herself a dream. There was much evidence from the content of her fantasies that in going to sleep it was the return to sole possession of her mother's lap that she sought. In a session, for instance, in which she both had a wish to be on my lap and another that I should be absent from the room, and just let her be alone, she drew attention to the fact that her favourite going-to-sleep fantasy was of being a baby in a cot beside a rose-covered cottage. She wondered why she never put anyone else in the picture. She wanted not only no one else in the lap with her, but also nothing but a lap, and indeed, the fantasy, like the session, would be spoilt if she could see her mother, since, as she explained, 'you can't see your mother if you are really close to her'. Her most satisfying sort of dream report, therefore, was one in which she not only lost the external object dimension, but became herself the internal imago of her mother. In sessions she hated me to make any sound or sudden movement, or to meet her gaze. Sounds outside the consulting room never disturbed her, so long as I was still. Though wanting this state of being symbolically in my lap, its dangers would soon emerge and she would have to alert me to the destructive child there; demands for my stillness would presently give way to attempts to make me move – she would jump off the couch, throw cushions, try to tip up my chair and so on, for fear that my stillness should become the stillness of the dead. While not wanting me to meet her gaze or look in her direction she panicked if she turned round and happened to find me with my head resting back or my eyes closed. Then I had to be both warned and shaken back to life.

In telling oneself a dream, one can relax the diplomatic functions of mediating between internal imagos and external objects, and establish a direct relation between oneself and internal imagos. This directness is a source of satisfaction particularly for schizoid patients, so much of whose waking life is taken up with the maintenance of an iron curtain between their internal imagos and external objects. Such a patient felt that her dreams, though awful for her to endure, were by far her most authentic experiences.

Although the teller may assume a psychic position as being 'dream contained' within the internal imago, as well as of containing it, both these forms of dream report represent the loss of one object dimension only – that of the external object world. The dream is never a solitary internal experience. As Kanzer (1955) puts it: 'Sleep is not a phenomenon of primary but rather of secondary narcissism, and the sleeper shares his slumbers with an introjected object.' In very young children, when the relations between internal and external objects are still very fluid, the sleeper may on waking imagine that he has shared his dream experience with another. For instance, a three-year-old patient could distinguish between reports and other thoughts, but he used to interrogate his mother for further information about the events reported in his dreams, on the assumption that they had been 'dreams à *deux*'. But nevertheless, he imposed some restrictive frame around his dream reports, because he never asked his father or his sister about them!

Can we take the idea of reduction of dimensions further, and ask whether this occurs within the self as well as between the self and the possible range of objects? Here we have the answer beautifully worked out by Lewin (1958) in his discussions of the body—mind split in dreaming. In the most untroubled dreams, he said, 'the perceiving dreamer was nothing more than that little weightless, immaterial being, vaguely located behind the eyes' (p. 50). In separating mind from matter, the self as observer loses the reflexive self-dimension – the touch of self by self, the look at self by self and so on. These reflexive elements, withdrawn from the self as observer, become dissociated and projected onto the dream picture of the self as observed. The maximal loss of self dimensions occurs in the blank dream when, as Lewin (1958) says: 'the dreamer does not separate himself as spectator, merges with the pure feelings of the dream' (p. 54). And of course, merges with the internal breast imago, so that in this exceptional type of dream, we have the reduction of the three dimensions of self, internal imagos and external objects, to the one dimension of the blank screen. A good example of a hypnagogic image approaching, but not quite reaching the blissful, tension-denying blank dream was given by a patient who experienced a recurrent drowsing fantasy that he was a mere point, in the presence of a large cloudy mass. As he awoke, the point self became spiky, like a thin line, and the mass more solid and cheesy: a point has position but no dimension; a line has one dimension; a body, three.

The idea of variations in dimensionality has significance in the theory of symbolization. De-differentiation between the thing symbolized and the symbol is the basis for the concrete thinking of the schizophrenic: for the cathexis of words, for instance, as if they were objects, as Freud argued. In more mature forms of symbolization a curtailment is effected of the omnipotent infantile greed which required the ego to treat the symbol as no less than what it symbolized. In accepting less, the symbolizer gains both in sense of mastery, since his symbol is his creation, differing from the original in ways he has effected, and in the applicability of the symbol to serve as a substitute for missing imagos. The range of application of the symbolic representation is much wider than that of the symbolic equation, and like Winnicott's (1953) concept of the transitional object, an early and concrete form of it, can be used as a substitute in many different bad moments. You can suck, stroke, kick, sit on or dismember a teddy bear, and you can be sure he is yours, and no one else's. So it is with the dream text: what the ego loses in its not being veridical, it gains in its power of possession, privacy, flexibility, ambiguity, reversibility and multiplicity of condensed meanings.

Now I think you will see why I took the trouble to define dreaming as telling a dream, for this conceptual starkness allows us to examine our primary datum divested of the attributions in which, as one of nature's dream theorists, the dreamer always clothes his experience and our data. Because the dream teller says that he had a dream last night, we are no more obliged to take his choice of medium for granted, than we should, from other vantage points of Freudian sophistication, believe that the manifest content of a dream is all there is to its meaning.

By assuming less, we discover more, and so we take the dreamer's notions about the act of dream telling as important secondary data to be read as seriously as the primary text of the dream. So it should be in the exhaustive psychological analysis of all actions; to understand what someone thinks requires us to be curious about what he thinks he is doing when he thinks. The most difficult secondary data of this kind to detect are those, of course, that are culturally shared by observer and subject alike, of which dreaming is a good example.

The psychoanalytic approach is phenomenological in the deepest sense, for we do not require that these reflexive data qualify as items of consciousness — we do not require a person to know what he thinks he is thinking for us to be able to infer a modulating effect on his ego-functions. Indeed, if we know that he does *not* know what he thinks he is doing when he thinks or dreams, then we can predict that he will utilize this reflexive knowledge according to different principles than if he were aware of it.

These are the principles of unconscious mental function, and the basics of our inference to them is essentially paradoxical. We assume that the outcome of actions provides the clue to intentions, and that the features of unconscious mental function derive from what the person does in order to remain ignorant of this very criterion. He attempts to maintain subjective, private, defensive meanings of his actions, so that he can spare himself the aversive superego consequences of knowing what he is up to.

It is central to the theory of the unconscious that we assume a dissociated state in which the person at the same time knows and does not know what he is doing. In this state of unconscious cognitive conflict, ego-functions mediate towards optimal management of contradictory intentions. Pre-eminent among these is H. Hartmann's organizing function that embraces differentiation and synthesis. If we apply to the detection of unconscious ego-functions the same logic we use in detecting

unconscious fantasy content, then we are justified in using the outcome of an action as one essential criterion of intention. Doing so,
we must not only endorse all those developments in psychoanalytic
dream theory which show how dream telling can symbolize infantile
fantasy themes, including the attribution to the dream text of the status
of 'a thing in itself' (Khan 1974), but in my view, we must go further
and attribute, via the observation of outcomes, unconscious ego intentions
with respect to the utilization of this specific mode of action or medium
of expression.

Conclusion

I have asked the question why patients insist on reporting dreams
when other aspects of the subtly analysed transference provide such
excellent play and battlegrounds for fantasy and resistance alike. After
all, there are other ways to reach these goals, including the defensive
goal of disclaiming that these are the goals they wish to reach. I have
suggested in answer that there are some special features of dream
telling which offer great advantages to the ego in its task of recognizing,
en route to reconciling, the two sides which are intrinsic to any argument
in the unconscious. On the one hand, we can characterize these as
the benign aspects of dissociation in which, within limits, two goals
can be had for the price of one: a secret both kept and revealed; a
current act given the protection of the past tense; a pictorial image put
out of bounds to others by the apparent hiatus between seeing and
telling; an unbearable truth both told and denied by locating it for the
time being in the context of an unveridical thought form which is
commonly not taken too seriously. And yet on the other hand, for every
dissociative aspect we can find a corresponding integrative function —
a new, differentiated whole emerges by the process of sacrificing the full
dimensionality of the conflictual state. Nowhere do we see this more
clearly than in the use of symbols in the dream text, and in my extended
version of this argument, in the very use of dream telling as a medium
for communication between internal object, self and other; in the
expression of the conflict between acknowledged and disclaimed intentions; and finally in the detection, not only of what the person wants
in his life, but also and perhaps pre-eminently, if we pay sufficient
attention to it, of the capacities of a given person's organizing function
at a given time.

Notes

1 I have a purpose in explicitly drawing attention here to the contribution of learning theory, in so far as the recognition of the *process* of this transformation is concerned. Too often, writers on ego psychology attempt to make psychoanalysis carry explanatory burdens which its methodology makes it extremely difficult, if not impossible, to handle in a successful way. These inappropriate impositions draw force and attention away from the tasks which the psychoanalytic method is uniquely designed to perform — namely, the capturing of the dynamically hidden content of past stimuli and responses (including drive stimuli and response-produced stimuli) whose psychological presence intrudes so anachronistically and often tragically into the individual's present life space. Learning theory can establish prospectively and with precision the laws of generalization across species; it provides no method for the discovery of retrospectively significant contents. Here psychoanalysis comes into its own.

2 For recent re-evaluations of these themes, together with references to relevant earlier literature, see the papers by Blum (1976), Khan (1976), Hartmann (1976), Plata-Mujica (1976), Curtis and Sachs (1976), presented in the Dialogue on 'The Changing Use of Dreams in Psychoanalytical Practice' at the 29th International Psycho-Analytical Congress, London, July 1975.

3 Freud (1916: 85): 'whatever the dreamer tells us must count as his dream'.

4 Since Wittgenstein's day we have learned that there is a high probability that if someone tells a dream, then he must have displayed the physiological indicants (if anyone was there to record them) of D-state in a prior sleep period. But the evidence of a high correlation, or even of complete functional equivalence, should this ever be established between psychological action and physiological function, gives us no brief to disclaim the difference in data base and level of explanation between the fields of physiology and psychology. Only complete concomitance in all phenomenological as well as functional features could do that. At best we can hope to establish the nature of the physiological sleep state which is a necessary prior condition for dream telling. All that we can confidently assert at present is that dream telling is more frequent on awakening from periods of REM than of NREM sleep. It is commonly assumed that this proves that the psychological act we report as dreaming takes place during the physiologically defined REM period. An equally plausible but more conservative inference would be that the experience of dreaming is the waking response to an unconscious perception of state change, such a response being a cognitive act of integration serving to rationalize the sensed discrepancy between the waker's pre- and post-REM states. It goes without saying that this act

would also supply the channels for conjoint expression of unconscious fantasy.

5   These features of dream telling apply also to the telling of those quasi-dreams, hypnagogic and hypnopompic fantasies, although they are less clearly segregated from other actions.

6   Or some forms of stage-4 sleep arousal disturbances (Fisher *et al.* 1973).

7   'So far as I can at present see, dreams that occur in a traumatic neurosis are the only *genuine* exceptions and punishment dreams are the only *apparent* exceptions to the rule that dreams are directed towards wish-fulfilment' (Freud 1923: 118).

References

Blum, H.P. (1976). The changing use of dreams in psychoanalytic practice: dreams and free association. *Int. J. Psycho-Anal.* 57, 315–24.

Breger, L., Hunter, I. and Lane, R.W. (1971). *The Effect of Stress on Dreams.* New York: Int. Univ. Press.

Curtis, H.C. and Sachs, D.M. (reporters) (1976). Dialogue on 'The changing use of dreams in psychoanalytic practice'. *Int. J. Psycho-Anal.* 57, 343–54.

Erikson, E.H. (1954). The dream specimen of psychoanalysis. *J. Am. psychoanal. Ass.* 2, 5–56.

Fisher, C., Kahn, E., Edwards, A. and Davis, D.M. (1973). A psychophysiological study of nightmares and night terrors. *J. nerv. ment. Dis.* 157, 75–98.

Freud, S. (1900). The interpretation of dreams. SE 4–5.

—— (1916). Introductory lectures on psychoanalysis. SE 15.

—— (1920). Beyond the pleasure principle. SE 18.

—— (1923). Remarks on the theory and practice of dream interpretation. SE 19.

—— (1925). Negation. SE 19.

—— (1933). New introductory lectures on psychoanalysis. SE 22.

Greenberg, R., Pearlman, C.A. and Gampel, D. (1972). War neuroses and the adaptive function of REM sleep. *Brit. J. med. Psychol.* 45, 27–33.

Hartmann, E. (1976). Discussion of 'The changing use of dreams in psychoanalytic practice': the dream as a 'royal road' to the biology of the mental apparatus. *Int. J. Psycho-Anal.* 57, 331–4.

Hartmann, H. (1947). On rational and irrational action. *Psychoanal. soc. Sci.* 1, 359–92.

—— (1950). Comments on the psychoanalytic theory of the ego. *Psychoanal. Study Child* 5.

Kanzer, M. (1955). The communicative function of the dream. *Int. J. Psycho-Anal.* 36, 260–6.

Khan, M.M.R. (1974). *The Privacy of the Self.* London: Hogarth Press.

—— (1976). The changing use of dreams in psychoanalytic practice: in search of the dreaming experience. *Int. J. Psycho-Anal.* 57, 325–30.

Kris, E. (1952). *Psycho-analytic Explorations in Art.* New York: Int. Univ. Press.

Lewin, B.D. (1946). Sleep, the mouth and the dream screen. *Psychoanal Q.* 15, 419–34.

—— (1958). *Dreams and the Use of Regression.* New York: Int. Univ. Press.

—— (1968). *The Image and the Past.* New York: Int. Univ. Press.

Malcolm, N. (1964). The concept of dreaming. In D.F. Gustafson (ed.), *Essays in Philosophical Psychology.* New York: Doubleday, Anchor.

Parkes, C.M. (1972). *Bereavement. Studies of Grief in Adult Life.* London: Tavistock Publ.

Plata-Mujica, C. (1976). Discussion of 'The changing use of dreams in psychoanalytic practice.' *Int. J. Psycho-Anal.* 57, 335–41.

Schafer, R. (1976). *A New Language for Psychoanalysis.* New Haven: Yale Univ. Press.

Stein, M.H. (1965). States of consciousness in the analytic situation. In M. Schur (ed.), *Drives, Affects, Behaviour,* vol. 2. New York: Int. Univ. Press.

Winnicott, D.W. (1953). Transitional objects and transitional phenomena. In *Collected Papers.* London: Tavistock, Publ., 1958.

Psychoanalytic phenomenology of the dream

ROBERT D. STOLOROW AND GEORGE E. ATWOOD

The extension of psychoanalytic treatment beyond the classical psychoneuroses to other forms of psychopathology has, in recent years, greatly enriched both the theory and practice of psychoanalysis. In concert with this 'widening scope of psychoanalysis', important new conceptualizations of personality development and pathogenesis have been offered — theoretical contributions that, in turn, have held critical implications for psychoanalytic technique. The theory and practice of dream analysis, by contrast, has in general not kept pace with the conceptual and technical advances occurring within our field. While certain authors have examined the communicative aspect of dreams (Ferenczi 1913; Kanzer 1955; Bergmann 1966) and others have attempted to update the theory of dreams to accommodate the tripartite structural model (Arlow and Brenner 1964; Spanjaard 1969), there have been few new major contributions to the psychoanalytic understanding of dreams since those of Freud (1900).[1]

It is our intention in the present paper to elaborate a theoretical point of view that we think holds great promise as a source of important new insights into the meaning and significance of dreams. This point of view has evolved in the context of ongoing efforts to construct the foundation for a new psychoanalytic theory of personality (see Stolorow and Atwood, in press). Our efforts have been guided by three general considerations. First, we have believed that any new framework should be capable of preserving the contributions made by the classical analytic theorists and of translating them into a common conceptual language. Second, it is our view that the theory of psychoanalysis should be formulated on an experience-near level of discourse, closely anchored in the phenomena of clinical observation. And third, we believe that an adequate psychoanalytic theory of personality must be designed to illuminate the structure, significance and origins of personal subjective worlds in all their richness and diversity.

Our studies in the foundations of psychoanalysis have accordingly led us to propose a 'psychoanalytic phenomenology' which takes human subjectivity as its principal domain of enquiry. As a depth psychology of human subjectivity, psychoanalytic phenomenology is devoted to unveiling the meanings and structures of personal experiencing. Its particular focus has been the concept of the 'representational world' (Sandler and Rosenblatt 1962; Stolorow and Atwood 1979) – the distinctive configurations of self and object which can be shown to shape and organize a person's experiences. We conceptualize these representational structures as systems of ordering or organizing principles (Piaget 1970) – cognitive-affective schemata (Klein 1976) through which a person's experiences of self and other assume their characteristic forms and meanings (Stolorow 1978a). Thus, the term 'representational world' is not equivalent to a person's subjective world of mental imagery. Rather, it refers to the *structure* of that world as disclosed in the thematic patterning of his subjective life.

Any new psychoanalytic approach to the dream must include a re-examination of the concept of the unconscious. In psychoanalytic phenomenology, repression is understood as a process whereby particular configurations of self and object are prevented from crystallizing in awareness. Repression is thus viewed as a *negative organizing principle* (Atwood and Stolorow 1980) operating alongside the positive organizing principles underlying the configurations which do repeatedly materialize in conscious experience. Accordingly, the 'dynamic unconscious' – pivotal in Freud's theory of dream formation – consists in that set of configurations which, because of their association with emotional conflict or subjective danger, consciousness is not permitted to assume. Particular memories, fantasies, feelings, and other experiential contents are repressed because they threaten to actualize these dreaded configurations.

In addition to the dynamic unconscious viewed as a system of negative organizing principles, another form of unconsciousness has increasingly assumed a position of importance in our general theoretical framework as well as in our thinking about dreams. The organizing principles of a person's representational world, whether operating positively (giving rise to certain configurations of self and object in awareness), or negatively (preventing certain configurations from arising), are themselves unconscious. A person's experiences are shaped by his representational configurations, but without this shaping becoming the focus of awareness and reflection. We have therefore proposed to characterize the structure of a representational world as *pre-reflectively unconscious* (Atwood and Stolorow 1980). This form of unconsciousness is not the product of

214

defensive activity. It results from the person's inability to recognize how the personal reality in which he lives and moves is constituted by the structures of his own subjectivity.

It is our contention that an understanding of the form of unconsciousness that we have designated as 'pre-reflective' sheds new light on the unique importance of dreams for psychoanalytic theory and practice. In general, the structure of a person's representational world will be most readily discernible in his relatively unfettered, spontaneous productions, and there is probably no psychological product that is less fettered or more spontaneous than the dream. As human subjectivity in purest culture, the dream constitutes a 'royal road' to the pre-reflective unconscious – to the organizing principles and dominant leitmotivs that unconsciously pattern and thematize a person's psychological life (Stolorow 1978b).[2] In the remainder of this paper, we shall explore some clinical and theoretical implications of this close proximity of the dream to the unconscious structures of experience. We offer first some general remarks on the nature of psychoanalytic dream interpretation.

The nature of dream interpretation

In classical psychoanalysis, the technical procedure for arriving at the meaning of a dream is to decompose the dream into discrete elements and then to collect the dreamer's associations to each of these elements. The rationale for this procedure is found in the theoretical idea that the associative chains provided by the dreamer, supplemented by certain connections and additions suggested by the analyst, will retrace the mental processes which gave rise to the dream and will lead the way back to the dream's latent content or unconscious meaning. It is assumed that the meaning of a dream, as determined by this method, is identical to the dream's causal origin; that is, the latent thoughts and wishes disclosed by the analyses are regarded as having been the elemental starting points of the dream's formation.

From the perspective of a framework that takes human subjectivity as its central focus, the determination of the meaning of a dream is a matter of elucidating the ways in which the dream is embedded in the ongoing course of the dreamer's experiencing. By restoring dream symbols and metaphors to their formative personal contexts, interpretation rebuilds the links between dream imagery and the salient concerns of the dreamer's subjective life. In developing a phenomenological approach to the psychology of dreams, we seek understanding of how dreams encapsulate the personal world and history of the dreamer. The utility of collecting free associations, from our standpoint, is thus not to re-trace

215

the presumed causal pathways of dream formation, but rather to *generate contexts of subjective meaning* in terms of which the imagery may be examined and understood. In addition to the discrete elements of a manifest dream, the distinctive thematic configurations of self and object which structure the dream narrative may also serve as useful points of departure for associative elaboration (Stolorow 1978b). Such themes, when abstracted from the concrete details of the dream and presented to the dreamer, can substantially enrich the associations that are produced and represent an important source of insight into the pre-reflectively unconscious structures of experience which organize a person's subjective world.

At the heart of the conceptual framework of psychoanalytic phenomenology is a set of interpretive principles for elucidating psychological phenomena in their personal contexts. With regard to dreams, these principles provide ways of viewing dream imagery against the background of the dreamer's subjective universe. Many such interpretive principles are implicit in the classical Freudian theory of how dreams are formed. We believe this theory is most profitably viewed as a hermeneutic system of rules of interpretation rather than as a causal-mechanistic account of the processes of dream generation. Freud (1900) argued that interpretation reverses the dream-work — that the activity of dream analysis moves backward along the paths of dream formation. It would be more accurate to say that the *theory* of the dream-work reverses the pathways followed by psychoanalytic interpretation. The dream-work 'mechanism' of condensation, for example, is the theoretical reverse of the interpretive principle that a single element in the dream text may be related to a multiplicity of subjective contexts in the dreamer's psychological life. Similarly, the mechanism of displacement inverts the principle that one may transpose and interchange the affective accents on various elements in the dream narrative in order to identify subjectively dangerous or conflictual configurations of images which the dreamer may be attempting to prevent from crystallizing in awareness.

Ths classical notion that dreams represent (attempted) wish fulfillments can also be viewed as an interpretive principle guiding the quest for a dream's connection to the subjective concerns of the dreamer. By giving the analyst an initial bearing in confronting the complexity of a particular dream narrative, this premise provides an orienting focus in relating the dream to emotionally significant issues in the dreamer's life. We would expand the classical conception of the centrality of wish fulfillment in dreams into a more general and inclusive proposition that dreams always embody one or more of the dreamer's *personal purposes*. Such purposes include the fulfillment of wishes as discussed by Freud, but also a number of other important psychological purposes which we shall delineate in the next section of this paper.

The interpretive principles of psychoanalytic phenomenology as applied to dreams operate as aids to the interpreter in approaching the content of a manifest dream and its associations. They enable the analyst to construct a complex map of the various lines of symbolic expression which connect a dream to the personal world of the dreamer. The utility of these principles for examining a particular dream lies in the degree to which they lead to an interpretation that convincingly illuminates the various features of the dream text as embodiments of the issues and concerns having salience in the dreamer's subjective life. The correctness or adequacy of a particular dream interpretation, in turn, is assessed by the same hermeneutic criteria that govern the assessment of the validity of psychoanalytic interpretation in general (Stolorow and Atwood, in press) – the logical coherence of the argument, the compatibility of the interpretation with one's general knowledge of the dreamer's psychological life, the comprehensiveness of the explanation in rendering the various details of the dream text transparent, and the aesthetic beauty of the analysis in illuminating previously hidden patterns of order in the dream narrative and in connecting these patterns to the background structures of the dreamer's personal subjectivity.

Let us now turn from this general discussion of dream interpretation to a consideration of a particular attribute of the dream experience – concrete symbolization.

The purpose of concrete symbolization in dreams

Among recent critiques of Freudian theory, some of the most constructive have been those that rest upon George Klein's (1976) clarifying distinction between the metapsychology and the clinical theory of psychoanalysis. Metapsychology and clinical theory, Klein held, derive from two completely different universes of discourse. Metapsychology deals with the presumed material substrate of human experience, and is thus couched in the natural science framework of impersonal mechanisms, discharge apparatuses and drive energies. In contrast, clinical theory, which derives from the psychoanalytic situation and guides psychoanalytic practice, deals with intentionality, conscious and unconscious purposes, and the personal meaning of subjective experiences. Klein wishes to disentangle metapsychological and clinical concepts, and to retain only the latter as the legitimate content of psychoanalytic theory.

In this section of the paper we shall first comment briefly on Freud's two theories of the dream-work – the metapsychological and the clinical. We shall then offer a clinical psychoanalytic theory of the purpose of concrete symbolization in dreams, based on the framework of psychoanalytic phenomenology.

Freud's metapsychological theory of the dream-work finds its clearest expression in chapter 7 of *The Interpretation of Dreams* (1900). There the dream-work (with the exception of secondary revision) is conceptualized as a non-purposeful, mechanical consequence of a process whereby preconscious thoughts receive an energic charge from an unconscious wish 'striving to find an outlet' (p. 605). The dream-work occurs as the preconscious thoughts are 'drawn into the unconscious' (p. 594) and thereby automatically 'become subject to the primary psychical process' (p. 603).

In contrast with this mechanistic view of the dream-work, germs of a clinical theory emphasizing its intentional and purposeful quality appear in an earlier chapter on 'Distortion in dreams'. There the dream-work is seen 'to be deliberate and to be a means of dissimulation' (p. 141) and disguise, serving the purpose of defense. In these passages, we can readily recognize the dream censor as being the dreamer himself, actively transforming the content and meaning of his experiences in order to protect himself from direct awareness of forbidden wishes.

This germinal clinical theory of the dream-work, emphasizing its defensive purpose, applies principally to the process of displacement and perhaps also to condensation. It does not shed a great deal of light on what we regard as the most distinctive and central feature of the dream experience – the use of concrete perceptual images endowed with hallucinatory vividness to symbolize abstract thoughts, feelings and subjective states. Freud's explanation of this feature of dreams was an entirely metapsychological one: a 'topographical regression' (p. 548) of excitation from the motor to the sensory end of the psychic apparatus was thought to result in 'a hallucinatory revival of . . . perceptual images' (p. 543). Thus, in Freud's view, the pictorial and hallucinatory quality of dreams was a non-purposeful, mechanical consequence of the discharge path followed by psychic energy during sleep. In contrast, our psychology of the representational world leads us to propose that concrete symbolization in dreams and their resulting hallucinatory vividness serve a vital and fundamental psychological purpose for the dreamer, and that an understanding of this purpose can illuminate the importance and necessity of dreaming.

In order to develop this thesis, it is necessary first to touch briefly on the problem of human motivation. We have conceived of psychoanalytic phenomenology as a methodological system of interpretive principles to guide the study of meaning in human experience and conduct. Rather than formulating impersonal motivational prime movers of a mental apparatus, it seeks to illuminate the multiple conscious and unconscious purposes (Klein 1976) or personal reasons (Schafer 1976) which lead a person to strive to actualize the configurations of self and object that constitute his representational world. These configurations may, in varying degrees, fulfill cherished wishes and urgent desires, provide moral guidance and self-punishment, aid adaptation to difficult realities, repair or restore damaged or lost self and object imagos, and also serve a defensive purpose in preventing other dreaded configurations from crystallizing in awareness. Any or all of these personal motivations can contribute to the construction of a dream, and it is essential to the therapeutic use of dream interpretation to determine the relative motivational salience or priority of the multiple purposes that the dream has served.

Our studies of the representational world have also led us to propose an additional, more general motivational principle, supra-ordinate to the personal aims discussed above: namely, that the *need to maintain the organization of experience* is a central motive in the patterning of human action (Atwood and Stolorow 1981). And it is here that we can discover the fundamental purpose of concrete symbolization in dreams. When configurations of experience of self and other find symbolization in concrete perceptual images and are thereby articulated with hallucinatory vividness, the dreamer's feeling of conviction about the validity and reality of these configurations receives a powerful reinforcement. Perceiving, after all, is believing. By reviving during sleep the most basic and emotionally compelling form of knowing – through sensory perception – the dream affirms and solidifies the nuclear organizing structures of the dreamer's subjective life. Dreams, we are contending, are the *guardians of psychological structure*, and they fulfill this vital purpose by means of concrete symbolization.[3]

Our claim that dream symbolization serves to maintain the organization of experience can be understood to apply in two different senses to two broad classes of dreams (with many dreams, of course, combining features of both classes). In some dreams, concrete symbols serve to actualize a *particular* organization of experience in which specific configurations of self and object, required for multiple reasons, are dramatized and affirmed. Dreams of this first class appear most often in the context of firmly structured intrapsychic conflict. With these dreams there is usually a wide gap between their manifest imagery and latent meaning, because the aims of defense and disguise have been prominent in their construction. Our approach to such dreams incorporates what we earlier referred to as Freud's clinical theory of the dream-work, particularly as this was later updated to include the principle of multiple function (Waelder 1936; Arlow and Brenner 1964). As we discussed in the preceding section, we also supplement the classical approach with a focus on dream themes and their associative elaboration, as a further means of discovering the specific configurations of self and object that the dream symbolism has both actualized and disguised.

In another class of dreams, concrete symbols serve not so much to actualize particular configurations of experience, but rather to maintain psychological organization *per se*. Dreams of this second class occur most often in the context of developmental interferences and arrests, whereby structuralization of the representational world has remained incomplete, precarious and vulnerable to regressive dissolution (Stolorow and Lachmann 1980). With these dreams the distinction between manifest and latent content is much less germane, because the aim of disguise has not been prominent. Instead, the vivid perceptual images of the dream serve directly to restore or sustain the structural integrity and stability of a subjective world menaced with disintegration. For persons with severe deficits in psychological structure formation, concretization may serve a similar purpose in their waking lives as well, not only in the form of delusions and hallucinations but also in the concrete behavioral enactments, often of a destructive or sexual nature, that are required to sustain the cohesion and continuity of a fragmenting sense of self or other (Kohut 1971, 1977; Stolorow and Lachmann 1980; Atwood and Stolorow 1981).

An important subgroup of this second class of dreams, in which concrete symbols serve to maintain psychological organization *per se*, are the 'self-state dreams' discussed by Kohut (1977). These dreams portray in their manifest imagery 'the dreamer's dread vis-à-vis some uncontrollable tension–increase or his dread of the dissolution of the self' (p. 109). Kohut suggests that the very act of portraying these archaic self-states in the dream in a minimally disguised form 'constitutes an attempt to deal with the psychological danger by converting frightening nameless processes with namable visual imagery' (p. 109). Socarides (1980) has discovered a similar purpose fulfilled by dreams that directly depict perverse sexual enactments similar to those performed by the dreamer in his waking life. The hallucinatory visualization of the perversion during sleep, like the perverse enactment itself, shores up an imperiled sense of self and protects against the danger of its dissolution.

The principal purpose of the perceptual imagery of self-state dreams is not, in our view, to render nameless psychological processes nameable. By vividly reifying the experience of self-endangerment, the dream symbols bring the state of the self into focal awareness with a feeling of conviction and reality that can only accompany sensory perceptions. The dream images, much like hypochondriacal symptoms, both encapsulate the danger to the self and embody a concretizing effort at self–restoration (Stolorow and Lachmann 1980; ch. 7). Thus, self–state dreams represent a most important instance of our general thesis concerning the central role of concretization in maintaining the organization of experience.

Clinical illustration[4]

The case we have chosen to illustrate our conception of the structure-maintaining function of concrete symbolization in dreams is that of a young woman whose sense of self had become fragmented into a set of separate, quasi-autonomous personalities. The dreams to be discussed, as will be seen, reflect various aspects of her lifelong struggle to maintain the organization of her subjective world and achieve unity and cohesion in her self-experience. A feature of this case making it especially well suited for this discussion is that the patient engaged in specific concrete behavioral enactments which served a purpose closely paralleling that of her dreams. Viewing her dreams in the context of these enactments will bring the organization maintaining function of her dream imagery into sharp focus.

The family environment in which the patient grew up was one of extreme physical and emotional abuse. Both parents treated her as an extension of themselves and as a scapegoat for their frustrations and disappointments in life. Violent physical beatings represented a frequent form of interaction with the parents, and throughout her early childhood she thought they wished her dead. A sense of profound personal disunity had haunted the patient all her life, appearing even in her earliest recollections. For example, she recalled from her fourth year an obsession with the issue of how it could be that her mind controlled the movements of her body. A disturbance in mind–body unity was also indicated by quasi-delusional journeys outside of her body which began during that same year. These journeys commenced on the occasion when she was visited by the benevolent ghosts of two deceased grandparents. The ghosts taught her to leave her body and fly to a place she called 'the field', a peaceful expanse of grass and trees somewhere far removed from human society. She felt safe in the field because she was alone there and no one could find her.

The psychological disintegration implicit in the patient's out-of-the-body journeys was embedded in a broader context of self-division resulting from the violent abuse and rejection she had received in her family. Beginning at the age of two and a half, when her parents abruptly ceased all affectionate bodily contact with her, and continuing through a series of pivotal traumatic episodes over the next several years, she was successively divided into a total of six fragmentary selves. Each of these fragments crystallized as a distinct personality, possessing its own individual name and unique personal attributes.

When the patient was seven years old she developed a brain tumor, causing agonizing headaches. The need to escape the pain generated by her neurological condition became an additional motive underlying the journeys outside of her body. It was two full years before her illness was correctly diagnosed and the tumor finally removed. The surgery itself was handled with brutal insensitivity by her parents and doctors, and she experienced it as an overwhelming trauma. The impact of all these circumstances on her precarious selfhood was symbolized in a set of recurring nightmares which began during her recuperation from surgery and continued throughout her adolescent years. In these dreams she stood alone in the small train station of her town as flames sprang up all around her. Soon the whole building was engulfed in fire. After the station had burned to the ground, two eyeballs lay quietly in the smoking ashes and then began to quiver and roll about, conversing with each other by means of movements and glances. This dream of burning down to two small fragments concretely depicted the disintegrating impact of a world persecuting her both from without and from within.

What psychological function can be ascribed to the patient's recurring dream of being burned down to isolated fragments? The repeated transformation of the experience of self-disintegration into an image of the physical incineration of her body enabled her to maintain the state of her self in focal awareness and encapsulated her effort to retain psychological integrity in the face of the threat of total self-dissolution. By utilizing concrete anatomical imagery, she was giving her disintegrating existence tangible form, replacing a precarious and vanishing sense of selfhood with the permanence and substantiality of physical matter. The image of the interaction and communication between the eyeballs at the end of the dream symbolized a further restitutive effort to reconnect the broken fragments and restore a measure of coherence to her splintered self. The specific symbol of the eyeballs captured an essential feature of what became her principal mode of relating to her social milieu. She assumed the role of an ever-watchful, often disembodied spectator, perpetually scanning her environment for desirable qualities in others which she hoped to appropriate and assemble into a re-built self. Thus, both her self-restorative efforts and what remained of her vanishing self became crystallized in her waking life in the act of looking and in her recurring dreams in the imagery of the eyes.

The central salience in the patient's subjective world of the need to maintain selfhood and recover a sense of personal unity was also indicated by an array of bizarre enactments (discussed in greater detail in Atwood and Stolorow 1981) which appeared concurrently with the onset of the recurring dream of being burned.[5] These enactments included the self-administration of severe whippings with a leather belt, delicate cutting and puncturing of the surface of the skin on her wrists and arms, gazing tirelessly at the reflected image of her face in pools of water, scratching and rubbing at cracks and crevices in hard physical surfaces such as walls and sidewalks, stitching the skin of her separate fingers together with needle and thread.

Among the various functions served by these patterns of behavior was the central purpose of strengthening the patient's conviction that she was alive and real and restoring unity to her shattered self. Reassurance that she was surviving and real was obtained in the case of the self-whipping through the strong sensations of pain distributed on the surface of her skin. In the pattern of delicate cutting and puncturing, a similar effect was achieved. By violating the physical boundary of her body she dramatized the very existence of that boundary and strengthened the feeling of her own embodied selfhood. In addition, the stinging sensations and the droplets of blood produced by the cutting provided concrete sensory evidence of her continuing aliveness. The patient's behavior in relation to her reflected image in pools of water played an analogous role in stabilizing her sense of existing as something definite and real. She recalled always having been fascinated by how the image of her face would disappear and then magically reappear when she disturbed the water's reflecting surface. The reappearing image gave her reassurance that while her sense of self (concretized in a visual reflection) might be made to vanish on a temporary basis, it could not be annihilated permanently. A sense of self-continuity was thus tenuously achieved.

The enactment involving scratching at cracks and crevices and sewing her fingers together pertained to the patient's experience of being an assembly of disjointed parts. With regard to the scratching patterns, she explained that crevices and cracks in the external environment 'itched' unbearably and compelled her to scratch them. The locating of the subjective sensation of itching in physical objects represented a transposition onto the plane of material reality of her feeling of inner fragmentation. She described herself as being like a jar filled with small spheres or cubes with concave surfaces, and as a checkerboard filled with round checkers; even though the constituent elements might be packed together very tightly, they still would not form an integrated and smoothly continuous whole. The itching cracks and crevices in the external environment corresponded to the subjective interstices between the various fragmentary entities comprising her self-experience, and the scratching represented her effort to find relief from her distressing lack of inner cohesion.

Closely similar was the function of her pattern of sewing her fingers together with needle and thread. This ritual began with holding her hand up to the light and gazing at the spaces between her separate fingers. Then she would push a needle and thread just under the skin of her little finger, then under the skin of the next one, and the next and so on, and then back and forth several times until they were all tightly interconnected and pressed together. The act of weaving the fingers together was one in which separate parts of her physical self were actually joined and made to appear whole and continuous, concretizing her effort to fashion an internally integrated identity out of the collection of part-selves into which she had divided during the course of her traumatic early history.

The enactments in which the patient engaged are functionally parallel to her recurring dreams of being burned to fragments. The essential feature the two sets of phenomena share in common is the reparative use of concretization to give an experience of self-disintegration a material and substantial form. In the dreams the emphasis appears on the concrete symbolization of the experience or self-dissolution, and the additional reparative trend of reassembling the broken pieces is hinted at in the image of the communication which develops between the eyeballs. In the enactments one finds analogous symbolizations and also the vivid expression of the patient's need to mend her broken self by reconnecting the separate fragments into which she had disintegrated.

The function of dreams in maintaining the organization of a person's subjective world is to be seen not only in situations wherein structures are breaking down, as was the case with the patient at the time of the onset of her nightmares; dreams may also play an important role in consolidating and stabilizing new structures of subjectivity which are in the process of coming into being. Let us turn now to a consideration of another dream of the patient we have been discussing, this one having occurred midway through the long course of her psychotherapy. The context of this dream in the treatment was one of intense conflict and struggle over the issue of self-unification. Two of the initial six part-selves had at this point been assimilated into the remaining four, but the next steps of integration were being approached by the patient with trepidation and reluctance. Specifically, she feared that becoming one would render her vulnerable to being destroyed, either by attack from the outside world or by unendurable loneliness. At the same time, however, she had come to abhor the prospect of a life spent in continuing disunity.

In her dream she walked into the living room of her house and saw on the mantle above the fireplace four cement boxes resting side by side. There seemed to be bodies inside the boxes. The scene terrified her and she awoke, but then fell back asleep and the dream continued. Now the four boxes were replaced by just one box, with four bodies arranged inside with their backs against the cement walls and facing inward toward a central point. The box seemed to be a coffin. In discussing this dream with the therapist, the patient spontaneously associated the four boxes with the four remaining part-selves still requiring integration. A great deal of progress toward this goal had already been achieved, principally through the four parts growing less and less distinct from one another in the facilitating medium of the therapeutic relationship. The patient was oscillating, however, between experiencing herself as a single person with multiple facets on the one hand, and as a recollection of separate persons who happened to resemble one another and share the same body on the other.

The dream concretizes one phase of this oscillation by replacing the image of four separate boxes with the image of just one that contains four bodies. The patient offered the interpretation that the shift from four to one could be understood as a prelude to the integration of her personality, with the exterior boundaries of the final box representing the developing structure of a unitary self. The danger felt to be associated with her impending integration is also concretely symbolized in the dream, by the identification of the box as a coffin. The patient frequently expressed deep anxiety that becoming one would end her life, and she once even suggested that she was coming together as something dead.

The dream of the transformation of four boxes into one box buttressed the patient's evolving self-integration by giving her developing unity a concrete form. In the same way that the earlier dream of being burned encapsulated her need to maintain her self-experience as she underwent psychological dissolution, this second dream expressed her need to maintain and consolidate the new but still unsteady structure of integrated self-experience which was gradually crystallizing. An enactment sharing this latter function appeared some nine months after the dream of the boxes. During the interim the patient had continued to wrestle with the problem of unifying herself, with each of the residual fragmentary personalities making a common commitment to a shared future as one individual.

In the subsequent context of such statements as 'We are me!' and 'I am one now – we voted last night and we all agree,' the patient began a therapy session by bringing out twelve small pieces of paper. On six of the slips were written the six names of the part-selves, and on the other six were short phrases designating the pivotal trauma she considered responsible for each of the self-divisions. After asking the therapist whether he thought he could match the selves with their appropriate traumas, she cleared off his desk and assembled out of the twelve pieces of paper two closely juxtaposed columns displaying the temporal sequence of her shattering psychological history. The act of arranging the names and experiences into a single ordered structure clearly concretized the patient's increasingly successful efforts to synthesize an internally integrated, temporally continuous self. By giving the newborn self a tangible form and demonstrating its unity and historical continuity to the therapist, she consolidated the structure of her experience more firmly than had been possible heretofore. Following the integrating enactment involving the twelve pieces of paper, the patient came to feel her own subjective integrity on a consistent basis, and the focus of the therapeutic work shifted to issues other than that of mending her self-fragmentation.

Summary

A psychoanalytic framework bringing into focus the unconscious structures of human subjectivity holds great promise as a source of new insights into the meaning and significance of dreams. While all dreams can be shown to embody multiple personal purposes, their most distinctive feature is the use of concrete symbolization that serves to crystallize and preserve the organization of the dreamer's subjective world. Analyses of two dreams from a clinical case demonstrate that the structure-maintaining function of dream imagery can be observed not only when existing structures are threatened, but also when new structures of subjectivity are coming into being and are in need of consolidation.

Notes

1 An important exception to this generalization is Kohut's (1977) concept of 'self-state dreams', to be discussed later.
2 From a different theoretical perspective, Erikson (1954) has suggested that attention to the dream's 'style of representation' can reveal the dreamer's modes of experiencing himself and his world.
3 Lerner (1967) has presented evidence that dreams, through their kinaesthetic elements, function to strengthen the body image. This, if true, would be a special, circumscribed instance of the broader thesis we are proposing here. Formulations of the problem-solving (Freud 1900), focal conflict-resolving (French and Fromm 1964) and trauma-integrating (de Monchaux 1978) functions of dreams may also be seen as special instances of the role of dream symbolization in maintaining the organization of experience.
4 Since dreams of the first type, in which the perceptual images serve to actualize a particular organization of experience required for multiple reasons, are very familiar to analysts, they will not be exemplified here. We will illustrate only dreams of the second type, in which the imagery serves principally to maintain psychological organization *per se*. We are aware that a clinical case could never 'prove' our thesis concerning the role of concrete symbolization in maintaining the organization of experience; it can only demonstrate that

the application of this proposition provides a coherent framework through which clinical data can be ordered and rendered intelligible. Aspects of the case not pertaining directly to our thesis concerning the function of dream symbolization, such as the establishment and working through of the archaic self-object transference, will not be covered.

5 Since the appearance of the bizarre enactments coincided precisely with the onset of the recurrent nightmare, we have regarded these enactments as 'associations' embedded in the same contexts of meaning in which the dream imagery took form.

References

Arlow, J. and Brenner, C. (1964), *Psychoanalytic Concepts and the Structural Theory.* New York: International Universities Press.

Atwood, G. and Stolorow, R. (1980), Psychoanalytic concepts and the representational world. *Psychoanal. & Contemp. Thought*, 3: 267–290.

—— —— (1981), Experience and conduct. *Contemp. Psychoanal.*, 17: 197–208.

Bergmann, M. (1966), The intrapsychic and communicative aspects of the dream: Their role in psychoanalysis and psychotherapy. *Internat. J. Psycho-Anal.*, 47: 356–363.

Erikson, E. (1954), The dream specimen of psychoanalysis. *J. Amer. Psychoanal. Assn.*, 2: 5–56.

Ferenczi, S. (1913), To whom does one relate one's dreams? In: *Further Contributions to the Theory and Technique of Psycho-Analysis*. London: Hogarth Press, 1950, p. 349.

French, T. and Fromm, E. (1964), *Dream Interpretation: A New Approach*. New York: Basic Books.

Freud, S. (1900), The interpretation of dreams. SE 4 & 5. London: Hogarth Press, 1953.

Kanzer, M. (1955), The communicative function of the dream. *Internat. J. Psycho-Anal.*, 36: 260–266.

Klein, G. (1976), *Psychoanalytic Theory: An Exploration of Essentials*. New York: International Universities Press.

Kohut, H. (1971), *The Analysis of the Self*. New York: International Universities Press.

—— (1977), *The Restoration of the Self*. New York: International Universities Press.

Lerner, B. (1967), Dream function reconsidered. *J. Abnorm. Psychol.*, 72: 85–100.

Monchaux, C. de (1978), Dreaming and the organizing function of the ego. *Internat. J. Psycho-Anal.*, 59: 443–453.

Piaget, J. (1970), *Structuralism*. New York: Basic Books.

Sandler, J. and Rosenblatt, B. (1962), The concept of the representational world. *The Psychoanalytic Study of the Child*, 17: 128–145. New York: International Universities Press.

Schafer, R. (1976), *A New Language for Psychoanalysis*. New Haven, Conn.: Yale University Press.

Socarides, C. (1980), Perverse symptoms and the manifest dream of perversion. In: *The Dream in Clinical Practice*, ed. J. Natterson. New York: Aronson, pp. 237–256.

Spanjaard, J. (1969), The manifest dream content and its significance for the interpretation of dreams. *Internat. J. Psycho-Anal.*, 50: 221–235.

Stolorow, R. (1978a), The concept of psychic structure: Its metapsychological and clinical psychoanalytic meanings. *Internat. Rev. Psychoanal.*, 5: 313–320.

—— (1978b), Themes in dreams: A brief contribution to therapeutic technique. *Internat. J. Psycho-Anal.*, 59: 473–475.

—— and Atwood, G. (1979), *Faces in a Cloud: Subjectivity in Personality Theory*. New York: Aronson.

—— —— (in press), Psychoanalytic phenomenology: Progress toward a theory of personality. In: *The Future of Psychoanalysis*, ed. A. Goldberg. New York: International Universities Press.

—— and Lachmann, F. (1980), *Psychoanalysis of Developmental Arrests: Theory and Treatment*. New York: International Universities Press.

Waelder, R. (1936), The principle of multiple function. *Psychoanal. Quart.*, 5: 45–62.

Name index

Abraham, N. 141
Adler, A. 153–4, 191
Alexander, F. 42, 73, 154, 161
Altman, L. 65, 84
Annual Survey of Psychoanalysis 84
Anzieu, A. 142, 149
Anzieu, D. 11, 16–17, 90, 137–50
Arlow, J.A. 51–2, 68–9, 155, 172
Atwood, G.E. 19–20, 152, 213–28

Balint, M. 50, 61
Benjamin, J.D. 69
Bick, E. 132–3
Bion. W. 10–11, 14–16, 89–90,
    102–3, 107, 131–4, 146
Blitzsten, L.N. 155
Bonime, W. 156, 191
Borges, J.L. 139
Breger, L. 190, 202
Brenner, C. 13, 20, 22, 49–63, 65,
    68–9, 155, 172
Breuer, J. 3, 49
British Society 8

Chicago Psychoanalytic Literature Index
    84

David, C. 132, 135
Dement, W.C. 66
Dora case 49, 169

Eissler, K.R. 30, 69, 73, 84, 156, 165,
    173
Elmhirst, I. 132

Erikson, E.H. 9, 17–18, 65, 151, 156,
    165, 195

Fain, M. 132, 135
Fairbairn, W.R.D. 42
Federn, P. 33–4, 155, 158, 169, 171, 175
Fenichel, O. 68–9
Ferenczi, S. 5, 17, 155, 158
Fisher, C. 66, 69
Fliess, R. 31, 84, 91, 138, 155, 158,
    163, 191
French, T. 156, 170–1, 182, 190
Freud, A. 18, 50, 68, 91
Freud, S. 1–9, 12, 14, 17, 18, 20–2,
    29–33, 35, 37–9, 41–2, 49–55, 64–9,
    75, 84, 90, 96, 100–1, 104, 107–12,
    114–15, 119, 134, 138–41, 151–3,
    154–9, 161–4, 166, 169–75, 181–91,
    195–9, 201, 203, 213–14, 216–18
Fromm, E. 170, 182
Frosch, J. 155

Gammill, J. 10, 16, 90, 127–36
Gill, M. 69
Gitelson, M. 41
Green, A. 1
Greenberg, J.R. 9, 18, 22, 151, 202
Greenberg, R. 181–94
Greenson, R.R. 13, 17, 22, 64–88,
    182
Groddeck, G. 117
Grotjahn, M. 33, 158
Guillaumin, J. 137
Gutheil, E.A. 156

Subject index

acting out 99, 15–16, 198
actualization, and dream-space 96, 99
adaptation, dream as mechanism of
181–3, 190–2
aggression 11, 153–4
alpha function 11, 103–4, 134
analyst, the 20, 81–2, 83–4
analytic situation, concept of 36–9, 42
anxiety: clinical examples 76ff., 124,
142ff.; control of 199–200; dreams
139, 173; mastery of 22; and trauma
5–6, 139; and unpleasure 57
anxiety envelope 141
arousal, in dreaming 9–10, 33, 166
association(s): of analysts 81–2; clinical
examples 76, 79, 81–2, 104, 167–8;
confirming interpretation 75; as
'disintegration products of verbal
thinking' 170; to features of analysis
other than dream 61–2; free 66, 68,
76; Freud on 161–2; intellectualized
71–2; interpretation without 164–5;
rationale for, in dream analysis
215–16, 219–20; theoretical view-
points 21–2

beta elements 103
binding 19, 119
bizarre enactments 222–4
bizarre fantasies 122, 124
bizarre objects 103
blank dreams 114, 130, 156, 207
bodily ego 143
bodily zones 149

body: and Freud's dreams 112; image
142, 143; maternal/mother's 16, 90,
101, 111, 120; part, dream as 196;
shed in sleep 66
body ego 17
body image 142, 143
body–mind split, in dreaming 207
borderline cases 15, 40–2, 102–3, 105,
122
boundaries 10, 11–12, 15–16, 90; see
also safety
breast: and alpha function 134; in
clinical examples 70–2, 146; and
dream-screen 9–10, 125, 130, 135;
good 132, 144; internalized 9–10,
125, 130, 133, 134–5, 207; toilet
132; see also maternal; mother

case studies see clinical examples
catharsis 32
cathexis 140–1, 146, 148
censorship, of dreams 138–9, 159, 164,
171
claustrophobia 61–2
clinical examples 58–60, 69–83, 96–8,
102–6, 122–4, 127–30, 142–8,
165–71, 184–9, 204–6, 221–6
cognitive-affective schema 214
communication, intra-psychic 91, 134,
139
communicative function of dream see
function of dreams
compromise formation 53, 60, 100,
138, 158–9

dream-telling 198–9, 203, 207, 209
dreaming ego 9
dreaming, mechanism of 30, 96, 110, 163
dream-screen: and analytic listening 127ff.; and dream-space 99; extensions of original concept 90; and internalized breast 9–10, 125, 130, 135; and pictorial representation 67; and REM research 114; and skin 16–17, 90, 133, 138; as a surface for protection 119
dream-space 14–15, 88–99, 114–15, 117, 126
dream-telling 9, 12, 197, 198–9, 203, 208–9
dream-work 114–15, 171, 216, 218 *passim*
drive-discharge theory 181

ego: body 17; demands on, in dreaming 163; development 6, 12, 16, 20, 22, 39, 41, 213; differentiation 41, 199; disintegration 19; dreaming 9; feelings 169–70; functions in dreaming 9, 52–8, 151, 171; gratification *see* wish fulfilment; ideal 139; integration 55, 124, 198; mastery 199ff.; modality 169–70; organizing function of 152, 198, 208; role in dreaming 7, 154, 155; skin *see* skin ego; synthesizing 22
ego auxiliary 37
ego psychology 17, 18, 22, 151–4, 175, 182, 198
ego-distancing 125–6, 158
ego-overwhelming 124–6
ego-rating system 125–6, 158
ego-specific defect 40
elaborated content 197
emotional development 9, 14, 20–1
envelope: of anxiety 141; of excitation 149–50; psychic 11, 12, 17, 140; visual 17, 90
erogenous zones 146
evacuation 15, 19, 102, 107
exhibitionist 159, 169
expulsion 89, 103

fantasy: bizarre 122ff.; conscious 53; grandiose 187, 189; and manifest

dream content 154; meanings and cognitive processes 196; oral 197; and reality 54; recounting 198; sadistic 200; spelling of word 23n; *see also* phantasy
form, of dreams *see* dream(s)
formation, of dreams *see* dream(s)
free association *see* association(s)
function of dreams: as adaptation 190, 192: as containment 11; in disturbed patients 12, 107; and dream as object 109; French work on 135; and function of play 10; as integration 6; and hallucinatory vividness 19; as maintenance of structure of representational world 152; potential of 12; as problem-solving 6; and REM research 190, 192
functions of ego in dreaming *see* ego

generalization, principle of 196
good analytic hour 35
good breast 132, 134
good dream 35–6, 91, 100
guilt 57, 131

hallucination: and dream 102; in dreams 3, 109, 113, 138, 166, 170, 173; and perversion 220; and vividness of images 19, 152, 218
holding 10
hypnotic situation, the 31–3
hysteria 49, 149–50, 159
hysterical personality 149

id: differentiation of 13; and dreaming 7, 57–8, 62, 67–8, 139, 154; and ego psychology 17; and hysterics 39, 53; and latent dream thoughts 161
identity, maintenance of 22
imagery, dream 8, 19, 67, 75, 216, 218
incestuous dreams 172
infantile mental processes in dreaming 56–7, 58, 196, 209
instinctual aspects of psyche 8, 17, 22, 57, 138, 139
integration: and disintegration, a clinical example 221–5; and dreams 6–7, 19, 22–3; and dream-telling 209; and ego 55, 124, 198; failure of 89; and REM 181, 192; of self 31; and trauma 202–3

interplay with id and ego 52, 53, 62, 78; revealed in dream 67; role in dream 154
symbolic elaboration 89
symbolic equation 15, 101, 207
symbolic processes 10, 14, 89
symbolism: concrete 217–26; of play 14, 18
symbolization: capacity for 21, 36, 100–1; concrete, purpose in dreams 217–21; and dimensions of dreams 199, 209; process of 123
symbol(s) in dreams 4, 152, 209, 215

thinking: capacity for 134; in clinical example 200; concept in psychoanalysis 196; dream as form of 110, 156; psychotic 11
topographic theory 51, 64, 69, 139, 141, 218
transference: and dream 111, 124, 132–3, 195; and dream analysis 7, 10, 12, 38, 132–3; and dream-screen 132; limits of 16; mirroring 143–5

transference neurosis 20, 31, 37, 40, 41, 91, 117, 169, 174
transformation, maternal 131, 133
transitional dream 118
transitional object 11, 207–8
transitional space 11, 98, 103
transitionality 151–2
trauma: cumulative 140; and dreams 5–6, 21, 140–2, 155–6, 173; and self 202–3; and sleep 5
traumatic dreams 5–6, 115, 139–41, 155–6, 201

wakefulness 33–5
wish fulfilment: clinical example 95–6; and dreamer 117; Freud on 5, 7, 22, 41, 100, 109, 138, 139; hallucinated 52, 173; and infantile wishes 19, 58, 62; and integration 192; Lewin on 130; and personal purposes 216; problematic of 163ff.; and splitting 202; undisguised 159–60
working through 100